Put the Knife in Gently!

Donald Zec

Put the Knife in Gently!

Memoirs of a life with Legends

ROBSON
BOOKS

First published in Great Britain in 2003 by Robson Books, The Chrysalis Building, Bramley Road, London W10 6SP

An imprint of Chrysalis Books Group plc

British Library Cataloguing in Publication Data
A catalogue record for this title is available from the British Library.

ISBN 1 86105 697 4

Typeset by FiSH Books, London WC1
Printed by Butler & Tanner Ltd., London and Frome

For Joanna

Contents

Acknowledgements

Writing memoirs is essentially a memory test. Scavenging the recesses of the mind for incidents and anecdotes over sixty or so years becomes harder as the decades flow but the memories do not. Images are clawed back into the mind, but precise times, dates and locations resist all attempts to pin down. My shelf-load of newspaper clippings dating back to the mid-1940s are as faded and as crumbling as the Dead Sea Scrolls. The years 1950–51 for example can now be read only in powder form. I was therefore obliged to turn for help to a variety of sources, technical and human, all of which were as crucial as the brandy-carrying St Bernard to a stranded mountaineer.

Primarily, I wish to thank the editor of the *Daily Mirror*, Piers Morgan, for permission to quote from previously published columns, pictures etc. This was instantly granted with the paper's customary goodwill. In particular, I am grateful to Malcolm Harding and Steve Wightwick of the *Mirror* library, both of whom were cheerfully tolerant of my persistent emails and occasional invasion of their archives. I received the same excellent response at the *Mirror* picture archives at Watford where John Mead and my former colleague Peter Cook gave generously of their time and expertise. I refer to Otto Friedrich's *City of Nets* in the Bibliography. However it must be added that this was the definitive account of Hollywood in the 1940s and an essential guide to anyone probing the industry's earliest beginnings. I am grateful to Dana Broccoli for permission to use the photograph of her late husband Cubby Broccoli and to Eon's Anne

Bennett for additional information on the 007 phenomenon. I am grateful to my friend, the gifted scriptwriter Roger Marshall, who probed with me the gruesome history of John George Haigh, the 'acid-bath murderer'.

Inevitably, other valuable contributions may have been overlooked. This was quite unintentional and I apologise for any such omissions and for any errors and inaccuracies contained in these pages. I have made every effort to locate the copyright holder(s) of some photographs, without success. Should I receive any information that identifies the copyright holder(s) I will rectify the omission(s) in any reprint or subsequent edition of this book. In this area, John Mead at the *Mirror* picture library at Watford was particularly helpful.

More personally I would like to thank my son, Paul Zec MA. His expertise as a university lecturer and fine jazz musician made his comments on the text incisive yet always easy on the ear. I owe much to my wife, Frances, for her tolerance and good humour, despite being caught up in the frenetic world of deadlines and headlines and phone calls in the middle of the night. She was a charming hostess to the stars who sauntered across our threshold. She provided a sympathetic ear if not shoulder to a reminiscing Cary Grant; discussed potty training with an ecstatic new mother, Audrey Hepburn; and, after dancing with Gene Kelly at the Savoy, conceded that the genius of *On the Town*, *An American in Paris* and *Singin' In the Rain* wasn't at all bad on his feet. But it is the legends themselves that I acknowledge with much respect and affection. They gave the world, and this observer, the best years of their lives. I hope these memoirs will be regarded as a fair token of my appreciation.

London, July 2003

What rage for fame attends both great and small.
Better be damn'd than mentioned not at all.

John Wolcot (1738-1819)

Introduction

This is not an autobiography in the sense that skeletons rattle out of cupboards and slighted blood relatives swear they will never speak to you again. It is more a memoir of a journalist's life and the variety of scene changes that preceded it. The last thirty years were dominated by close encounters with celebrities, several of whom became legends. Inevitably, many of these are dead. But precisely because they are legends they're still up there, centre stage – relished by those who lived through their times but just as fascinating to later generations eager to know what they were like as flesh and blood. The classic films that featured many of them are reissued generation after generation: *Citizen Kane*, *All Quiet on the Western Front*, *Casablanca*, *It's a Wonderful Life*, *Sunset Boulevard*, *Some Like It Hot*, *The Apartment*, *Gone With the Wind*, *From Here To Eternity*, *African Queen* – these and many others seem always to be with us. Phrases like 'rounding up the usual suspects' (from *Casablanca*, 1942) is part of our everyday language sixty years later. However, it is not the films, but the unique personalities featured in them, that loom large in these recollections. On walls throughout the world you will still see posters of Charlie Chaplin, Humphrey Bogart, Clark Gable, Marilyn Monroe, James Dean, Montgomery Clift, Spencer Tracy, Frank Sinatra, John Wayne, Elvis Presley, The Beatles, Louis Armstrong and other treasured icons. This is as close to immortality as it gets. I was fortunate to have known them all with varying degrees of intimacy. The purpose of this book is to recall their considerable impact upon millions, including

1

this interrogator. The job of interviewing living legends is not always the thrilling experience one imagines it to be. Sometimes it is as tough as drawing teeth. Conversely, upwind of a particularly garrulous movie star one just sits back and waits for the onslaught to subside. It is a vocation that tends to make more enemies than friends. I've always imagined that the less celebrities approved of me the more likely I was doing a fair job. Thus when a displeased Frank Sinatra wired to inform me that 'As of this morning you blew it' I blushed with self-esteem. Similarly, to be told by Elizabeth Taylor in the back seat of her Rolls, 'You know you are a shit, dear' was equally reassuring.

I did not, in fact, choose to write about celebrities. I just drifted into the film world after serving time as a crime reporter. This turned out to be a valuable apprenticeship, since sin, along with sex, has long been Hollywood's most saleable and enduring commodity. Fortunately for the world's media, few of the prime players in the game have demonstrated any noticeable coyness at seeing their darkest secrets luridly revealed. 'I don't mind what you write,' Kirk Douglas once said to me, 'just put the knife in gently' – a variant on Hollywood's famous dictum, 'I don't care what you say, just spell the name right.' It is hard to fault that logic. After all, where would dear Joan Collins be in her beautifully retouched middle age but for her relentless flirtation with headlines?

Researching the mountain of gossip columns and the burgeoning archives of cover photos – miles and miles of lip-glossed smiles – is all in a year's work. Still, no one can say that Hollywood (and some of its most virile actors) have not served Joan Collins well. Yet, though the camera appears to keep a respectful distance and she pouts a little less than of late, she still goes on, a sixty-nine-year-old phenomenon of her trade. The fact that her husbands seem to get younger as she gets older is irrelevant. Good luck to her. In the kingdom of the purblind, the shrewd-eyed superannuated sex-symbol is queen. She and '*Hello!*' magazine are a partnership made in heaven. But then, stories revealing the intimate lives and loves of the famous have obsessed generations since D W Griffith created the very first movie stars, sisters Lillian and Dorothy Gish. Viewing Hollywood now from the perspective of misty nostalgia, it's obvious that I had the best years of its life. When I arrived, Clark Gable was king with the finest set of upper and lower dentures that a grateful MGM could supply. Frank Sinatra had all of his own hair. John Wayne was saluting the American flag in his backyard every morning. Humphrey Bogart held court at Mike Romanoff's restaurant, needling anyone and everyone within earshot. Marilyn Monroe was alive and well and generously distributing her way through a variegated contingent of lovers. Cary Grant was doing press-ups, and a high-pitched Hungarian named Zsa Zsa Gabor was cornering the market in rich, long-suffering husbands, a couple of whom used to meet occasionally to compare eardrums.

Meanwhile, Elizabeth Taylor was beginning her own sumptuous banquet of husbands (twice married to Richard Burton). The whole intoxicating atmosphere was animated by self-indulgence on a scale that had to be seen to be disbelieved. Careers rocketed and plummeted at the speed of light. But with all its dangers – or maybe because of them – Hollywood was the Playground of the Western World. To find oneself, as I did in the 1950s, virtually embalmed in its seductive, subtropical maw was actually no particular hardship. The fact that I was welcomed with almost indecent largesse was not, as the late entertainment czar Lew Grade used to say, 'because of my pretty face'. As a film columnist on the *Daily Mirror*, then the world's biggest-selling daily newspaper (five and a quarter million sales a day) I was, in their eyes at least, a sizeable gift to the Hollywood publicists.

Things are different now, with hard-edged accountants and not profligate producers controlling the budget. But, when the Lion roared at MGM and Harry Cohn bellowed at Columbia and Darryl Zanuck cracked the whip at Twentieth Century-Fox, the red-carpet treatment was the order of the day for what the trade papers called 'visiting firemen'. To arrive at the famous Beverly Hills Hotel from a Britain where food rationing had barely ended was an eye-opener of some magnitude. The decor of my hotel suite – overtones of crushed-pink, palm fronds, bougainvillea and a console of locks on the door – would have satisfied even the most demanding Saudi Arabian sheik. In the bungalows outside, secluded by lush jungle-thick foliage, favoured guests on the level of Howard Hughes entertained selected playmates, or sat in a fug of cigar smoke talking about percentages, residuals and sex. The contrast between the wintry, war-worn Britain I had left and this wall-to-wall opulence in Beverly Hills was exotically highlighted by the gifts on display all around the room. Close inspection of the goodies on offer confirmed that the film studios had been well briefed about my arrival.

'Welcome to Hollywood', said a card from Howard Strickling, the powerful PR chief of Metro-Goldwyn-Mayer together with a bottle of bourbon, a bottle of Scotch, pineapple, grapes and candy. 'Hi!' said Hal from United Artists with champagne and a small bowl of caviar – with a postscript: 'Anything you need, you just call!' 'Welcome!' declared Louie from Universal, with similar 90-proof goodies wrapped in pink bows and Cellophane. A jeroboam of champagne gleamed alongside a message from Republic Studios, which informed me that I had merely to lift a phone and a flattery of fixers would appear like genies to gratify any wish or requirement. The whole suite appeared to be awash with the best liquor from the Scottish highlands to the plains of Kentucky. Some of the secretaries in charge of the arrangements had clearly misread the boss's scribbled instructions. I was addressed as 'Mr Zel', 'Mr Zeek' or 'Mr Lek' but the overall message was unmistakable. Hollywood was at my feet (some of its leading players would later be at my throat, but that entertainment was still to come).

Called everything from 'Tinseltown' to 'The Village of the Goddamned' the Hollywood of that era was resonant with sex, profligate with money and licked its lips over the choicest scandals of the day, or night. The mix of characters on offer on any given day could have come straight from the pages of F Scott Fitzgerald, Raymond Chandler, Damon Runyon or Mario Puzo's *The Godfather*.

As Hollywood's Hall of Infamy has frequently demonstrated, the town's most celebrated filmmakers were scarcely nature's gentlemen. They had no need to be. As colourful as un-hanged highwaymen, they were ruthless, controlled vast sums of money, terrorised their stars, but were capable of squeezing out a crocodile tear now and again if the situation so required. Most spoke in mangled English, cursed inventively in Yiddish, but were the fiercest patriots in town. No one sang 'God Bless America' with more patriotic fervour than Sam

Goldwyn, born Schmuel Gelbfisz in Warsaw, Poland. Likewise, Adolph Zukor from Hungary; Carl Laemmle from Germany; Nicholas and Joseph Schenck; Jack and Harry Cohn from Russia; the Warner brothers, from a place called Krasnashiltz, Poland – all would one day become a fraternity of moguls ruling an empire of unfathomable wealth. Uncouth they may have been, but they compensated with an uncannily shrewd understanding of what the paying public would laugh over, weep at and queue eagerly for around the block. Mixing Slavonic schmaltz into the cornball innocence of straw-chewing America, they distilled the magic of universal dreams.

Short on Ivy League credentials themselves, they bought the talent of others. Their skill lay in hiring the great writers of the day with a fistful of dollars and the firm handshake of the born persuader. These were the founding fathers of motion pictures. The totality of their studio output underpinned all that has lasted in Hollywood. The stars they created still dominate the industry's roll of honour. And if, like those predators the late Harry Cohn and L B Mayer, they chased starlets round their Louis XV desks, only the churlish would have denied them first call on the available merchandise. Admittedly, one or two of them found themselves in dubious company, dazzled and fêted by the sort of gentry who make offers you can't refuse. Some played tennis with the immaculate but infamous gangster Bugsy Seigel. Others threw the dice in exclusive Las Vegas haunts, unaware, or unconcerned, that their charming and attentive host was a past or present racketeer of some renown. The bent-nosed hoodlums whose patois was 'dees, dem and dose' have long disappeared, replaced by Brooks Brothers style and Harvard courtesies. One fine day in New York I lunched at the Oak Room of the Plaza Hotel with an urbane, twinkling philanthropist behind a red carnation who told me everything about himself except one minor detail – his one-time association with the notorious crime syndicate, Murder Incorporated. I ought to have suspected something by the way certain functionaries approached him merely to enquire whether it was OK if they continued to breathe. I returned to my room and consulted a paperback I'd bought about the Mob. This same gentleman occupied a sizeable chunk in the index. (My reluctance to name him is because on balance I preferred my overcoats to be made of cashmere rather than concrete.)

The steamy indiscretions of screen idols have long been the unfailing meal ticket of the media. Columnists and other vagabonds hired to chronicle the behaviour of the exotic inhabitants are never short of material, scandals in particular. In an industry sustained by sin, pith and myth, those determined to scratch beneath the veneer were – still are – scarcely welcome in the village. Naturally, if you fell on your knees adopting an attitude of prayerful adoration, all doors were open to you. But the largesse came at a price. The unspoken caveat is carved in stone: there is no such thing as a free lunch. But, for those who 'go with the flow', there is no joyride like the Hollywood experience. A friend of mine arriving in his hotel suite in Beverly Hills one night found one such companion waiting for him with nothing on except the greeting HAPPY BIRTHDAY neatly deployed across her buttocks and WELCOME emblazoned over the corresponding area in front. The enterprising press agent who had discovered the fact of my friend's birthday has since parlayed his talents into politics. The switch involved no noticeable change in working practices. The other problem newcomers encountered – and still do – was actually finding the Hollywood as perceived by the outside world. They arrive, look around, and are instantly disappointed. Thronging along boulevards called Wilshire, Sunset or Santa Monica, they look in vain for passing celebrities. Not an Eastwood, Streisand, Schwarzenegger, Pfeiffer, Cruise or Madonna in sight. Street-corner hustlers sucker them into buying 'Maps of Film Star Homes', which they hope, naïvely, will point out the homes of living screen legends. They stream up Coldwater Canyon, along Mullholland Drive or on the beach at Malibu, hovering outside electrified gates hoping to glimpse a movie star in residence (or *in flagrante*). But more likely than not the door is opened by a startled Japanese transvestite or a spaced-out male model who is caretaking for the absent owner. Worse, they may be seen off by a Doberman pinscher with a diamante collar and a hundred-dollar pedicure programmed to kill with the first bite.

The fact is, Hollywood is only a place in the sense that it has a zip code, a traffic problem, and borders on Beverly Hills to the west,

San Fernando to the north, or sprawls south into the giant cauldron of Los Angeles. You will scarcely know you are in Hollywood unless you spot the sign or those familiar landmarks like Mann's Chinese Theater or the Brown Derby. Otherwise its drive-ins, diners, the Chinese laundries and strip joints are no different from those in Culver City, or the rest of LA's vast urban anonymity. But the Hollywood that has long tantalised the world, enriched many, destroyed some, exists largely in its manufactured celebrities and the totality of its myths.

Unarguably, Hollywood deserves its reputation as the undisputed film capital of the world. It is to films what Detroit is to automobiles. No other place can match it for the sustained quality of its product or for the genius of its filmmakers. But it is equally fabled for its unashamedly self-gratifying lifestyle. Everything about the place underscores the gibe, 'Nothing succeeds like excess.' As Sinatra sang, 'All or nothing at all'. The general assumption of the inmates is that everyone is in it for the power, the fame and the money.

And more money: breakfast at the princely Beverly Wilshire Hotel seemed to this observer to be mainly for dealing, not eating. Almost everyone collected a copy of the *Hollywood Reporter*, *Daily Variety* or both, and scanned the gossip before the menu. Those whose careers might be in the balance pored over the pages with a mixture of hope and dread. The Gideon Bible may have been in their hotel suite. But it is the 'trades' that they were fervently hoping would answer their prayers.

That morning the conversation was loud on residuals, buy-backs, percentages, or the latest boardroom mêlée at MGM. Since time is money, strangers become first-name friends in seconds linked by the soft intimacy of mutual avarice. They may also become partners within minutes, litigants within days, and enemies for the rest of their lives. By the third cup of 'decaff', film deals have been clinched, 'front money' finalised, a star born, or a reputation demolished. And all the while they're taking phone calls, popping vitamins and looking around to see who is looking at them. 'Who's that guy in the far corner? He looks familiar?' I asked my waitress. 'No idea,' she said. 'He wondered if I knew who you were.'

Across the street from the hotel, Hollywood becomes almost a parody of itself. Rodeo Drive, the richest thoroughfare on earth, displays the diamonds, the furs, the cashmere suits and the custom-made shoes of the most famous houses in Europe. But its patrons mooch around like Skid Row vagrants. The vogue then and now is 'scuffed chic'. The bearded young executive in the torn jeans, wide-open shirt and dirty trainers is probably a multimillionaire and part-owns a studio. Since 75 per cent of the town's acting talent is likely to be out of work 95 per cent of the time, no one dare lose an opportunity to make a pitch any time any place. The cop giving you a ticket for a traffic violation is just as likely to slip you his CV and the number of his answering service. If the face of the attendant at the car wash seems familiar, don't ask him, 'Haven't I seen you somewhere?' He'll drop the squeegee in your lap and cite walk-ons in *NYPD Blue* or the day he doubled for Eastwood. You brush him off at your peril. Come Thanksgiving or the next studio shake-out, he'll be running the store and he'll be asking *you*, 'Haven't I seen you some place?'

If the film city's prevailing mood is of uncertainty, an uncomfortable feeling that scene shifters are on their way to dismantle the place, remember that this is Hollywood. Security and contentment were never an option. As with its favourite desert playgound, Las Vegas, all the gambling clichés apply. The movie business is where producers 'press hunches', 'stake their shirts', 'go for broke', while only taking a short lease on that hacienda on Coldwater Canyon. With luck your picture will go into profit, you'll get your name in the 'trades', agents will chase you, and maître d's will clasp you warmly by the dollar. Fail, and rivals will avert their gaze and avoid a handshake for fear that failure is contagious.

This chronic sense of impermanence was long ago envisaged by one of Hollywood's favourite sons, David O Selznick (1902–65). The man who made classics like *A Star Is Born* and *Gone With the Wind* might have been expected to regard Hollywood as secure as Fort Knox. Instead he famously complained to the writer Ben Hecht, 'Hollywood is like Egypt, full of crumbling pyramids. It'll just keep crumbling until the wind blows the last studio prop across the sands.'

Wrong, of course. With a world hooked on the ecstasy pill of illusion, this place can never go out of business. There will merely be a faster turnaround of characters running the store. Mighty Japanese conglomerates, generating the energy to frighten the natives, have taken control of famous studios, their inscrutable gaze fixed on the easy billions to be made from digital TV and DVD.

Wealthy mid-eastern entrepreneurs have bought up some of the richest palaces around, whose outlandish decor sits well with the architectural frivolities of Beverly Hills. You can take your pick of such styles as French Colonial, English Rustic, Canadian Mountain, Louisiana Plantation, Mexican Adobe, Swedish Pine and Disney Chic. High up on Benedict and Coldwater Canyon, homes are built on stilts, apparently defying gravity, engineering logic, and the surly subterranean warnings of the San Andreas Fault. The fact that the Next Big One may send you and your home cartwheeling into the valley is the unwelcome ghost in every household. A glance at the sky-scraping magnificence of Century City, the mansions of Bel Air, let alone the concrete edifices of downtown Los Angeles, inspires chilling thoughts about What Would Happen If ...? It is Hollywood and beachside Malibu's misfortune to have been built over California's notorious earthquake fault line. No respecter of property or persons (least of all megastars), it shifts and rumbles, fracturing the designer stucco and Italian marble, reducing expensive plate glass into shivering fragments. When San Andreas lies dormant, other climatic eccentricities peculiar to the Pacific rattle the blinds and the nerves of the inhabitants. Mudslides, typhoons or 'twisters' have occasionally nudged film-star haciendas into somersaulting down the San Fernando Valley or toppling over onto the Pacific Coast Highway.

In an industry that cherishes its black humour and one-liners, the following earthquake anecdote is a collector's item. It seems that, after one sizaeble tremor, convicts from a nearby prison were shunted in to help sandbag some of the more vulnerable properties. Rapists, arsonists and other well-wishers went swiftly into action shoring up the properties of the wealthy. But the demand for inmates soon exceeded the supply. One distraught resident in platform heels and a classy negligée was seen running around screaming, 'Get me a convict.

Get me a convict!' They got her one too: a handsome charmer by all accounts. (It would have surprised none of the locals if they had subsequently fallen in love, married, and now owned a string of hamburger joints called The Big One.) Of course, eyebrows are rarely raised in a town where – aside of the respected analysts – soothsayers, mystics and all kinds of hocus-pocus merchants make a swift dollar out of the superstitious rich. Where else but in Bel Air would one hear a hostess lament that her Alsatian was suffering from a lack of self-esteem? As stars and company chieftains get ever younger, the corresponding shift of power from the maturely balding to the brash young whiz kids is an entertainment in itself. Once, only adult superstars in the Streisand class could dictate to a studio, reduce its bosses to stammering surrender. Now the child stars of record-breaking 'soaps' throw tantrums, fire their agents, and 'kick ass' in chortling imitation of their elders. They discuss scripts and talk percentages over chocolate malteds. They even have their own Therapy Group. Those old enough to own a driving licence arrive for their sessions in Ferraris, Porsches or BMW convertibles. Barely out of short pants, they wonder what went wrong with their lives. Asked on TV to explain his motivations and ambitions, one pint-sized interviewee responded gleefully, 'Money ...money ... moneeee...!' Behind exploding pink bubble-gum they complain that the industry isn't what it was. Armed security guards escort them everywhere. Closed-circuit cameras maintain an unblinking vigil over their beds at night. Almost everyone, especially those attending the exclusive schools in Beverly Hills, either carries a gun or knows where one is handy. It is all symptomatic of a place whose creators never believed was built to last.

Its history has never ceased to fascinate historians. The early film prospectors who were sent out from New York to scout a place to make movies went first to Arizona. They were disappointed. In December 1913, a very young Cecil De Mille – the middle B came with fame – wired the New York office of the Jesse L Lasky Feature Play company: 'Flagstaff no good for our purpose. Have proceeded to California. Want authority to rent barn in place called Hollywood for $75 a month. Regards to Sam.'

Sam, of course, was the former glove salesman born Schmuel Gelbfisz in Poland. He restyled himself as 'Goldfish', then 'Goldwyn' on becoming a producer of considerable self-esteem. And rightly so. At sixteen – the year was 1895 – he trudged hundreds of miles due west from his Polish ghetto to the Oder river. What little cash he had was spent on getting him smuggled out of his Russian-controlled homeland into Germany. He trudged another couple of hundred miles alone to Hamburg. Broke and hungry, he stood around the dockside toying with the notion of stowing away on anything sailing west. Learning glove making from a family contact named Liebglid, he finally raised the eighteen shillings for a ticket on the boat train to London. Penniless, his only other language Yiddish, he found himself way back at the end of a queue of thousands of other refugees from Russia and Poland. For three nights he slept rough in Hyde Park, existing on scraps and stolen food. How he managed to raise the paltry cash to travel steerage to America is difficult to answer, since Goldwyn rewrote the scenario over the years. But he had achieved the immigrant dream. In the US he swept floors and emptied garbage, before joining forces with a vaudeville hoofer named Jesse Lasky and the unknown De Mille, to make silent movies. The barn De Mille had his eye on was an old shack at a place called Vine Street. Good enough, he decided, for a workable film studio. But the far greater attraction was the breathtaking panorama outside the barn. Tall palm trees and desert cactus were set aglow by the blazing sun beyond the white-capped San Gabriel Mountains. The Pacific to the west, the towering granite of the Sierra Nevada to the east – to the awe-struck De Mille, this was God's gift to a hand-cranked camera.

So this was the 'place called Hollywood'. The woman who so named it was Daeida, the cultivated wife of a real-estate millionaire, Horace Henderson Wilcox, 'Hollywood' being the name of her country house back east. Wilcox had made a property fortune in Kansas. Arriving in California in 1885, he looked out across the barley fields and orange groves, the tall eucalyptus trees and the lofty cedars, and visualised a land for decent, pure-minded God-fearing people. To attract settlers of that calibre he offered plots of land gratis to anyone who would build churches on them. Saloons were banned. No one was allowed alcohol, to play pool or to drive sheep or hogs through the streets on Sunday.

Thus Sodom and Gomorrah was still a long way off when two shrewd entrepreneurs moved in – General Moses Hazeltine Sherman, a railway boss, and Harry Chandler, the future publisher of the *Los Angeles Times*. The Hollywood their syndicate bought in 1903 was little more than scrubland. But their lawyers shrewdly sketched out its limits on a map and had the area designated as an independent municipality. A smart move, since it gave the proposed real estate instant legitimacy. There was a run-down overgrown rail track, which they straight-facedly called the Los Angeles–Pacific Railroad. The Sherman and Chandler syndicate then went out on a sales pitch selling building lots at bargain prices. To twist prospective purchasers' arms, they put scores of SOLD notices on the plots. This was a piece of harmless chicanery the town would improve upon in the years ahead. De Mille was therefore delighted when Lasky and Sam Goldwyn responded to his telegraphed request with, 'Authorise you to rent barn but on month-to-month basis. Don't make any long-term commitment.'

This was the understandable caution of mid-European refugees who left their shtetls in the old country with just the shirts on their backs and a dream. But even in their most fanciful imaginings they could not have envisaged what that old barn on Vine Street and Selma Avenue would one day become. In vast studios decades later, Cecil B De Mille would saccharinise the Old Testament, cosmeticise the Cross and mesmerise hordes of native Americans into dollar-a-day ignominy as extras. The adroit adventurers who joined him instantly struck gold, and in the process created the Hollywood of popular myth. It would one day attract and nurture the best writers, directors, actors and musicians from a Europe devastated by war. And because the rewards on offer would make sheiks blush, it would also dangle a lifestyle to kill for. It would attract countless ingenuous wannabes who regarded a million-to-one shot as pretty good odds, considering. And, if few advanced further than the casting couch, many succeeded via that route with no noticeable dent in their self-esteem. Deluded by the promise of swift and easy money, hustlers and rogues would move in, investing their last dollars on cashmere suits, loitering with intent around the famed watering holes of Beverly Hills. They looked around at producers who had made it, convincing themselves they could just as easily do the same. Bereft of anything resembling talent, taste, ideas or hard cash, they still thought they could work the system.

The joke is, some did. In the Dream Factory, 'chutzpah', a Yiddish gem of a word roughly defined as 'shameless audacity', is often as crucial to a film deal as 'development capital' from the Bank of America. If you could not act, write, direct or raise 'serious money' chutzpah might still get you up if not running. To paraphrase George Bernard Shaw, 'Those who can, do; those who can't, produce.' But 'shameless audacity' has a limited shelf life. Eventually, parasites have no place to feed except off other parasites. Fortunately, for them, Hollywood is so rich in its creative talent it can accommodate its charlatans as a lion does its fleas. The Lion that once roared for Metro-Goldwyn-Mayer celebrated the greatest concentration of acting talent in the world. The studio claimed with tolerable hyperbole to have 'more stars than there are in heaven': Jean Harlow, Clark Gable, Greer Garson, Judy Garland, Fred Astaire, Ginger Rogers. The Lion was entitled to roar at the stars it created and the classics it produced: *Ben-Hur*, *The Wizard of Oz*, *Gone With the Wind*, *Ninotchka*, *Singin' In the Rain* – their combined audience is measured in billions. Fortunately, Louis B Mayer, the scrap dealer turned dream merchant, did not live to witness the grievous bodily harm inflicted on his legendary creation.

The rise and fall of United Artists, no less a studio giant, became umbilically linked to the fate of Metro. Its earliest pioneers were not exactly First Family paragons. But they look positively angelic when compared with some of the current spin doctors in the trade. On 5 February 1919 Charlie Chaplin, Mary Pickford, Douglas Fairbanks Sr and D W Griffith formed United Artists. The aim was to create a company that would give 'independent producers greater artistic freedom and flexibility'. And give themselves a greater share of the loot. It was a good idea doomed to strike a reef due to the flawed characters of the participants. Temperament, distrust and ego-jousting dogged the partnership from the start. No ship could sail safely with such loose cannons aboard. Charlie Chaplin, behind his lovable little tramp image, was a calculating loner with a predilection for wealth and the company of young girls. Mary Pickford, 'the world's sweetheart', was indecently rich and a tetchily unsociable drinker. D W Griffith, who had brought Pickford into films, matched her with his bourbon intake but was bad at handling money. Meanwhile, Fairbanks, who saw himself as an American aristocrat, detested Chaplin's radical politics.

Five years after the company was founded, Griffith was broke and gone. Joe Schenck, the former fairground showman, was brought in as chairman. He had come from the Loewe Corporation, where his brother Nick was company secretary. Others came in as white knights, but profits plummeted. The *coup de grâce* was delivered by the son of a rabbi named Asa Yoelson. Better known as Al Jolson, he brought talking pictures to the screen; their prime victims Chaplin, Fairbanks and Mary Pickford, were shell-shocked.

The company was virtually dying when the immigrant who had slept rough in London's Hyde Park moved in. Sam Goldwyn breathed life into the failing enterprise. The company revived. Its picture releases included the films of Howard Hughes, David O Selznick, Walter Wanger, Hal Roach and Alexander Korda. With a new genius at the helm, a financial guru of some taste named Arthur Krim, the company flourished: *Twelve Angry Men*, *Some Like it Hot*, *Around the World in Eighty Days*, *Network*, *Tom Jones*, *One Flew Over the Cuckoo's Nest* and, to phenomenal grosses, the James Bond films. United Artists, together with MGM, Twentieth Century-Fox, Paramount and Columbia, gave Hollywood the best years of its life. And the lifestyle that came with the package, in the words of America's most influential columnist Walter Winchell, 'had to be seen to be disbelieved'.

With television a mere upstart at the time, almost every motion picture made money. A favourite maxim at the time asserted, 'You'll never lose money underestimating the intelligence of the audience.' Film production was a licence to print money, the cameras whirring incessantly at Universal City, at Warner's, Disney, Fox, Republic, Paramount, Columbia and at the Goldwyn lot on Gower Street. Nowhere else on the planet were fortunes made so easily or squandered so lavishly. Hollywood, or more specifically its exotic dormitory Beverly Hills, evolved as a sensualist's paradise. Once within its confines you had nothing to lose but your inhibitions. Its very architecture was styled to reflect the seductive mood. The pink-splashed façade of the Beverly Hills Hotel, the Babylonian promise of the Garden of Allah, the chic sophistication of the Château Marmont – many of Hollywood's most intimate secrets were hatched within those walls. The secrets spawned into gossip on which Hollywood and the global media have mutually, and mightily, prospered.

With the blandishments and the financial packages on offer, few could resist the temptation. Even New York's celebrated literati eventually succumbed. S J Perelman, F Scott Fitzgerald, Raymond Chandler, Lilian Helman and others discovered that their cultural integrity was in no way compromised by being treated like visiting sultans. They just took the money and carped, salving their consciences with brittle put-downs of the Hollywood of their times:

- 'A flock of beetle-brained windsuckers with necks hinged so they can say yes to Darryl Zanuck' (S J Perelman)
- 'All the personality of a paper cup' (Raymond Chandler)
- 'Strip the phoney tinsel off Hollywood and you'll find the real tinsel underneath' (Oscar Levant)

But most of these same critics couldn't wait to exchange their New York pallor for California tans They relished their stretched limos, the lavish wining and dining and the more tactile delights that come with celebrity. Yet they were quick to distance themselves from the natives, biting hard on the hand that fed them. It's an old habit that hasn't changed. Hollywood should worry! In those ecstatic years, the Dream Factory and 'more stars than there are in heaven' were having a ball. Personally, I couldn't wait to catch the flavour of it.

CHAPTER ONE

Fiddling in the 'Street'

Hollywood may be an acquired taste. It's curious, though, how easily one can acquire it. The atmosphere of unabated luxury drenched in sun and sensuality seduces the senses the moment you touch down in LA. To your average uptight Englishman just in from the cold, the palms, pools and pulchritude combine to induce a languid sense of disbelief. Well so it was for this Englishman at any rate when first he fetched up in the City of the Angels. And later, when, for example, I found myself in the company of Humphrey Bogart on his yacht *Santana*, the thought inevitably struck me, 'How come this is happening to me?' Certainly there was nothing in my genes or genealogy that remotely presaged this kind of scenario. On the contrary. Any reasonably competent crystal gazer confronting the humble evidence would have yawned me out of the room.

I was born at number four George Street, London NW1. The house no longer exists, eliminated by the underpass that now links the Marylebone and Euston roads. Renamed Gower Street, it had a pub at one end called the Orange Tree. On Saturday nights the drunken clientele would emerge into the night singing with raucous nostalgia the music hall standards of the day. The star soprano of the saloon bar was a Mrs Coatier, who lived alone in the basement below us. She doubled (when sober) as a Pearly Queen, and her tormented recitals would drown the heavy rumble of the Circle Line trains, which rattled beneath the nearby Euston Square station. Occasionally there would be a crash of broken glass and foul language as she tried – and failed

– to unlock the door without spilling the jug of beer she hoped would see her through the night. Close by was an estate office whose name, Rutley, Vine and Gurney, was straight out of the pages of Dickens. As a child I sometimes delivered the rent, thirteen shillings and sixpence a week. Clerks dressed like pallbearers scratched away at massive ledgers. Sometimes when the rent was a mite overdue, I'd get the wagging-finger admonition – then a barley sugar to show there was no ill feeling.

My parents arrived from Russia on a cargo boat at Tilbury Dock before World War One. Two of my father's brothers were also aboard. A third, gambling on a better life in the United States, went westwards and we never heard from him again. His immediate descendant spoke like a revivalist preacher and made the best false teeth in Virginia. (He once introduced me to a naval attaché in Norfolk as a 'partial upper and full lower'.) All his nonpaying relatives wore his dentures with pride. He tried to coax my father to join him in the States. But one immigrant experience was enough for brother Simon. Justly self-styled as a master tailor, Dad had the piercing eyes, waxed moustaches and prodding finger of the archetypal despot. Oversexed, not overly cautious and over here, he sired children at an alarming rate. Well, it alarmed my mother. She regretted, privately, that her prolific husband's religious scruples had given him such an aversion to birth control. She lay back and thought of Russia.

My father was fiercely patriotic for his adopted land. He made the red, white and blue rosettes we wore to school on Empire Day. He was the first to stand whenever the national anthem was played. At thirteen, my sister Edith won a competition with a stirring essay entitled 'This Sceptred Isle'. She was presented with a velvet-covered box of chocolates by one of the great admirals of World War One, Viscount Jellicoe of Scapa. Viewing the presentation, my mother dabbed her eyes. My father stood twirling his moustaches and beaming a smile around the hall like Eddystone Lighthouse. On Sabbath days, he rose early and dressed fastidiously. El Cordobes donning the 'Suit of Lights' was nothing compared with my father's preparation for the solemnities of the day. First the white shirt with the formal tie and stiff collar. Then the pinstriped trousers and highly polished shoes. The mustard-yellow check waistcoat in place, watch chains dangling, my mother helped him into the black jacket that had been lovingly brushed like the Derby favourite. He then synchronised his heavy gold pocket watch with the grandfather clock bought at the price of a thousand or so Kensitas cigarette coupons and a dry cough. Finally, removing the tissue paper, he took out the black homburg and, facing the mirror, lowered it majestically on his head. The coronation was complete. He then went out to pray, walking the mandatory three paces ahead of my mother as befitted the head of the house and sole provider. With his high cheekbones, moustaches and piercing anthracite eyes he resembled Toscanini striding out towards the 'Met'. Behind him, my mother tittered geisha-like at the fine display. Charity being an immigrant imperative, my father broke Sabbath rules and carried loose change for any beggars encountered en route. Barrel organists, match pedlars and disabled veterans of the war touched their caps and said 'Thanks, guv' as the coins rattled into tin cups.

George Street was close enough to Bloomsbury to have ambitions. But it was closer still to Drummond Street market to know its place. Fortunately, all the requirements of the decidedly hard-up were close at hand: the public baths, the 'flea pit' cinema and particularly the Temperance Hospital, which was constantly overrun by those familiar epidemics of the working classes – scarlet fever and diphtheria. In the 1920s there were still visible reminders of World War One. The woman in the flat above ours had lost her husband at the Somme. She was rarely seen by her neighbours. But the soldier's Lee-Enfield rifle, bayonet fixed, leaned permanently against the landing wall. We were warned that we touched it at our peril.

George Street had its fair intake of immigrants, who slotted inoffensively into the social landscape. There were too few refugees at the time to attract the degree of prejudice that would bedevil the future. The bulk of them came to Britain in the first decade of the 1900s, mostly via Tilbury Docks. They ended up in the tenement buildings around Aldgate, Whitechapel and along the Mile End Road, or in the poorer quarters of Manchester or Leeds. Like their counterparts in the Bronx and Brooklyn, they laboured hard to send their sons and daughters to college. Survival was the universal imperative. The overwhelming ambition of all these refugees was that their sons and daughters should strive for a better life. Education was the key, university the ultimate prize. Competition was fierce. Denied access to the professions in their ghettos of Russia, Lithuania and Poland, the immigrants turned to the fret saw and the needle and thread for their livelihood. Thus cabinet making and fine tailoring were the two main skills that kept the East End workshops humming through the night. The tailors sold their beautifully finished garments to companies with showrooms in upmarket W1. My father, who proudly had the logo MASTER TAILOR embossed on a ground-floor window, produced ladies' suits and coats that were masterpieces worn by the titled hostesses of Mayfair and Belgravia. His workroom was over my bedroom. The assorted noises from above kept me awake into the small hours. I could identify the various stages in the making of a garment by the sounds of the implements. Long into the night I could hear the rhythmic scissoring of the cloth; the hiss of steam as the heavy-duty iron was cooled; the thud as it came down on the cloth; the steady pedalling of the Singer sewing machine; and the squeak of the tailor's dummy as it was manoeuvred on its stand. If I slept right through the night undisturbed, this indicated that orders were scarce, at which times my father took less trouble over his moustache ends. His helpers in the workroom were mostly hard-up relatives who sat cross-legged on tables stitching seams and humming Bing Crosby standards or Klezmer tunes from the schtetl. They paused occasionally for mugs of strong sweet tea and the odd drag on a scented Abdullah cigarette. The butts were trodden on, but I could still recycle them secretly at dawn for an ecstatically guilty smoke.

There seemed to be an intuitive reluctance among these Russian or Polish immigrants to talk about their former lives in their home countries. We assumed, correctly, that the experience was too painful for our parents to recall. They evaded all questions about their Russian past. That aspect of their lives had long been cauterised. But over the years we intuitively learned about the Cossacks rampaging through the villages; the rapes, pillaging and other diversions that were a regular feature of the ghetto experience. It was trauma enough being uprooted from their home; travelling by cart or freezing trains to the port of Odessa; sailing steerage into the unknown; summarily decanted into a strange and largely unfriendly environment. My parents saw no reason to share the nightmare with their children. But old fears surfaced with the rise of Nazism in Germany and its ugly offshoot in Britain led by Sir Oswald Mosley and his black-shirted British Union of Fascists. We had now moved within earshot of the riots, the police charges, and the counterattacks that hallmarked Mosley's appearance on the streets. My mother and father exchanged the pained unspoken reactions of those who had seen it all before.

In school holidays I was allowed to help the local greengrocer deliver fruit and vegetables along the street. The cart was pulled by an uncomplaining street-smart horse whose ability to defecate while at a fair canter seemed a minor miracle to me at the time. I got an extra ha'penny for jumping down and shovelling the manure into a bag. This was sold on to a policeman in Drummond Street, who grew tomatoes in his backyard. (Years later, in Hollywood, I told that great actor Lee Marvin that as a child I once shovelled horseshit. 'They've been doing that here for years!' said he.)

In one short-lived period of prosperity we seemed to have acquired a handyman-cum-butler by the name of Ernie. I believe he was a World War One veteran my mother took pity on. He was a stocky ex-bombardier down on his luck, and my father liked him. Mother reserved judgement. His duties ended abruptly one spring morning when he was discovered helping himself to my father's whisky. My mother ordered him out into the yard to announce his dismissal. Captain Dreyfus's public humiliation in front of the French military – the ripped-off epaulettes, broken sword and all – was nothing compared with my mother's dispatch of the shame-faced Ernie. He stood rigid. She full-faced him. She told him he was sacked and then ordered him to remove the black jacket (courtesy Uncle No. 1), the waistcoat (courtesy Uncle No. 2) and then the bowler hat (courtesy my grandfather, deceased). My sisters and I watched Ernie's disgrace in awe. An accompanying drum roll would have completed the drama. A week later he was back at work. The cast-off ensemble didn't fit anybody else.

Preparation for the Sabbath was a minor ecstasy involving all the senses. The smell of frying oil, metal polish and freshly baked bread merged with the devotional awe that preceded the lighting of the candles and the filling of the silver wine cup, a gift to my father from some obscure Freemasons' lodge. A stiff white lace cloth was spread diagonally over the mandatory tasselled velvet table covering. The two silver candlesticks, smuggled with other heirlooms from the Ukraine, gleamed in the candlelight. On a Friday evening, an hour before my father ushered the Sabbath in with a prayer, my mother would exchange an apron for the customary black dress on which she pinned her sole item of jewellery (artificial), shaped like a butterfly.

On the morning of one such Friday she went into shock. My sister Mary, then twelve, had gone to a circus with her friend Winnie Twitchin. Same age, but Christian. Drawn into one of the sideshows, the two inseparables had somehow managed to win a prize, which turned out to be a live piglet. Flushed with understandable excitement, they rushed to display the piglet to their nearest and dearest. Geographically, this put my mother first in line. Those with an understanding of Jewish customs and all things kosher will know that to bring a pig within touching distance of a Jewish home – and on the Sabbath, no less – puts Armageddon in the shade. But Winnie, Mary and the piglet were naturally oblivious to such considerations. Mary swung the cast-iron knocker on the side door, eyes shining, pig squealing. My mother stood there wiping her hands. 'Look what we won!' they trilled. Mother recoiled from the pig like a rabbit from a snake. Guilt, fear and nausea made her weak at the knees. But good nature plus an echo of some Biblical imperative about the stranger at the gates demanded a measured response. 'Oh what a lovely pig!' my mother lied with an ashen smile. This response was misread by Winnie Twitchin. She experienced a burst of Christian generosity. 'You can have it if you like.' 'Oh, no!' Mother choked, backing away from the prize piglet. 'You give it to your mother, she'll be so happy. She'll be so proud of you.' She shut the door and sank to her knees with a violent shudder. 'Who was that at the door?' enquired my father. 'The insurance collector,' finessed Mother. It was a minor deceit. She knew that to tell him that a pig was on the porch on the Sabbath was to court disaster. The pig was taken squealing to its rightful destiny.

I grew up believing, absurdly, that I could become a professional violinist. The seeds of that idea had entered the bloodstream courtesy of my Ukrainian ancestors, whose idols were Stokowski, Caruso, Chaliapin and the greatest fiddler ever, Jascha Heifetz. My mother, born Leah Oistrakh, claimed kinship with the great David of that name. I instinctively empathised with performers – actors, singers and musicians, fiddle players in particular. Not the stern stuff of Bach and Mr Kreutzer. More the musical saccharin played at seaside hotels to frail and decidedly hard-up gentlefolk. The Lyons' Corner House at the south end of London's Tottenham Court Road offered the best grub-and-culture deal in town: spaghetti Bolognese served on gingham-draped tables with a Hungarian Gypsy band playing the schmaltzy standards of the day. Sandor Horvath was the leader. He tore into Monti's 'Czardas', then played the Russian 'Otchi Tchornia' (Black Eyes) with a vibrato to break your heart. To top that act the cellist doubled on a musical saw, with 'The Swan' by Saint-Saëns. In 'palm courts' along countless seafronts, the violinist in white tie and frayed bobtails sawed at 'trees', accompanied most often by a Joyce Grenfell lookalike straddling a cello.

My first fiddle was bought in a Soho pawnshop. I spotted it in the window suspended on a piece of string among antique bed warmers and glass-eyed stags' heads. Apparently ancient, the belly dusted with old resin, it was marked by me as the Stradivarius the world had somehow overlooked. I was twelve years old at the time. The salesman hooked it down. I peered inside the 'S' slots and froze. It was just possible to discern the faint logo, 'Antonius Stradivarius, faciebat anno 1721'. My ears hammered with excitement. 'How much?' I asked in the casual tone of the born hustler.

'Twenty-five shillings} (£1.25 pence today).

I counted out the hoarded pocket money, trying to keep the William-like smirk off my face. My feet barely touched the ground as

I raced to J and A Beare, the celebrated dealers in Soho. I slid the masterpiece over the counter.

'Can you tell me what this is worth?'

'Certainly.'

The expert gave the fiddle a five-second appraisal and smiled.

'How much did you pay for this?'

'Twenty-five shillings.'

'Worth it,' he said.

As a schoolboy I joined hundreds of other young fiddlers in a concert at London's historic Crystal Palace. It burned down soon after. A bit of an overreaction, it seemed to me. I soon learned that it takes more than a bleeding heart to master the fiddle. Moreover, there were far too many musicians chasing too few jobs at the time. Archer Street was to musicians what Warren Street was to car salesmen. You mingled on the pavement with other pale-faced contenders like the stevedores in *On the Waterfront*. I landed a few weddings and the like, but the going was rough. For my last gig I soloed 'Goodnight Sweetheart' at a half-empty dance hall in Ipswich. The lights fused midway through the number, followed by an explosion, then total darkness. There was mild panic as the dancers stampeded to the exits. Unapplauded and unpaid, I took the train home and tucked the fake Stradivarius away for good, 'Goodnight Sweetheart' having a special resonance at the time.

Deprived of one audience, I tried another. A brief triumph in the role of Cardinal Wolsey in an amateur showing of *Henry VIII* produced a rave notice by W A Darlington ('remarkable young actor...') in the *Daily Telegraph* and loud applause from all my relatives in the stalls at London's Sadler's Wells. The performance owed plenty to the director, whose gestures and inflections I had imitated to the last gulp. A teenage patriarch in ecclesiastical scarlet, I overplayed outrageously Wolsey's angst and disillusion, sobbing audibly on the agonised 'Had I but served my God with half the zeal I served my king...!' The curtains closed on my exit, and, as it turned out, on my acting ambitions. All attempts to repeat the triumph with other roles failed on the grounds that they all bore an uncanny resemblance to Cardinal Wolsey.

Two muses down, and out. A job as a negotiator with a dubious estate agency was similarly abortive. Issued with a bowler hat, umbrella and, oddly, a Raleigh drop-handled racing bike, I prospected London in the style of a real-estate salesman. At one house in Tottenham I tried to impress the owner and a prospective customer, with my knowledge of building construction. 'Sound as a bell,' I said, prodding the ceiling with the umbrella, and puncturing it. Plaster showered down on to a rosewood table and the ceiling light exploded. The owner, who had 'Ypres' tattooed on his arm and plaster on his head, propelled me towards the door. En route to the street I contrived a smile, assuring my client of my best endeavours at all times. The bowler hat and umbrella flew after me. I cycled home and reviewed the situation. With Archer Street and Shaftsbury Avenue no longer in the frame, Fleet Street entered into the reckoning.

Journalism may not have much in common with the 'Oldest Profession' except that enthusiastic amateurs have always been warmly welcomed by both vocations. A quick survey of our trade's most famous names demonstrates that there are no fixed rules on how to enter the fray. Some slogged it out in the parochial hinterland of provincial newspapers. Others, knowing somebody who knew somebody else, perhaps 'Bubbles' Rothermere or the late Lord Beaverbrook's colonic irrigator, might have been nodded in onto the ground floor.

In those days, the 'Street' housed most of the great national newspapers. Not any more. That Fleet Street is dead, its ashes scattered over Wapping, the face-lifted dockside pioneered by Rupert Murdoch. Now it is just another London thoroughfare descending from the Strand down to Ludgate Circus and the river. The nearest I had come to the printed word at the time was selling advertising space for *The Floor Coverings Review*, a pulse-quickener if ever there was one. My first and only contact, a linoleum company, having laughed me off the premises, I threw the sales literature into the nearest dustbin, phoned my resignation from a call box in Hatton Garden, and headed for the 'Street of Adventure'.

The shortest route, via Shoe Lane, EC4, proved to be the most fortuitous. It housed the London *Evening Standard*, which together with the *Daily Express* was the pride and joy of their buccaneering owner, Lord Beaverbrook. Newspaper buildings have a resonance all of their own. The subterranean roar of the monster print machines; the vans fanning out all over London with the early editions – it was heady stuff to an ambitious byline seeker. Architecturally cheerless, well distanced from its more powerful sibling in Fleet Street, the *Standard* was the most influential London evening paper of the 1930s. The received wisdom in those days was that a stint on a provincial newspaper was an essential baptism for Fleet Street. The great preponderance at the time of Welsh editors, Mancunian subeditors – or 'subs' – and brittle editorial executives with Tyneside accents underscored it. The alternative was to aim at the lowest rung of the ladder and hope that by guile and a touch of chutzpah one could short-circuit the system. I chose that route and landed a job with no recognisable status except mandatory membership of NATSOPA, the former National Society of Operative Printers and Assistants. The office branches were called 'chapels' which I innocently assumed implied some quasi-religious connotation: a direct line to the Almighty in the event of a dispute. I expected the FOC (father of the chapel) to look like Moses and speak like Solomon. That stained-glass reverence disintegrated when I arrived one morning to find the entire staff out in the street on a lightning strike. Still new to the game, I attempted to enter the building.

'Where're you going?' enquired an official.

'To work,' I said.

'Oh no you're not!'

'Who says I'm not?'

'The F-O-fucking-C, that's who!' he said.

The brief impasse was interrupted by the arrival of a shortish Edward G Robinson lookalike with intimidating eyebrows and what biographers called an 'impish' smile. A Canadian multimillionaire, Lord Beaverbrook was not grinning that day. Recognising him, the strikers respectfully drew back, allowing him to pass through to the front door. An unashamed propagandist, who used his newspapers to bludgeon those he disliked, he was in no mood to lose a day's publication. 'What do they want?' I heard him ask a subordinate.

'More money' was the answer. 'Give it to 'em' was the order (a surrender that years later pundits would cite to support their predictions on the death of Fleet Street).

The excitement generated in a newsroom at full pelt is a particular rapture. In the dinosaur days of hot-metal typesetting, subeditors scribbled with thick black pencils on dull grey copy paper. They shouted 'Boy!' to the messenger concerned who was often twice as old as they were. As deadline time approached, the tension and momentum increased. There were plenty of splash headlines to be written at the time: the rise of Hitler, the abdication of Edward VIII, Munich, the Spanish Civil War ... Journalists worked with a passion reinforced by what seemed to be the greatest concentration of pubs in a single street. I attended more funerals for prematurely deceased colleagues than I care to recall. The alcoholic intake of some of them is still talked about in their favourite hostelries. (The expected life span of journalists was once announced by the actuarial profession to be $52\frac{1}{2}$, which caused a split-second run on tomato juice.)

Since I looked as though I could be trusted to run a serious errand, I was given the job of collecting the day's political cartoon from David Low – the greatest political cartoonist of his day. Creator of the legendary Colonel Blimp, Low was admired, respected and feared not least by whoever was at Number 10 Downing Street at the time. He was a marvellous draughtsman, achieving devastating effect with immense economy of line. He savaged Mussolini, ridiculed Hitler in the most relentless series of cartoons of the 1930s. (He was on Hitler's short list of those to be 'dealt with' once Storm Troopers were marching down Whitehall. My late brother, Philip Zec, wartime cartoonist of the *Daily Mirror*, was added to that list in the early forties.) Few premiers, union bosses or other public figures escaped Low's genial mischief. His ability to raise hackles in high places particularly delighted him. It showed in the roguish grin on that pink and cherubic face with the little goatee beard. Nothing amused him more, as I recall, than some of his own cartoons. On arrival at his first-floor studio in Hampstead, I was directed to sit stage left while he put the finishing touches to the day's masterpiece. I was instructed not to move, cough, burp or otherwise interrupt the genius at the drawing board. He would labour long and silently until he was satisfied. Clearly he found himself hard to please. He would brush or pen a line, scrape a razor-blade over another, finally standing back like a benign mandarin. Once in a while he invited me to view the work. 'What do you think, son?'

'It's good,' I would mumble.

'Good? It's bloody great!' declared the master.

The cartoon frequently shared space with the 'Londoner's Diary', a mischievous platform for political gossip, upper-crust scandal, and His Lordship's vendetta of the week. Its contributors included important political and literary figures like Michael Foot, Malcolm Muggeridge, Howard Spring, Robert Bruce Lockhart and Harold Nicholson. They generally wore horn-rimmed spectacles, hairy tweed jackets and corduroys and called each other 'old boy' a lot. Just to hover in the room where they worked – or plotted – was instructive. I hovered and learned a lot. I graduated from intelligent messenger to editorial dogsbody.

Promotion to the 'racing room' introduced me to the Maharajah of Baroda, who in turn introduced me to his favourite horses. I visited stud farms and reported which stallion had serviced the most mares; in the process I learned more about sex than anything my prolific father was prepared to impart.

European Fascism polarised political attitudes. I read every paper I could lay my hands on and joined the Left Book Club (Gollancz; half a crown a time) and talked exhilarating nonsense with other aficionados late into the night. Now and again friends would quietly disappear. We learned eventually that they had joined the International Brigade fighting Franco in the Spanish Civil War. Some never returned home.

I was still not a real reporter. I decided to take a chance elsewhere. The father of the chapel sent me away with the benediction, 'You're bleedin' mad, my son.' It was just a short walk through narrow passageways to Fetter Lane, and the London *Daily Mirror*.

Geraldine House, the *Mirror*'s headquarters, rose in tiers like the decks of a passenger liner – the printing machines in steerage, the bosses in the staterooms above. By the time I joined as a reporter in

1938, the paper had given up imitating its racy American counterpart the New York *Daily News*. But not without some reluctance. War was little more than a year away, but the headlines of those days scarcely reflected the fact.

> EX-TYPIST CRUSHED ME LIKE A WORM ... KING'S COUNSELLOR
>
> 6FT 4IN WIFE BOUNCED 3FT 11IN MIDGET ON HER KNEE TOO OFTEN...
>
> STARS WEEP AS $60 A DAY CHIMPANZEE IS BURIED IN SATIN COFFIN
>
> GIRL IN DUSTBIN – THEORY OF BLOODLUST
>
> PUPIL, 22, WEDS HER TUTOR, 83

Thus in the lively prose of popular journalism, the dramas of everyday life were recorded. Like this straight-faced collectors' item:

> Sleeping on a sofa over which there was a large mirror, Mrs. Fanny Peacey, eighty-nine, of Worthing, dreamed that it [the mirror] was falling on her. The nightmare woke her up. She jumped up from the sofa in a daze, lost her footing, fell over a fender and never recovered. The story of Mrs. Peacey's dream was told at the inquest yesterday.

The front page may have railed against the growing threat of Nazi Germany. The day's opinion column may have scorned the appeasement policy of the Chamberlain government. But it was the bouncing midget and the chimp lying in state that gripped readers most as they rode their buses, bikes and trains to work. To satisfy the curiosity of its more genteel customers (who claimed they bought the paper only for their servants) a gossip column was introduced. There was this item on a fancy-dress party: 'The best costume of the lot was Mr. Derek Hall-Caines. The two most amusing were Miss Diana Cook's – she was in bicycling bloomers – and Mr. Jack Profumo's, who wore a red nightshirt and carried a candle.' (A more innocent display than the one which would eventually lead to his downfall.)

The paper had come a long way since its immaculate conception in 1903 as the 'first daily newspaper for women'. It was staffed at the time by well-educated ladies head-hunted from the glossy magazines. The influential paragon who created it was Alfred Harmsworth, the first and only Lord Northcliffe. (This solitary status was due to all his children having been born illegitimate. Buttressed by wealth, they found this no handicap whatsoever.) Having already founded the *Daily Mail* and *The Times*, he rejoiced in the title of 'The Napoleon of Fleet Street'. But, initially at least, he was a shade less successful than the little general. The *Daily Mirror* collapsed and showed all signs of expiring. Its circulation plummeted from 265,219 to 24,000 within three months. That hurt his lordship far less than the loss of £100,000 of his own money, an intolerable breach of the Harmsworth tradition.

He decided that the paper's coy, genteel image, aimed at the dewy-eyed clientele of Fortnums and the like, had to go. On 21 May 1910 it created its first journalistic sensation, publishing a photo of the dead King Edward VII lying on his bed at the Palace, eyes shut, hands folded. Public reaction was predictable: shock, horror, outrage and a stampede to buy copies at the newsagents. The coup revealed the public's morbid fascination for celebrated corpses. Marilyn Monroe and Elvis Presley would, years later, command an even more avid audience.

The paper was now in the less fastidious hands of Northcliffe's brother, Harold, the first Lord Rothermere. Alfred could have the glory. Harold preferred the cash. From that day forth, the paper would be run for profit. But not for long. By the mid-thirties the paper was in crisis. It was rescued by Guy Bartholomew, regarded as the father of Britain's tabloids. His formula was roughly sex, sincerity and sensation. The man he chose to execute his design was Hugh Cudlipp, a brilliant journalist who would steer the *Mirror* to becoming the largest daily paper in the world. A flamboyant Welsh genius, he was every serious newspaperman's guru. His mind worked at the speed of light. He could deliver an inspired headline while applying a match to his eight-inch Bolivar cigar. Ash would hardly be forming for him to have designed the entire centre spread. A full-blooded campaign might just occupy his inventive mind before the Cuban missile needed to be relit. He was a hands-on editor who conducted rather than dictated, encouraging virtuoso performances from some of Fleet Street's best-known names like Keith Waterhouse, 'Cassandra' (the late Sir William Connor), the multi-award-winning John Pilger and the late legendary agony aunt, Marj Proops. All the surviving pupils have cited Cudlipp as the catalyst, the Great Inspirer of their exceedingly successful careers. He was the dominant figure of a journalistic phenomenon – three brothers, Hugh, Percy and Reginald, all at one time editors of national newspapers. But he was then only a name to me when I landed a three-day trial on the paper, at the end of which – no decision forthcoming – I stayed for forty years.

My first assignment was a disaster, but instructive. There had been a fire at a night club in Soho. I returned from the scene and clacked out two hundred words on an old Underwood typewriter, which began as I recall with the turgid introduction, 'Firemen were called to extinguish a blaze at a night club in Old Compton Street yesterday ...'

The news editor read no further and slowly shook his head. 'This is shit,' he said not unkindly. 'Let Dudley Hawkins have a go at it.' Five minutes of interrogation by this old campaigner produced the following rewrite: 'Clad only in her scanties, a blonde 22-years-old night club hostess climbed along a 30ft parapet in a Soho fire last night to rescue her pet cat Timothy.'

Here, in a single sentence of soaring hyperbole, were all the elements of popular journalism: sex, heroism, drama and pet worship. On those lively imperatives, popular journalism (and not a few noble proprietors) have prospered mightily over the years.

I was still to learn all that – and was sent up to Manchester to speed up the process. But it was also as part of a plan to introduce 'new blood' into the northern office – mine and that of another reporter, Ian Fyfe (who would die as a war correspondent in the D-Day landings). We were given £25 each, first-class railway vouchers, sternly briefed to go up and make a name for ourselves. The money was to cover immediate expenses. That caveat meant different things to the two recipients. I suggested we go straight to our prearranged digs at the Theosophical Society of Great Britain, an ancient mansion which accommodated sinners at the time. Fyfe, a pale, hard-edged Scot the size of an average jockey, insisted we go straight to a preselected bar, his thirst more pressing than theosophy. By 9 p.m. we had spent two fivers apiece, and were visibly canned.

There is a class of drunk who, released of all restraint, will lurch onto any stage determined to outperform the performers. He can be seen on the Costa Brava with a flower between his teeth, rear cleavage exposed, in a heavy-footed attempt at flamenco dancing. My effort was marginally more upmarket. A violinist was performing on a dais at the other end of the bar. He was playing the dreamy melodies of my youth. I became maudlin and dangerously mobile. He saw me coming and backed towards the pianist. I reassured him in words of slurred syllables that I could play the instrument. He hesitated. 'Let the booger 'ave it!' roared a well-wisher from the back of the hall. The musician capitulated. 'Sorrento?' I enquired of the pianist. Moonlighting from the town's symphony orchestra, he winced at the choice but played the introduction. By the time I had reprised the chorus the customers were joining in at full pelt. Pints of beer were sent up to the soloist from boozed Andy Capps who were queuing with requests. Fyfe decided the recital deserved a wider audience. He pulled me to a telephone booth in the bar and dialled the Manchester news desk (where we had yet to present our credentials.). 'You gotta hear this – it's focking marvellous,' he insisted. The listener at the other end was the paper's northern editor. A stocky, diffident character with rimless glasses, he had dropped by the desk to check the stories of the night. He got 'Sorrento'. And then once more with feeling.

Like an old Groucho Marx routine, Fyfe grabbed the phone. 'Hey, whaddaya think o' that then, hey? Hey whaddaya think hey? Hello? Hello?' Silence.

The following morning, the editor was not unkind. He felt obliged to remind us, however, that we were there to boost the paper's sales in the north. On the other hand, if my musical inclinations were so strong, I was free to approach the Hallé Orchestra.

The point taken, we returned to our rooms at the Theosophical Society, only to be asked kindly to pack and leave. Clearly the round-the-clock lifestyle of a newspaper reporter did not blend well with the essential serenity of the establishment. Its mission, to achieve 'an intuitive insight into the divine nature' required a sober response. This was not immediately apparent in the two gentlemen from London. We left with much mutual goodwill.

I found rooms above the Elton School of Dancing in the Oxford Road. The landlady doubled as the school's principal. An amplified gramophone barely drowned out the noise of the trams and traffic on the Oxford Road. The other paying guests were mainly company reps whose crumpled suits and lifeless smiles were straight out of *Death of a Salesman*. In the 'classroom' below, the shrill-voiced madame instructed an awkward squad of pupils, which included a detective, a Hoover salesman and an unfrocked priest. A formidable brunette of uncertain vintage, she suggested after supper one night that we both go downstairs and have a lesson on the house. After supping on a tepid shepherd's pie followed by jam roly-poly awash with custard, I did not care to foxtrot. Not with Madame. But she had already cranked the gramophone. She waited, arms outstretched, a heavily corseted stand-in for She Who Must Be Obeyed. Her chosen record was 'Lovely lady, I'm falling madly in love, with...yee-oo'. Whether this was wishful thinking or coincidence was academic. She pulled me to her like a sumo wrestler. I would have preferred a sumo wrestler. She steered me through the basics, adding a few interesting innovations of her own. How that session might have ended was never tested. In the middle of a ninety-degree turn, one of the guests put her head round the door. 'Where's the cocoa, love?' she enquired. The spell broken, Madame released me. 'Another time?' she murmured, straightening my tie. 'Of course,' I said. I left the next day, found new lodgings, and dived into the deep end of journalism.

CHAPTER TWO

Bad News is Good News

Manchester's closeness to coalmines, steelworks, the mills and the mountains produced the dramas that made the news. Insinuating myself, as reporters must, into the lives of the northerners reinforced the belief that people north of Crewe tend to have some admirable qualities not immediately apparent down south. 'Blunt but honest' roughly identified most of the characters whose lives I reported on for the *Mirror*. Great company, too, in the pubs, fish-and-chip shops and on the football terraces where the dramatis personae of popular journalism spent their leisure hours. Manchester was up to its raised eyebrows in culture. Its famous Hallé Orchestra, the renowned *Manchester Guardian* (it dropped the 'Manchester' on acquiring national status), its art galleries and famous grammar school gave it the prestige it retains today.

But culture rarely makes news. The big stories centred on the *Coronation Street* scenarios of everyday existence. And, since life was tough and dangerous, there was never any shortage of 'human interest' stories. Pit disasters, factory blazes, mountain rescues, rail crashes, bizarre murders and tragic suicides – I found I needed a strong stomach as well as an observant eye, reporting on the unceasing dramas of the day. Reporters, like doctors, are supposed to be able to witness major disasters or disfigured murder victims without flinching. But some of the assignments I covered still haunt me. The suicide of a gifted young doctor in Wigan more than sixty years ago remains a chilling memory. Directed to the victim's home, I was

34

greeted by his wife, whose icy calm but too bright eyes should have warned me. She took my hands and pulled me into the surgery. The dead man had not been moved. He sat stiff in a chair, eyes open. The woman then emitted a shriek that must have echoed along the narrow street. In the doorways of the terraced houses women in curlers and aprons huddled together, whispering. One person's tragedy united them all. No one could explain why the doctor had taken his life. But one of the women, as canny as a gypsy, pulled me aside. What she had to say reflected the bizarre superstitions of that age.

Some months before the tragedy, the doctor's wife had given birth to a child, a boy. Tragically, the infant was born with no fingers to his right hand. Various theories were offered in explanation. But none had the eerie rationale of this knowing housewife from along the street.

'I told the doctor's wife to be careful with their dog,' she said. 'He was a big beast dragging her for miles over the fields. I kept telling her, "He'll have your fingers off if you're not careful." But she laughed. Well I'm not saying anything, but the strangest things can happen. When that child was born without fingers it must have broken the poor doctor's heart.'

A weird theory perhaps in the cool light of the early twenty-first century. But not to those Lancashire neighbours, who in those less sceptical years clung stubbornly to their superstitions.

Tragic as that episode was, misfortune constantly made the headlines. The problem for the young hack was how to ring the changes on the clichés and platitudes slotted remorselessly in his stories. Tragedies brought forth such well-attested phrases as 'she sobbed uncontrollably', 'his voice faltered' or 'she bit on a trembling lip'. For happy laughing situations, this uninspired correspondent could draw on such staples as 'he whooped with joy', 'shook with laughter', 'beamed', 'chuckled', 'grinned' or 'chortled'. Babies were doomed to 'coo contentedly'. Detectives 'swooped', police 'combed the area', and mystery always 'surrounded' the death or disappearance of the story's leading character. (Once, when I was deputising as northern news editor, a correspondent phoned in from some hamlet up in the Pennines where a robber was on the run. 'The police are combing a vast area in the hunt for the criminal,' said a hoarse excited voice at the end of the line.

'But according to the gazetteer,' I said, 'less than a thousand people live there.'

'Oh...' His voice took on a more modest tone. 'Well how about changing it to "Police are combing the area with a small-tooth comb"?'

It is a paradox of popular journalism that bad news is good news. Disaster sells. Much of a tabloid's raw material can be unearthed in police stations, hospitals and magistrates' courts, which tend to feature the monopoly of the frail, flawed or fallen humanity. Blame my tear-diluted bloodstream but I somehow cornered the market in 'trembling-lip' situations. If four weddings and a funeral were listed on the day's assignments, I would land the black-edged invitation. But it was success of a kind and I was posted to Stoke-on-Trent in the Potteries to see if the formula could work there. This move coincided with a policy change on the paper of some significance. It featured me and the paper's chairman, Harry Guy Bartholomew.

Bartholomew was the undisputed supremo of Britain's tabloid journalism. He was a volatile, intimidating character with the strong passions and menacing sentimentality of your average Mafia don. Emerging from the famous wine bar El Vino's one fine spring afternoon, his thick silvery hair fluttering in the breeze, he returned to the office having made the Big Decision. The paper was for Youth. It was for the Thrusting Generation of Tomorrow. *Ergo* the paper would no longer feature stories about Old People. That instruction, delivered personally to the editor, carried the awesome finality of God's briefing of Moses on Mount Sinai. The editor pinned the notice up in the newsroom. No old people. Period. *Verboten*. Unaccountably, promulgation of the ban did not extend beyond the outskirts of London. Overlooked were reporters and other exiles in the paper's far-flung outposts – like Stoke-on-Trent. If the Manchester office was the paper's Siberia, Stoke was its most distant and discounted gulag. It was therefore not deemed necessary to inform the man in the Potteries of Mr Bartholomew's 'No Old People' edict.

Stoke, on that particular Sunday more than fifty years ago, was not merely quiet but irreversibly brain-dead. The courts closed, the police stations deserted, I made the routine enquiry at the local hospital. 'Just an old lady found ill in a doorway,' a matron said. I investigated, then, switching into my sentimental mode wrote this story about an 84-year-old woman who lost her precious Sunday hat in a gust of wind, then, heartbroken, lay down in a shop doorway and composed herself to die. The epic was duly teleprinted via Manchester to London. The news editor scanned the opening sentence skidding to a halt at the primary statistic. Eighty-four years old! He read no further and promptly impaled the copy on the spike. A shadow fell across his desk. By coincidence, Mr Harry Guy Bartholomew was making one of his rare appearances in the newsroom. He enquired of the news editor man whether anything was happening and was told, 'Nothing in particular.'

It was an unsatisfactory reply. Something was always happening somewhere. 'Anything from Manchester?' 'Nothing you'd want to read, sir!' smirked the obedient servant at the desk. 'I spiked this piece about an old crone of eighty-four.'

'Let me see it,' declared the Godfather. He began reading, a shade too intently for the news editor's comfort. 'Bart' read how the old lady had gone to church in a three-and-sixpenny hat, a birthday gift from her older sister; how a sudden gust of wind sent the straw hat with the cherries on top whistling down the high street and out of sight. Faced with the dreadful prospect of returning home and reporting the loss to her sister, the hapless lady wandered the streets, finally collapsing in the doorway of a shoe shop named Freeman, Hardy and Willis. It being Sunday, she was not discovered until the following day, shivering and suffering from exposure. The chairman slowly turned a page. The news editor shifted uneasily in his chair. The story was now approaching its Heavenly Angels denouement – albeit with a spike hole in the middle. It told how a dustman finding the hat in some distant gutter handed it to the police, whose enquiries led to the elderly patient in the hospital ward. Cap in hand, his old army boots polished, the dustman placed the hat on the bed. It only required a doctor to murmur, 'She's going to be all right' for Guy Bartholomew to stifle a gulp. According to informed sources at the time, tears actually filled his pale-blue eyes. (Admittedly the story was not the stuff of Pulitzer prizes but on a wet and blustery Sunday in Stoke we clutched at straws.)

'This is what our paper is all about,' declared the tear-streaked tycoon. 'Humanity. Heart. *Real life*.' He then noticed that the trembling prose had a hole in the middle.

'Did you spike this?'

'Well actually...I mean...you said no old people, so...' The news editor's explanation choked into a cul-de-sac.

'I know what I *said*,' Bartholomew sighed wearily. But any fool could obey orders. The story made the centre spread. Old people were back in the paper. I had bucked the system and was brought back to London as a reward.

August 1939, and World War Two was only weeks away. A handful of us hauled ourselves away from a pub called Number Ten in Fetter Lane and took a taxi to the Duke of York's headquarters in Chelsea to join the Territorials. I found myself posted to the London Irish Rifles, whose parent regiment, the Royal Ulsters, would soon add more battle honours to its distinguished record in war. 'Are you Irish?' the recruiting officer had asked. A memory of a faded portrait of my father and uncle, who resembled the brothers Karamazov, indicated caution. Many of my Fleet Street colleagues were in the London Irish. 'Not as far as I know,' I said trying to sound like a cheerful leprechaun. It worked, and I soon looked the part. I wore an up-slanted beret (a caubeen) bearing a silver harp and a green feathered hackle on top. All this in place, I felt I could address the Irish Question with some authority.

War was a fortnight away. But I was still a reporter. I was sent to Churchill's London home near Hyde Park for a statement. The great man was taking a bath. I stood outside the door shouting questions above the splashing. The response was indistinct but the defiance unmistakable. He was eager to light his cigar and take on the Nazis. I received a more cautionary response from the then British foreign secretary, Lord Halifax. He was among the 'common sense may yet prevail' fraternity. I interviewed him at his home in Eaton Square, SW1. A tall, sombre diplomat (Eton and Christ Church), he greeted me with all the courtesy expected of the third viscount in the dynasty. He selected his platitudes elegantly, expressing the belief that Hitler 'may even now be persuaded to step back from the brink'. This did not square with the considered opinion of Sergeant Major Susands, of F Company, London Irish, who recommended we keep our uniforms ready and boots polished. He decided it would be war within a fortnight and he was right. The Territorials were immediately called to headquarters.

It just so happened that the billet earmarked for our company was also in Eaton Square, a short march up the road from the Halifax home. Ironically, I was now back marching up the square behind the pipers, my green Irish hackle rustling in the wind. The bagpipes and the drums brought the foreign secretary out onto his doorstep. Incredibly, our eyes met. His widened in fleeting recognition, dissolving into a frown of disbelief. Mine challenged, 'If "common sense may yet prevail" why am I wearing a uniform and a hat with a feather on top?' But the message had now bounced off a well-polished door. Prime Minister Neville Chamberlain announced over the radio that we were at war with Germany. And I was guarding one end of Putney Bridge, wearing a bus driver's overcoat and sneakers, and slinging a rifle stamped 'Demonstration Purposes Only: Do Not Fire!'

Soldiering is presumed to be a great leveller. This was literally true of F Company of the London Irish Rifles, whose Other Ranks were required to sleep on the floor. Our billet was in *Upstairs Downstairs* territory embedded between Chelsea and Belgravia. It was one of those mansions from which the well-heeled residents had swiftly departed, their priceless furniture and *objets d'art* snug and safe – mostly in the air-conditioned security of the Harrods Depositories close by. The mansion was resonant with history and gracious living. Our scratchy straw palliasses insulted the well-waxed parquet floors. The morning after we arrived, a butler returned to collect some forgotten items from an upstairs attic. He paused to take a last look at the drawing room. And like a fastidious Jeeves, he was visibly unamused. He looked disdainfully as the men engaged in the standard elemental functions peculiar to army barrack rooms: coughing, spitting, farting and complaining. 'Disgusting,' the butler said. 'Piss off!' responded the congregation in unison.

Expectations of actually emerging from the war alive – in F Company particularly – were zero. We arrived at that conclusion after a careful appraisal of our equipment. Some uniforms were second-hand. A few of us wore World War One puttees. We threw rocks instead of grenades in training. Although I had to guard Putney Bridge with a dud rifle, I did have a whistle in A1 condition. My orders were to blow it if the standard challenge did not produce an acceptable reply. It was midnight when a tall figure approached in the moonlight, preceded by a whiff of exotic aftershave. The colonel was testing the defences.

'Halt! Who goes there?' I challenged.

'Friend,' drawled the colonel.

'Advance, friend, and be recognised.'

The figure closed in. A tall aristocrat with a trimmed moustache and riding boots, the colonel beamed, 'That really was awfully good, y'know. You sound like officer material to me. What's your name?'

'Rifleman Zec, sir!'

'Spell it.'

I spelled it.

'Ah. That's bloody unfortunate.'

'Sir?'

'Obvious, y'fool. Not likely to come out of this war alive, neither of us. And how d'you think they put the names up on the war memorials, eh? Alphabetical order! Yours will be right at the bottom to be peed on by every dog in the street. Pity. Dismiss!'

The alphabetical curse plagued me and all those Zunzs, Zolas and Ziffs who sailed, soldiered or flew in the service of the Crown. When vests and pants (winter issue) were being handed out, the Adamses, Archers and Tommy Atkinses were snug and laughing while teeth chattered at the other end of the line. The ritual stabbing which the army describes as inoculation is no great hardship if you are an Arbuthnot, a Burton or a Chambers. You get the sharp needle, the steady eye, and the careful aim that favour the First of the Few. They do not have to witness the weak and the shriekers collapsing like ninepins, clutching their arms and baying at the moon. After a while, we at the wrong end of the line perceive that the doc is beginning to yawn. He looks at his watch and is pushing the needle in like an umbrella into its stand. Finally you offer your arm and settle for septicaemia.

Pay day was the ultimate indignity. The company commander sat there, a Midas behind the trestle table (wooden) on which the shillings and pence rose at different heights like a distant view of the New York skyline. To have to wait in line for the derisory reward that passed for soldier's pay in World War Two was amusing enough. But to be the end man, striding towards the last nine and fourpence in the world, was a special humiliation. I recall marching the distance, observed by the battalion, drawing up in front of the officer, stamping to attention and saluting. He could see the joke. He slid the money towards me with the tips of his manicured fingers . 'Hardly worth the walk, was it, Zec?' he drawled.

Life expectancy in Britain's big cities during World War Two was not discussed. Londoners and their counterparts in Birmingham, Manchester, Liverpool and elsewhere lived one night at a time and brewed a lot of tea. The dawn search by rescuers through the rubble required a strong stomach rather than a stiff upper lip. The aim of Goering's Luftwaffe was above all to destroy the morale of the British people. The total failure to achieve this, despite the civilian death toll and the shortages, mystified the chief perpetrator of the terror, Adolf Hitler. He had, of course, expected the traditional backs-to-the-wall stoicism for which the nation is famous. But not the bloody-minded, stuff-you defiance. Despite the appalling losses to U-boat torpedoes in the North Atlantic, and the military reverses on the continent of Europe, the British still cracked jokes and sang of hanging their washing on the Siegfried Line. They made clothes out of old curtains and lipstick from recycled beetroot juice. Historians have long given this phenomenon serious thought. The consensus is that the great morale boosters of the time were Winston Churchill, the RAF, Vera Lynn and not least the *Daily Mirror's* pert-breasted strip cartoon heroine in the see-through lingerie named Jane. Bomber squadrons regarded it as a good omen if Jane stripped off on the days they took off. Most barrack-room walls and submarine lockers featured a Jane strip wearing little between her smile and high stilettos. The distinguished historian, the late A J P Taylor (*English History*

1914–1945) listed Jane as one of the main reasons for the paper's success as a brash yet 'serious organ of democratic opinion'. He added, 'The English people at last found their voice, and the historian is the more grateful for this voice...'

The most incisive aspect of that 'voice' was the paper's daily political cartoon. Drawn by my late brother Philip, it became one of the most influential political weapons of World War Two. Powerfully drawn, provocatively captioned, the cartoons were regarded as being crucial to the nation's morale. Except for one particular cartoon – notoriously misunderstood – which so infuriated Winston Churchill that the paper was almost closed down. It was published 6 March 1942. It showed a torpedoed sailor adrift on a dark and desolate sea. The caption read, 'The price of petrol has been increased by one penny – official.' It achieved an immediate, though scarcely merited, notoriety. To my brother's astonishment Churchill was enraged. The then home secretary, Herbert Morrison, sneered, 'Very artistically drawn, witty – Goebbels at his best. It is plainly meant to tell seamen not to go to sea to put money in the pockets of the petrol owners.' Questions were asked in Parliament. The *Mirror*'s chairman Guy Bartholomew and the editor were summoned to the Home Office.

The cartoon's intention was plainly not subversive: 'All I wanted to do,' my brother explained, 'was to alert the millions of readers that the petrol they were using, perhaps wasting, cost not only money but men's lives.' The irony was that the offending caption was not my brother's idea. He had written, 'Petrol is dearer now.' Reading it over his shoulder, his friend and colleague 'Cassandra' (Bill Connor) recommended the more astringent caption. Meanwhile my brother carried on with his devastating daily attacks on the Hitler clique. So successfully, in fact, that this 'filthy, lying, hyena', as Goebbels described him, was put on the 'hit list' once Germany had won the war. My brother was delighted. The cartoons had struck their target.

For the first year of the war, F Company of the London Irish Rifles played token war or, more aptly, trivial pursuits. The French Army relaxed on the Maginot Line. The RAF dropped leaflets on Germany, to 'rouse them', said Churchill, drily, 'to a higher morality'.

Chamberlain called this stand-off 'the Twilight War'. Others dubbed it 'the Phoney War'. Either way, the hiatus invited mischief. At the time we were briefly led by a captain who, according to the received wisdom at the time, was immaculately equipped in all areas – south of his brain. Stories have been told of soldiers being required to whitewash the rough stonework outside Nissen huts, and other idiotic caprices of the brain-dead military. I present the following personal experience to the archive.

In this particular winter, a heavy snowfall in the Malvern Hills (where we were stationed) totally blanketed the countryside. Nothing between our billet and the far horizon but a vast, smooth duvet of white. Our captain, aware of an impending visit by the brigadier, decided to surprise him. F Company would be different from the rest of the battalion, if not the world. He ordered the snow to be swept from the rooftop, windowsills, driveway, the front steps and the wrought-iron railings in front of the company headquarters. 'Focking lunatic' was the considered but not unfriendly verdict of grown men as they shovelled the snow outwards from the billet. For the more delicate work on the railings we used a brush and pan finished off with an exaggerated flick of a finger. The assignment completed, the company area resembled a black oasis in a vast white desert. The company commander stood back from his masterpiece and, in the manner of the Almighty at the Creation, saw that it was good. The captain could barely wait out the fifteen minutes before the brigadier's arrival. Even we who had contributed to the lunacy felt a shade different from ordinary men. But then, as happens to the best-laid schemes, it began to snow. I mean heavily. Paralysis seized our leader. The assembled company chuckled inwardly behind expressionless faces – a rare gift known only to actors and old soldiers. The captain regained speech. 'S'arn' Major', he shouted, 'get the men at it double-quick!'

'To do what, *sah*?' enquired the warrant officer, purple-faced beneath his caubeen.

'The snow man, the *snow*! Get 'em at it, brooms, brushes, anything – I want no snow on F Company!'

Out in the real war, the 13,500-ton passenger liner *Athenia* had been torpedoed by a German U-boat with the loss of 112 lives. Not long after, the *Bosnia*, *Royal Sceptre* and *Rio Clara* were sunk off the coast of Spain.

But, here in the Malvern Hills, I and the others were frantically brushing the snow away even as it fell. The brigadier arrived in good time to see men leaping in all directions, some catching the falling snowflakes in their helmets. He studied the burlesque with the merest tightening of the jaw. 'I have made some interesting inspections in my time,' I heard him murmur to the escorting colonel, 'but I think I have now seen everything. Perhaps you would invite this captain to join us later in the mess, eh...hm...what?'

In the early part of the war at least, our battalion were the New Contemptibles. Heroes there would be. But not yet. Thus while our parent regiment, the Royal Ulster Rifles, was treated with the reverence it deserved, our mob foraged for favours and of course had to provide its own entertainment. A notice in company orders required any soldier who could demonstrate what Noël Coward called 'a talent to amuse', could play an instrument, juggle or otherwise hold an audience, to report to the entertainments officer. My modest talents as a fiddle player had got around. My repertoire, as previously stated, originated two thousand or so miles east of the Blarney Stone. The pure-blooded Irish in the battalion were indifferent if not hostile to anything but their native music. The dreamy gypsy airs I was raised on particularly grated on their nerves, though I never knew why. My attempts to bridge the cultural divide by offering variations on a theme of 'Wit' a shillelagh onder me arm and a twinkle in me oi' fooled nobody. I asked the officer what kind of music he had in mind. He was evasive. I suggested some unaccompanied Bach. He dismissed me, and the suggestion. The regimental concert would take place at the local cinema, to which soldiers' families would be invited. Since my fiddle playing was a part-time caprice I was scarcely concert-ready. Some practice was called for. I decided the battalion butcher shop provided the necessary isolation. This was situated in a marquee presided over by a rifleman everybody called 'Mad Paddy'. A thickset stocky character with yellow hair, he could dismember a carcass of beef as skilfully as a Tower Hill executioner. I decided it would be prudent not disturb him as he slashed away at his work and positioned myself midway behind a side of pork and a wall of tinned galantine. It was not inspirational. I limbered up on some Kreutzer studies and soared, I mean sawed, into the ascending octaves of Kreisler's *Praeludium*.

'Shot that focking screechin!' commanded a voice from behind a bleeding carcass.

A dilemma. As a lance corporal, should I pull rank? As a musician, should I press on regardless? I compromised with a disarming smile and a short placatory chorus of 'Phil the Fluter's Ball'. Not disarming enough.

'You focking asked for it!' exploded the enraged butcher. He made a menacing sweep with the knife. Closer than he had intended. The vein severed, blood spurted out in a crimson arc onto the sawdust. I staunched the wound in my wrist with muslin ripped from a frozen pig, and reported to the MO's tent. A peacetime gynaecologist, he was not favoured to stay the course owing to massive overweight and an enthusiasm for Irish whiskey, which accounted for his comatose slumbering at the time of my arrival. The orderly was a five-feet-nothing Irish gnome instructed not to awaken his master unless the Germans invaded, and then gently. Nevertheless, he took a strand of surgical thread from a container and placed it in the lid of a Cherry Blossom boot polish tin, into which he poured some water. He placed a lit Bunsen burner underneath. By then I calculated I had bled about a pint of blood and suggested he might care to waken the MO.

'I tink that's favourite', he agreed and shook the bulky figure on the camp bed. One bloodshot eye opened. And closed. Another shake. 'Whatsammarrer...who wants...eh?'

I released the muslin to let him see the wound. 'Ah, yes,' he sighed, rolling off his bunk. 'Suturing, I think.' He gripped my arm. 'Great shtrength ringsh the bell!' he wheezed encouragingly and managed to get the needle in at the fourth attempt. I prayed he wouldn't breathe too close to the Bunsen burner. The operation completed, he fell back on the bunk and snored.

The entertainments officer saw the bandages and frowned at this apparent threat to his arrangements. I wasn't very happy either. Twenty-four hours later on a forty-eight-hour pass I collapsed on

Millbank and was hospitalised with a lively case of septicaemia, boot polish apparently being inimical to the bloodstream. But I returned to duty in time for the concert. 'Can you still perform?' the officer asked urgently.

'Of course,' I said, wiggling my fingers to prove it. 'But naturally nothing too demanding.'

'Good. Now this is what I want. We have this sketch about the Blitz. It's a very dramatic sequence. You stand in the wings and when I give you the signal I want you make a sound like an air-raid siren.'

'A what?'

'An air-raid siren, man! Yer brains gone or something?'

I felt destroyed. I was not a soloist. Just a simulated sound effect.

'I don't think I can make that kind of sound.'

'Yes you can,' he said wickedly. 'Mad Paddy said you could. He heard you.'

That night behind the curtain, on the given signal, I slid two fingers up and down the fiddle's E and A strings into a microphone. It sounded like an air-raid siren. There were no encores. And no applause. Now and again when I glance at the scar on my wrist I become quite misty-eyed. They played real music in those days.

For a while I was a sergeant major instructor at a weapon training school. It updated officers and NCOs on the latest teaching methods. Clearly, military training manuals are not meant to be literary gems. Their simple function is to acquaint all minds, from the officer potential to the marginally deficient, with the serious business of killing. It is not until sane men actually articulate the instructions, hearing their own voices loud and clear, that serious doubts set in. One sunny afternoon on the slopes of the favourite beauty spot of Boxhill in Surrey, I took a mixed bag of soldiers through bayonet practice. Straw-filled dummies stood extended towards the trees. They represented the enemy. Bayonets were fixed. I stood in front of a dummy, raised my voice from profundo to alto and heard my words echo back from the slopes: 'A penetration of two inches in a vulnerable part of the body is sufficient to kill. I will give the order "Throat" "Stomach" "Left groin" "Right groin", like this.' I penetrated a left groin. 'And you will simultaneously intimidate the enemy with an appropriate shout: "Grooaargh!" The primeval scream bounced back off the hilltops. Birds flew and the squad eyed me with some pity. 'Withdraw...Left groin. Groaargh!'

I stopped in mid-frenzy to ask gentlemen officers and a truculence of NCOs, 'Any questions?'

An awkward silence. A starling twittered down on the well-bayoneted dummy. A warm breeze rustled the distant trees. Cowbells rang from a nearby farm. The sun shone, the scene idyllic. A thoughtful character beneath a steel helmet confronted me with a quizzical smile.

'Yes?'

'The thought occurred to me, Sergeant Major,' he began, so gently, 'that of all the literary forms poetry is by far the most rewarding. Don't you agree?'

I had no answer to that. 'Squad – dismiss!' I said.

Hitler's *blitzkrieg*, Dunkirk and the threatened invasion of Britain of course changed everything. We were now in Haverfordwest on anti-invasion manoeuvres when news came over the radio that France had fallen. Hearing Churchill's defiant 'we will never surrender' speech over scratchy radios, F Company, like the rest of the world, stood enthralled. Churchill's words soared over the rhythm of the waves. Emotional reactions were profound. Men stood by their machine guns gazing silently out to sea. A messenger ran up: 'Emergency meeting in the mess hall,' he shouted. We filed in. The pervading mood: nervous anticipation tinged with a sense of excitement. 'This is *it*!' I heard one riflemen mutter as RSM Begbie stood on a small balcony, which overlooked the hall. He struck the balustrade with his baton. A hush. We waited.

'I have an announcement to make,' he said gravely. A long pause as he weighed his words. Finally: 'Twenty-eight spoons, twelve knives, three forks and a salt cellar are missing from the mess. I am giving the culprit twenty-four hours to own up. If he is not man enough to do this, all of you lot can expect trouble. *Dismiss!*'

Behind me, Rifleman McKenzie Porter, former colleague and news editor of the *Daily Mirror*, grinned behind his spectacles. 'Wonderful stuff,' he said. 'After that there's just no way we can lose this war.'

CHAPTER THREE

The Man in Room 404

I was finally discharged from the army in 1945 with the rank of company sergeant major and a demob suit that was just as laughable. War being noisier than peace, I was left with a hearing disability my comrades alluded to in rhyming slang as 'Mutt and Jeff'. An additional nicety was a condition known as 'tinnitus', an interminable noise in the ears known only too well to ex-artillerymen. The upper reaches of a Paganini caprice I do not hear at all. But I can pick up basso profundo, Frank Bruno and the Voice of Doom.

I reported for duty at Geraldine House in London to discover that six years is an epoch in Fleet Street. I rejoined a newspaper vastly different from the journalistic frolic I'd left in 1939. If, as the historian A J P Taylor asserted, 'In the Second World War the British people came of age', so too had the paper I returned to. All the old political debris of 1939–45 was swept away in a Labour Party election landslide. Work began to create the Welfare State and clear the moonscape of rubble in the blitzed towns north and south. Stories had a harder edge. The paper's political voice was being listened to and quoted. Circulation began to soar. The *Mirror*'s logo, 'Forward with the People' was an apt claim. But the old gilt-edged imperatives of tabloid journalism – entertainment, crime and royalty – were still the staples of the paper's success. Royalty in particular. For a brief and bizarre period I became the *Mirror*'s court correspondent. 'Too good to be true' was my immediate reaction. I was dazzled by the opportunity but deluded as to the benefits supposedly on offer. I envisaged cocktails with the Beautiful People in 'royal circles', or informative chats at, say, Royal Ascot with top-hatted sources 'close to the Palace'.

In fact, the Mafia's vow of *omerta*, instant death to those who spill the beans, was nothing compared with the tight-lipped secrecy surrounding the monarchy at the time – hilarious in retrospect, compared with the amounts of embossed royal dirty linen being laundered in public half a century later. Once the late Princess Diana had stripped her soul for the biographer Andrew Morton – the breakdowns, the bulimia, the well-heeled boyfriends and all – royal reticence was blown out of the water. The final nail in the coffin of confidentiality was the near-farcical trial of Paul Burrell, the late Princess Di's butler. Once he had blown the gaff in Britain and the United States, damage limitation by the Palace became a failed and forlorn exercise.

(A footnote to this sad saga concerns Dodi Fayed, killed with Princess Diana in the Paris tragedy in 1997. Some of the 'rich playboy' comments in the obituaries scarcely matched my impression of him. I was introduced to him at dinner one night in Los Angeles by Dana Broccoli, whose late husband Cubby masterminded James Bond into legend. A quiet, courteous young man, Dodi came over as a serious-minded, hard-working filmmaker refreshingly different from some of the self-serving characters who had latched onto the late princess. One thing is for certain: any letters Diana may have written to him would never have been bartered around the media.)

That whole episode and its aftermath – not to mention the speculation about Charles and Camilla Parker Bowles – hit the House of Windsor like a hurricane. Not in the whole history of the British monarchy had the private life of royalty been so brazenly thrust into the world's headlines. Only the astute intervention by the Queen – who learned much from her most adroit mother – saved the monarchy from ridicule, or worse, irrelevance.

But in the euphoric aftermath of World War Two, the 'royals' were treated with forelock-touching reverence. Their upper-crust press officials treated newspapers and their reporters with disdain if not contempt. The royal wives were never pregnant. That disgusting descriptive was for the masses. Royal mothers-to-be were either in an 'interesting condition' or were 'cancelling all engagements'. No information remotely concerned with reality was ever allowed to escape the ring of steel that protected the monarchy's age-old myths. The press secretary I dealt with at the time was an aloof and inscrutable mandarin named Commander Colville. Just a whit less majestic than his employers – George VI and Queen Elizabeth – no one revealed so little with more charm. Court correspondents were therefore required to search elsewhere for crumbs off the royal table. This brought me into the unsolicited company of a character I knew then only by his chosen pseudonym of 'Harry Moon'.

It happened after I had written a fairly innocuous piece about some trivial goings-on at the Palace. My phone rang that same morning. A hoarse Cockney caller informed me that I had apparently got certain facts wrong. Slightly miffed, I challenged him to disclose his credentials. 'I ought to bleedin' know,' said he. 'I work there, don' I?'

He was a boilerman at Buckingham Palace. Low down on the totem pole, but crucial nevertheless.

As all the recent revelations have confirmed, there has always been a powerful urge among those who humbly work in palaces to reveal what goes on beneath the ornate ceilings, or duvets, of their royal masters. Some do so, unashamedly, for the money. Others who valet, cook, fetch or carry for the greatest monarchy on earth simply covet a share of the limelight. Harry was in that category. A shortish, stocky informant, with an uncontrollable habit of talking out of the corner of his mouth, he had a genuine sense of playing a part in the great constitutional dramas of the day. To this Yeoman of the S-bends, keeping the royal bath-water at a tolerable temperature wasn't exactly small beer. The knowledge that his hot water gurgled upwards into direct and intimate contact with the Skin Imperial pleased him considerably. But it lacked the vital additive of recognition. And so now and again he would phone me with harmless but fascinating insights into the everyday life of the monarch. But on the eve of Princess Elizabeth's wedding – 20 November 1947 – Harry decided he had a major scoop. And he was eager to unleash it, albeit in the same conspiratorial tone: 'I have some information.'

'Yes?'

He lowered his voice as if the world were listening. 'I have been ordered to put six hot-water bottles in the state coach. These are of aluminium, three foot long... Are you gettin' all this?'

'Of course.'

'And on the return journey they will be filled with boiling water and placed under the seat and the floorboards in the same way.'

The first edition of the *Daily Mirror*, 20 November 1947, led its front page with:

HOT BOTTLES FOR BRIDE'S TWO COACHES

My informant pocketed the fiver and a mole was born. Further harmless revelations were published and Harry now saw himself as a royal correspondent *manqué*. Success went to his head. Imprudently, he was given to whistling up taxis outside the Palace, flicking a Woodbine into the wind before entering. His final communiqué was in November 1948. He was ten minutes ahead of the agencies with the news of the birth of Prince Charles. He later volunteered the additional snippet that Dr Jacob Snowman, a leading exponent of the art, had been called in to circumcise the infant. How this informant could acquire such intimate details intrigued the Palace sufficiently to dismiss him a few weeks later.

That dismissal, according to the chirpy informant in question, might have been straight out of *Hancock's Half Hour*.

> The scene: a room at Buckingham Palace. An immaculately dressed figure sits behind a large desk. Standing stiffly to attention before him, Harry the Mole.
> OFFICIAL: I have to tell you that we are dispensing with your services as of today.
> HARRY (puzzled): Oh, sir. Why, sir?
> OFFICIAL: It has come to our attention that you have been giving information to gentlemen of the press contrary to rules. (We were all gentlemen in those days.)
> HARRY (in a fair attempt at looking aghast): Me, sir? No, sir! More than my job's worth.

OFFICIAL (drily): Aptly put. But could you please explain
the several taxis you have been observed taking outside
the Palace over a considerable period, in order to make
these clandestine meetings?

HARRY (short pause for his brain to take it in; finally):
Fair cop. Didn't mean any harm.

He came over to my home to say goodbye. 'Don't worry about me,'
he smiled. I felt sorry for him and gave him some cash and a suit I'd
worn that he'd admired and was roughly his size. 'Get out of the
informant business,' I advised.

'You're dead right', said he.

He walked out onto the Bayswater Road, the suit under his arm,
and hailed a taxi. Old habits die hard. A month later my phone rang.
The same hoarse unmistakable voice: 'I'm working in the casualty
department of a hospital. We get a lot of interesting cases, suicides,
murders, lot of celebrities. Interested?'

'No.'

'Just thought I'd ask.'

(I remember telling the late Peter Sellers all about Harry. The
actor's eyes gleamed as he immediately latched onto the comedic
possibilities of the character. He thought it would make a great film.
But then he became Princess Margaret's friend and was frequently
invited to her private soirées. He decided that playing Harry the Mole
might cause embarrassment. When one is invited to sail in royal
waters, one does not rock the boat.)

As today's monarchy desperately tries to reinvent itself it is hard
not to empathise with the hapless victims. Especially the Queen. A
glance through the Royal Book of press cuttings must be a chilling
experience. Not merely does it point to the threatened destruction of
a supposedly indestructible image, but the subtext underscores a
persistent failure to read the massive mood change of the British
people. When these words were being written, a leading cleric
suggested the possibility that the Queen should actually put herself
forward for election – a notion that must have made earlier monarchs
spin in their mausoleums. But the fact that the idea was actually raised

was an indication of the nation's scrutiny of what had always been beyond the public's gaze. That constitutional guru Walter Bagehot, a hundred and fifty years ahead of Barbara Cartland, spoke of the monarchy's 'mystique and reverence', adding the stern warning, 'One must not let daylight in on magic.' What price that 'mystique and reverence' today? Is there any magic left to expose?

Paradoxically, making Her Majesty more 'available' doesn't seem to work either. Mystique and matiness cannot coexist. Flirting with the media has frequently resulted in the wrong party being seduced. As Melanie Phillips once wrote in the *Observer*, 'The misguided idea that the media can be neutralised by dealing with them on their own terms has caused the Royal Family to come to grief.'

As happens in our trade, the role you play often depends upon the last good story you wrote. I had covered a murder case with reasonable competence and was posted to the crime section. That role began – and ended – with one of the most grisly cases in criminal history. At the end of it all, John George Haigh was hanged for one murder, though he was credited with six and confessed to nine. But the case had momentous repercussions for newspapers and, in particular, for the editor of the *Daily Mirror*, Sylvester Bolam. The whole sensational affair was the major crime story of 1949. In those days the crime reporter all newspapermen revered was Percy Hoskins of the *Daily Express*. Resembling Alfred Hitchcock, he had the same avuncular manner and mischievous humour. A great story teller, he was the most popular habitué of El Vino's, the Fleet Street tavern where editors, QCs and other egos competed to be the wit of the day. Hoskins's police contacts were the envy of the Street. He brought them occasionally to El Vino's, pouring champagne for bulky men whose plain clothes and confidential nose-tapping unmistakably signalled 'the Met'. The received wisdom was that Hoskins learned about murders and other serious crimes almost as swiftly as the detectives themselves. Watching Hoskins was therefore the crime reporter's first imperative. For Hoskins suddenly to leave his Bollinger and exit the bar in mid-anecdote was significant. On the occasion I saw this happen I discovered that he had been tipped off about the strange disappearance of an elderly widow from the Onslow Court Hotel in London's South Kensington. Immediately suspected was her unlikely companion, a dapper fraudster named John George Haigh. A well-dressed, plausible charmer with a clipped moustache and an Alvis sports car, he could have passed for a successful Mayfair car salesman.

Mrs Olive Durand-Deacon was the widow of a colonel in the Gloucestershire Regiment. She was 69 and weighed 196 pounds. With her furs and broad-brimmed hat she bore a strong resemblance to the Marx Brothers' famous leading lady, Margaret Dumont. She led a tranquil existence at the hotel, with other genteel widows whose tight pensions barely covered the hotel's weekly rate of five pounds, fifteen shillings and sixpence a week. Haigh was staying at the same hotel. Haigh's charm and Lovat green suit blended well with the hotel's ambience, which was straight out of *Separate Tables*. Clement Attlee was at Number 10. Errand boys were whistling 'Slow Boat to China'. The MCC were cricketing in colonial South Africa. And Britain's most beloved radio comedian, Tommy Handley, had just died. His famous signing off line 'TTFN' – ta-ta for now – was the jokey style in which Haigh would end some of his letters from the condemned cell.

By the time I was interviewing Haigh at the hotel it was suspected that he had already murdered a London doctor and his wife. A trusting gentlewoman, Mrs Durand-Deacon would not have known that the gold-rimmed spectacles with which Haigh studied the hotel menu had belonged to one of his victims. So too had the crocodile handbag he sold to her for ten pounds. A petty crook, he had always been short of money. His table hopping in the hotel dining room now had an increased urgency. Soon, 'that nice young man in room 404' was sharing after-dinner mints and coffee with the widow. He had admired her hands. She was flattered and mentioned that for some time she had been interested in earning some pin money, manufacturing artificial fingernails. 'What a coincidence!' declared the deceptive Mr Haigh. He had just the right facilities at his workshop, in Crawley, Sussex. Perhaps she would care to visit it. She would. She did. In the storehouse, ever the gentleman, he removed her fur coat and sat her in a chair. Then shot her in the back of the head.

It had been a tedious drive and he was hungry. He left the body in the chair and crossed the street to Ye Olde Ancient Prior's Café and ordered poached egg on toast with a pot of tea. He returned to the storeroom, stirrup-pumped a large drum with acid, and dumped her body into it. That chore completed, he tidied up, brushed his hair, and later went to the George Hotel in the town and ordered the set dinner. By now the police had focused on the Sussex storeroom, and had found gruesome evidence of the crime and its victim. Haigh would not have known that false teeth and gallstones are stubbornly resistant to certain acids. But the detectives knew that, and briefed me accordingly, adding the thought that Haigh probably had a list of nine murders to his credit. It was that thought I took with me when I had my last meeting with Haigh at the Onslow Court Hotel. He complained about the persistent police questioning, insisting he knew nothing about the widow's disappearance. But he observed all the courtesies over afternoon tea.

'Shall I be mum?' enquired the serial killer.

'By all means', said I, thinking about the stirrup pump.

I had been informed by a 'source' that an arrest was imminent. An eleventh-hour interview would be a bonus. The rest of the 'pack' had similar ideas. Reporters and photographers crowded the pavement outside the hotel. Haigh had had dinner and gone back to his room. I phoned him from the lobby. 'Come on up,' he said. Room 404 was small and dimly lit by the single bedside lamp. 'I'm sorry I can't offer you anything,' he apologised with a tired smile. 'I'm not quite sure why you want to see me. I've told you and the police all I know. There's really nothing more that I can say.' I went to the window and looked down on to the square below. Light from the street lamps gleamed on the shiny black police cars that ringed the square. Police were marshalling onlookers away from the hotel entrance. In minutes they would be tapping on the door.

'I accept what you say, John,' I said, 'but look out here. They don't seem to be convinced.' He joined me at the window. There was a twitch of the eyebrows. A long silence. He rubbed his lips. Finally he said, 'I've got something for you,' and went to a drawer. He slowly reached inside and, considering his colourful CV, I measured the paces between myself and the door. He took out a framed portrait of himself. 'I think you may find this very useful in the next twenty-four hours.' A killer's vanity. Notoriety or celebrity, it was important for him to look his best. The picture made the front pages. That same vanity accompanied him to the death cell. He protested mildly at having to surrender his favourite lovat green suit, silk woven tie and patent-leather shoes. He did the next best thing. He willed the suit to Madame Tussaud's with the request, 'I would be obliged if the trousers were immaculately pressed.'

He had other concerns. He had told me once that he had always been a perfectionist. He was worried now that there might be some technical foul-up in the execution. 'My weight is deceptive,' he told the governor of Wandsworth Prison, Major A C N Benke. 'I have a light springy step and I would not like there to be a hitch. Perhaps we could have some kind of rehearsal.' The request was noted but not granted. The governor reassured him that there would be no hitch and, who knows, may well have told him not to worry. The hangman, Albert Pierrepoint, did not make mistakes. The night before the execution he left his pub Help the Poor Struggler, and went straight to the prison. His ropes were made by the same Southwark establishment that had made the flags for Nelson's ship at Trafalgar.

Haigh was executed on 10 August 1949. Afterwards, Pierrepoint bought a restaurant and called it (subtlety eluding him) the Last Drop. There were few tears shed when the notice that the hanging had taken place was posted outside the prison gates. But there was plenty of sympathy around for Sylvester Bolam, the editor of the *Daily Mirror*. 'Bish' Bolam was a quiet, slightly built graduate of Durham University. He was a hands-on editor, particularly when a big story was breaking. On the night of Haigh's arrest, all Fleet Street knew the full horror of his crimes. Journalistic zeal overrode professional caution. The *Mirror* published two stories. One carried the headline VAMPIRE: A MAN HELD. (The vampire label referred to Haigh's confessed fascination with the taste of blood.) The second item, on the same page, showed Haigh leaving a police station having been charged with murder. The juxtaposition of the two stories was clearly prejudicial and led to a charge of contempt of court.

On 25 March, Sylvester Bolam appeared at the Royal Courts of Justice, London, close enough to the *Mirror* offices for Bolam to stroll his way to court. 'Bish' arrived looking paler than usual. If he imagined that it would all end with a weighty fine plus a stern rap over the knuckles, he was soon jolted into reality. The judge who sentenced him, Lord Justice Goddard, leaned forward, his face reddening beneath the wig. 'Sylvester Bolam, you will be taken into the custody of the tipstaff and you will be committed to Brixton prison for a term of three calendar months.' The shock waves reverberated along Fleet Street. The paper's sensitive north-country editor was of course devastated, bewildered and humiliated. A classical pianist with a fondness for Corelli, he found Brixton Prison an unwelcome switch from his apartment in London's Clifford's Inn. Now and again I'd taken my fiddle there and we'd play duets together, causing grievous bodily harm to J S Bach and Arcangelo Corelli. John George Haigh put an end to the soirées. It was the editor's bad luck to have been on duty on the wrong evening, landed with the wrong murderer, the wrong judge, at the wrong time. Three years later, while smoking a cigarette after breakfast, he died suddenly of a heart attack. Meanwhile, the crowds queued to view the wax lookalike of Haigh at Madame Tussaud's. The former choirboy had achieved a macabre notoriety far beyond his wildest nightmares. His eyes glittered over a fixed sardonic smile. In time he will probably be melted down into another monster.

Haigh's execution brought my role as a crime reporter to an abrupt and welcome finale. I had been exposed to the glitz of royalty and the venality of rogues. Ideal qualifications, in the paper's view, to take on the fun and the follies of show business. It was goodbye to Mr Moon and those bulky men eager to help me with my enquiries. Instead it was *Hello Dolly* and the Kleig-lit world of motion pictures. It was rich and enticing territory at the time.

Britain was then Hollywood's most profitable overseas market. The nation's 4,500 front-line cinemas played to a total audience of 25 million a week. The profits returned to US distributors, already indecently prosperous, were enormous. All their movies, other than the most dire, made money. There was little competition either from British films. Apart from Charlie Chaplin, a lightweight actor named Leslie Howard and other soft-centred matinée idols like James Mason and Robert Donat, British talent did not travel well. The stilted English accent that dominated our films at the time was lost on the audiences of middle America, and a joke in the major cities. Michael Wilding's unfortunate habit of delivering his lines as though his jaws were wired was rich material for American comics but poison at the box office. The fact that Wilding's favourite co-star, Anna Neagle, was voted Britain's top money earner of 1951 (the magnificent Bette Davis was second) indicates the chauvinism of British films at the time.

It was left to J Arthur Rank, a rich flour magnate with a vision, to put British cinema on the map. But he had neither the flair nor the wisdom of a Sam Goldwyn or a Louis B Mayer. A Methodist, he cherished an ambition to spread the message of Methodism, oblivious to Goldwyn's famous dictum, 'Messages are for Western Union'. Rank's familiar logo of a beefy character beating the giant gong did hallmark several successes. But the studio was dominated by accountants who had no feeling for cinema, nor an understanding of its magic. The Rank 'Charm School', created as a 'reservoir of talent', simpered into oblivion. At best, it merely produced cloned versions of Stewart Granger or Jean Simmons, those originals scarcely world-beaters themselves. Characters like Guy Rolfe and Michael Rennie may have caused the odd debutante to swoon over her pink champagne, but they did not stop the traffic in downtown Milwaukee.

What saved the British film industry at the time was a relaxation of the tax laws, which encouraged American producers and their stars to make pictures in Great Britain. It brought over filmmakers like Cubby Broccoli, whose twenty James Bond films have earned upwards of $3.6 billion worldwide. The cross-fertilisation of American-backed Hollywood stars with Britain's fine character actors and technical know-how instantly struck oil. Admittedly there were some embarrassing blips, such as for example, Errol Flynn apparently single-handedly winning the battle for Burma in World War Two. That apart, the fusion of American money with Hollywood stars and

British skills triumphed to the benefit of all parties. With the industry awash with money, much of it in sterling, Hollywood was enjoying the best years of its life. I couldn't wait to catch the flavour of it.

Americans are by nature among the most hospitable people in the world. In the 1950s, echoes of the Battle of Britain, Churchill and the Blitz heightened their admiration for the British. The English stiff upper lip, Cockney rhyming slang – the visiting Brits could dine out on those bonuses at the most exclusive parties in town. Spout three lines from Shakespeare and the ecstatic hostess would throw in the guest villa for as long as you wanted. (The talented British actor Laurence Harvey parlayed more hot dinners out of *Hamlet* than Olivier did in his prime.) But if, in addition, you worked for the largest daily newspaper in the world, then, in the parlance of the locals, you could write your own ticket. Nothing cynical about it. Hollywood always admired success. In the land of Barnum and Bailey, to be the world's largest anything commanded respect. So I did not delude myself that the lavish welcome I received on arrival was anything much to do with me; but a newspaper circulation of five and a quarter million copies a day was a statistic no self-respecting press agent could ignore.

Hollywood's jitters about the Fourth Estate had been conditioned by its most feared columnists of the day, Hedda Hopper and Louella Parsons. Two singularly forbidding matrons, they exercised an influence that went far beyond the remit of entertainment gossip. They held the reputations of leading film figures in their mottled grasp. They knew this and revelled in it. Hedda Hopper, a Margaret Thatcher in everything but Denis, had the inside track with politicians who courted her shamelessly. When the McCarthy witch hunt terrorised the studios, Hedda's far-right credentials soon became apparent. She intimidated most of the film magnates, using her column to parade her prejudices. Her sartorial trademark was an outrageously fussy hat. Beneath it, a shrewish mouth dispensed the exquisite bitchery that she knew would be quoted around the town. She glided around Hollywood in a vintage Rolls-Royce. Heads turned, or ducked, as she swept imperiously into restaurants. The more she was feared, the greater her sense of power.

On one Christmas visit to her home I had to sidestep the mountain of gifts sent by producers, directors, stars, hairdressers and the like. They rose like a tinselled mountain in the hallway and up the staircase. I was told of one Christmas eve when burglars broke in and removed the lot. Clandestine phone calls were made on her behalf to all the donors, who instantly replaced the gifts down to the last piece of Tiffany. Louella Parsons was treated no less generously, but more out of love than fear. She was, by contrast, a more benevolent operator. She wrote without malice, holding the sole franchise in the sort of material that drips from the pages of *Hello!* and *OK!* magazines. Celebrity births, marriages, separations and divorces were her speciality. Sobbing goddesses were on the phone to Louella even as their husbands were slamming the door behind them. Actresses of note on discovering they were pregnant would inform Louella, the doctor and their partners in that order. The competition between her and Hedda was fierce but never personal. Like two bejewelled parasites, they had waxed fat off this tasty carcass in California. When the star system died, they perished with it. But, at the height of their reign, all Hollywood's greats genuflected, asking only, as Kirk Douglas asked of me, that they 'put the knife in gently'.

CHAPTER FOUR

A Legend on the High Seas

'I see those assholes have got to you already!' Humphrey Bogart grinned. His creased eyes had quickly taken in the gallons of gift-wrapped liquor courtesy of Hollywood press agents interested in my health, and circulation. 'Bogie' was happy and it showed. It was a bright Saturday morning in January 1955. There was a strong Pacific breeze, perfect for sailing, and he was eager to drive down to the yacht basin in Los Angeles to board his beloved boat, the *Santana*. This sleek beauty of a vessel was his passion, stoically accepted by his actress wife, Lauren Bacall, as 'the other woman in their lives'. Hero worship can be a dangerous indulgence for journalists, critics especially. The reasons are obvious. But just occasionally along comes someone like Bogart and all those caveats like 'objectivity and impartiality' go flying out of the window. It was the man you discovered you were dealing with, not the celebrity. It had been six months since we had lunched together in London at Les Ambassadeurs, a much-favoured haunt of visiting Americans. I was supposed to be interviewing him but that ritual bored him, the shutters coming down one minute into the conversation. As ever with Bogart, he was less interested in himself, more interested in cheerfully needling his host. I had mentioned casually that I was planning a visit to the States, Hollywood in particular. 'Call me when you hit the coast,' he said. In show business, such invitations tend to be issued on reflex. Like 'darling, you were wonderful'. Doubly so, when extended in the afterglow of a couple of bottles of claret. So, on checking in at the Beverly Hills Hotel that weekend, Bogart's instruction to call him went unheeded. By me. The phone rang. The rasping tone unmistakably Bogart: 'I said for you to call me.'

'I only checked in twenty minutes ago,' I stalled.

'Thirty,' corrected the well-briefed Sam Spade. 'You got plans for the weekend?'

'Well...'

'What I thought!' he hooted. 'Newspapermen are like a social disease around here. Limeys especially. Pack a shirt and some sneakers. I'll be over within the hour. We'll go sailing.'

First lesson learned about Bogart. He did not toss out idle invitations. Following through, even six months later, came naturally to him. It was a matter of principle and of style. I readily confess to having been impressed at the time. In the Hollywood of those days, it was easier to get invited to the White House than on to Humphrey Bogart's boat. And here he was in my room, a cigarette drooping from his lip in a manner familiar in so many of his films. He stared at me quizzically beneath heavy brows. I guessed he was undecided whether to opt for small talk or engage in his favourite blood sport – barbed insults to test the defences. But there was time for that. Moreover, the sun was shining, the wind was up and Bogart was restless to get to sea.

I pointed to all the gift liquor in the suite and suggested we haul the lot onto his boat. 'Great idea!' he grinned, intrigued by the notion of filling his galley with liquor courtesy of Howard, Louie, Maury and the rest. 'Let's go,' he said and soon we were in his open sports car speeding west towards the ocean. Suddenly he braked. 'We forgot the booze,' he shouted on a fast U-turn. Ten minutes later we slurped out of the hotel lobby, the bottles cradled in our arms. The doorman was impressed. Even by the standards of Hollywood's prestigious tippler, this implied serious drinking. 'Have a nice weekend Mr Bogart,' he winked. 'You bet,' said Bogie.

Santana got under way, heading south for Catalina Island. The transformation in Bogart was total. Hands on the tiller, his eyes creased towards the horizon, the man was in his element. 'Well,' he said, looking back towards the coast, 'we've got rid of all that bullshit.

Who's gonna pour me a Jack Daniel's?' There was a good wind and we were sailing fast. Now and again Bogart roared over the screeching gulls, 'The skipper would like a little refreshment!' Sometimes it might have been his Danish crewman 'B S Pete' – the initials stood for 'bullshit' – who refilled his glass. Or maybe Carl the cook. A couple of rising young actors were also on hand. They were selected from a large queue only too eager to sluice out the bilges or stack the ropes, just to be near their idol. As powerful as any of the moguls who employed him, he had no need to surround himself with acolytes or career boosters. He had it all. And Lauren Bacall. His guest list for the *Santana* was therefore selective. Those invited were required to leave their egos and career preoccupations back on shore. By the time he handed the wheel over to me I had personally seen off all the liquor from Metro-Goldwyn-Mayer and started on Twentieth Century-Fox. 'Just keep her steady as she goes,' he said matily, though I noticed he stayed close enough for emergencies. Other yachts sailed by, their owners signalling respects to the captain. Vital nautical information was exchanged by bullhorn: 'Cocktails at five chez vous? Over.'

'Is Joe with you this weekend? Get the bum to call me. Over.'

That night we tied up off Catalina Island. Someone aboard played a guitar. The vocal accompaniment from the captain was strictly substandard but nobody ever hired Humphrey Bogart for his singing. A keen chess player, the cap'n drew me into a game. We played on a small board in a gently rolling saloon. Both players had drunk heartily at the studios' expense and were mentally well adrift of the concentration required. But national pride was at stake. On the surface at least. Bogart may have been a passionate Anglophile – but not over the chessboard. This was the War of Independence Mark II. Bogart went into his taunting mode. His genial insults rose in decibel ratio to the pieces he lost. Forced into an exchange he didn't want he acted out a snarl. 'Who needs this!' Steered into further trouble, he put on a ferocious act of attacking all things British. He railed against our colonial past, the coffee at the Savoy, 'your lousy teeth, lousy food, lousy upper-class accent and the bloody rain. Nothing personal,' he laughed. But the bogus tirade induced a loss of concentration.

'Checkmate,' I said.

'Yeah, well, you gotta have been cheating somewhere along the line,' glowered the master mariner, offering a handshake.

Jet-lagged and over the limit, I craved sleep. I keeled over in my cabin. The boat rocked languidly in the darkness. 'Hey, Limey,' cackled a voice from the shadows. 'Know whose bunk you're sleeping in? Betty's.' (The reference was to Lauren Bacall.) 'Don't puke on the fancy linen.'

At sun-up the following morning I expected Bogart to look ragged after the previous night's carousing. In fact the skipper was up, listening to forecasts and coughing on his third cigarette since awakening. This confirmed another much-admired aspect of the Bogart persona. No matter what revels had taken place the night before, the serious actor behind the image guaranteed that normal service would be resumed the following morning. The Hollywood accolade remained throughout his life: the man was always on time, knew his lines and was ready to shoot. Critics admired him, and though they may not have always liked his films they accorded him a kind of diplomatic immunity. There was always something to relish in his performances. Like that of Spencer Tracy, Clark Gable and John Wayne, Bogart's good luck was in the features he was born with. In an industry that bought faces, Bogart's was unique and totally compelling. It was basic to the powerful and intimate relationship he achieved with the camera. No other actor worked so assiduously at creating, and then sustaining, his screen image. The harrowed eyebrows; the basilisk stare through a cloud of cigarette smoke; the slow threatening smile and flat, lisping delivery – this was the blueprint memorably exploited across a range of classics. I referred to a few of them as the *Santana* rocked gently off Catalina Island. '*Dead End?* Yeah, that wasn't a bad one. George Raft turned it down and kicked himself afterwards.' *The Maltese Falcon*, *To Have and Have Not*, *The African Queen* and, of course, *Casablanca*: 'Now you mention it,' he conceded, 'they weren't at all bad those movies.' That was as far as Bogart was prepared to go in relation to his work. That much he owed those who hired him. And, come rain or come shine, he never gave less than his best. But, outside of that, his home on Mapleton Drive, and his boat, were off limits to the hustlers and the special pleaders who come with the Hollywood package. I remember Lauren Bacall, declaring 'He was the only man I have ever known who truly belonged to himself.' Much of what we saw on the screen was the extension of that persona: his basic decencies; his taste and moral certainties; his abrasive but not unkindly humour were subtly distilled in many of the roles he played.

A self-avowed Democrat politically, a dissenter by disposition and Episcopalian by upbringing, he detested gossip and those who lived by it. The restaurant owner Mike Romanoff, the bogus Russian 'royal', was always welcome because he played chess and tolerated Bogart's verbal onslaughts with a smile. It was a small price to pay for a priceless and memorable friendship.

Few screen heroes in their private lives remotely matched the image they confected on the screen. Errol Flynn was a bisexual drunk with a depravity all of his own. Bing Crosby's apparent meanness as a father hardly squared with his stained-glass persona of *The Bells of St Mary's.* Likewise Henry Fonda, ultimately revealed as a moody, complex, occasionally tyrannical father. Thus a fair test of a celebrity's measure as a man might be the degree to which his public and private images are at ease with each other, the one perfectly superimposed upon the other the way a camera's subject is held in perfect focus. This is not easily achieved in an industry that thrives on the manufacture of illusions. Leading the double life where the two personalities – the public and the private – are jarringly at odds can be damaging to the psyche. Those who found the strain unbearable were either notable suicides or famous incumbents of the Betty Ford Clinic in Palm Springs. But Humphrey Bogart was constructed of more resilient material. His father was a successful East Coast physician, Dr Belmont de Forest Bogart, who could trace his family back to the year 1500. His mother was a talented children's portrait painter who had studied with Whistler in Paris. That cultural heritage took some living down for the man darkly associated with the catchline 'Drop the gun, Louie!' But it was a crucial part of Bogart's character, informing his politics, his wit and his wisdom.

Much of what happened in Bogart's early life conditioned him for the consummate movie actor he was to become. He had turned to the theatre after failing in five subjects at school and reneging on the promise he had made to his father to go to Yale. He joined the navy instead and might have seen some action at sea had not World War One ended two weeks later. His first performance on the New York stage was described by one critic as 'trenchant bad acting'. According to another, his performance 'could be mercifully described as inadequate'. I reminded him of it. 'I agreed with them,' he said affably. His first two marriages having failed, he hoped for better luck with his third wife, Mayo Methot. Out of the frying pan into the inferno. A heavy drinker with an explosive temper, Mayo when drunk was daunting and dangerous. She taunted him about alleged affairs with his co-stars. One night, she chased him with a butcher's knife and stabbed him in the back. Discovering the damage to be minimal, Bogart ruefully shrugged the incident off with, 'I like a good fight.'

The best years of his life, he was eager to tell me (and anyone else within earshot) that weekend on *Santana*, began with his marriage to Lauren Bacall. Born Betty Perske of sturdy immigrant stock in New York, 1944, she displayed an astringent East Coast repartee and velvet sexuality that hit Bogart amidships on their first encounter. When they were on screen together (*To Have and Have Not*, *The Big Sleep*, *Dark Passage*, *Key Largo*) the chemistry was palpable. An intelligent and witty hostess, she was more than a 'Hollywood wife'. She was a forthright companion who shared Bogart's political beliefs, campaigning with him for the Democrat politician, Adlai Stevenson.

Now and again as the *Santana* raced for home, I tried to talk politics with Bogart. He was even more circumspect about that than he was about his celebrity. His one-time entry into the political maelstrom had left him disillusioned and a shade cheesed off with some of his fellow actors. He had joined forces with other celebrities in defence of writers, actors and directors caught up in the anti-communist hysteria of the late 1940s. (The ugly repercussions of that madness are dealt with later.)

Bogart's alignment with such figures as Ira Gershwin, Danny Kaye, John Huston, Frank Sinatra, Groucho Marx and others, was a matter of politics, not personal inclination. His intrinsic conservatism made him an unlikely champion at the barricades. He was merely supporting the right of characters he didn't necessarily love to 'think and say what they damn well please'. But in the end he was disappointed to discover that not all of the celebrated victims were politically unblemished: it emerged that some of them had not come clean about their political affiliations. Some were not the 'innocent martyrs' for whom Bogart believed he had given his name, his time and above all his influence in the defence of freedom of speech. He felt he had been betrayed, uttering the now legendary accusation, 'You fuckers sold me out'.

Loyalty was high on Bogart's list of essential virtues. One day, after sailing into Newport harbour, he brought his skipper into the yacht club bar for a drink. An official approached him, indicating crassly that members did not bring their 'paid hands' into the club. Bogart fixed the man with a glare and called for his bill. He signed it on the front, then wrote his resignation on the back. A few weeks later a contrite committee amended the rules. Bogart was equally supportive of young actors. To the ones with real talent he had this advice: 'Take the big part but hold off on the big house and the Cadillac for a while, otherwise you'll be in hock to the studio for the rest of your life.'

That weekend on the *Santana* had been a baptism of sorts. You get to know a man under sail, under canvas or under fire. All the appealing Bogart facets were in evidence sailing in the Pacific: his style, the finer sensitivities, and the essential good nature of the man. Back in Los Angeles we drove straight to the Bogarts' fourteen-room home on Mapleton Drive in Beverly Hills. Bogart, with his creased bloodshot eyes and two-day stubble, could have walked straight into his role as Charley in *The African Queen*. He turned the key and slowly swung open the door. Across a pristine landscape of white carpet we glimpsed the chic Mrs Bogart pouring tea for some of her elegant friends. A hint of Chanel wafted back towards us. A whiff of bodies and booze wafted back towards them. Against the backdrop of Dufys, Picassos, and Renoirs, we resembled a couple of skid row bums who'd invaded the Tate. A fastidious man, Bogie decided upon a cautious re-entry into the atmosphere. 'Keep your head down and follow me,' he hissed, creeping towards the stairs. 'Nice weekend honey?' enquired his alert-eyed spouse.

We met several times in London after that weekend. Bogart was no longer chain-smoking. By late 1956 he was receiving massive radiotherapy for cancer of the oesophagus. His frailty and the appalling loss of weight showed. Bogart knew he was dying but the old gallows humour was heroically maintained. Nobody was fooled. Everyone understood this was Bogart striving to lessen the ordeal for his wife and friends. When his legs began to fail him a chair was put in the service lift to hoist him up to bed. More jokes were shared with his special chums David Niven, Sinatra, Nunnally Johnson and, above all, John Huston (all together now in some Green Room Up Above). Betty Bacall never left his side. Her husband tried to persuade her to go out for a break. She brushed off the suggestion with an affectionate expletive. Secretly Bogart was delighted. 'Maybe that's the way you tell the ladies from the broads in this town,' he said with some pride.

A few days into 1957, I phoned Betty Bacall from London to ask about him. 'Bogie's going to be just fine,' she said, concealing the more obvious truth. He was dying. 'Goodbye, kid,' he said as she briefly left the room. 'Hurry back.' He died 14 January 1957.

Perhaps the litmus test of greatness in motion pictures is whether history, not merely Hollywood, takes serious note of the subject's work, his life and times. On this score Humphrey Bogart, who died with memorable bravery, has earned universal recognition in the story of our times.

CHAPTER FIVE

Venus Submerged

*'From my vantage point I had the uncanny impression that
Jane Russell was breast-feeding a carp.'*

While there may be many celebrities who are dazzled by the notion of
talking to the press, there are some who might just prefer to go
snorkelling in a sewer. This comes as a shock to your average self-
important hack raised on the concept that every door must be opened
to him or her. Both soon discover this fallacy, usually from the wrong
end of a barge pole. I confess to having been rebuffed by experts. The
formidable Bette Davis (*All About Eve*, *Whatever Happened to Baby
Jane?* and a string of other classics) decreed one day that she no longer
wished to speak to me, in a frosty telegram from Los Angeles. Before
that, another chain-smoking extrovert by the name of Tallulah
Bankhead, whom I'd momentarily forgotten to worship on cue, wired
me to the effect that my prose reminded her of the bottom of a
birdcage. There was a variation on that theme from the volatile singing
star, the late Mario Lanza. He signalled his displeasure by dispatching
to me a crate of toilet rolls with the handwritten inscription: 'These
foolish things remind me of you.'

All this is a preamble to a memorable incident – well it was
memorable for me – which occurred some time in 1948. It concerned
one of England's finest footballers at the time, Wilf Mannion. A
blond, shortish genius of an inside forward, he was the David
Beckham of his day, though without that wonder boy's hype and

highlights. Mannion was the hero of the sensational match in 1947 when Great Britain defeated the Rest of Europe 6–1 at Hampden Park in Glasgow. He was as dazzling with his feet as Fred Astaire, with the body-swerving brilliance of Muhammad Ali. Like Beckham, he had great mastery over the ball, enabling him to outfox his opponents and conjure magical, match-winning passes. For most of his nineteen years as a professional, he played for Middlesbrough. But towards the end he clashed bitterly with the management over pay and conditions. He accused the club of short-changing top players like himself. The controversy exploded into front-page headlines, when he stubbornly refused to re-sign with the club. He went on suspension without pay for six months. He became a virtual recluse in his home outside Manchester, incommunicado to the hordes of journalists, radio commentators and the like who laid siege outside his door. The drama was now far bigger than a sports story. It was now a national *cause célèbre*.

I was persuaded that I had the necessary guile and chutzpah to succeed where all others on the national press had failed. And so a first-class rail seat was reserved for me on the Euston-to-Manchester express. I was delivered to the station in a king-sized Daimler. My suite at the Midland Hotel, Manchester, was commensurate with the importance of the assignment. In the evening the northern editor had laid on a dinner at which leading pundits would fill me in on the story in general and Mannion in particular. Over limitless claret, the experts briefed me on the great footballer's career. They spoke in awe of the miraculous patterns he wove as he danced rings round the opposition. They placed him alongside such legends as Stanley Matthews and Tommy Lawton. They marvelled at his genius in the air, all the more brilliant for a player barely five foot five tall.

It was heady stuff. I returned to my suite, prepared a list of questions, and slumbered in the euphoria of anticipation and cigar smoke. In the morning a limousine swept me to the home of the great man. The uniformed chauffeur saluted me out of the car. 'I'll be about an hour,' I said.

I rang the bell. The door opened an inch, revealing a single hostile eye.

'Good morning,' I trilled.

'Fuck off!'

The door slammed shut. Bolts slid into place.

I returned to the car. Packed my things and caught the express back to London.

No limousine awaited the hero's return.

'What happened?' the news editor enquired.

'He told me to fuck off.'

'I thought he might,' said he.

My sympathies, I have to say, were with Mr Mannion. An occasional comeuppance of the two-word variety is a useful antidote to journalists' delusions of grandeur. Show business of course feeds these delusions with all kinds of blandishments, sweeteners, flattery and free lunches. This buttering-up intensifies when a film company is launching a film, particularly one that has all the indications of being an almighty flop. Faced with the prospect of millions of dollars going down the drain, the company's press agents resort to a variety of stratagems to get their dead duck to fly. The favourite is the 'junket' – a splurging extravaganza of a world premiere to which correspondents are flown first class from all parts of the cinema-going world. This kind of freeloading is frowned upon by most newspaper columnists. But one particular junket seemed too good to miss. It invited me to fly courtesy of Howard Hughes and the airline he owned at the time, TWA, to Silver Springs, Florida, for the opening of his film *Underwater*. More specifically, the invitation was to view Jane Russell underwater.

It could be fairly argued that any view of Jane Russell in her mammiferous prime was awesome, whether on land, sea or in the air. But here was the billionaire, Howard Hughes, a renowned breast fetishist, offering us the ultimate in the cult – the world's most famous bosom undulating in The Deep. On offer was a unique world premiere that would actually be screened in the pellucid depths off Silver Springs, Florida. An audience of critics would be flown from all points of the globe to a briefing rendezvous in one of New York's finest hotels, after which chartered aircraft would fly us south to Miami, where the dunked and scantily clad Jane Russell would wallow before our snorkelled eyes. Howard Hughes's obsession with breasts, Jane's in particular, led to his notorious film *The Outlaw*, which was banned, condemned and vilified so vehemently that the grateful Mr Hughes chuckled all the way to the bank. (A poster advertising Miss Russell and the film was recently auctioned off for $750,000.) It was Hughes who famously designed the cantilevered bra, cunningly constructed to enhance her already prodigious bosom. He had decided on this corrective after viewing a pivotal (his word) scene in the movie. This is where Jane Russell is tied between two trees by leather thongs. She writhes to free herself, the contortions accentuating the movement of her breasts. But not enough for Howard Hughes. Two senior government officials had arrived at his office to discuss a new secret military aircraft. Hughes kept them waiting. He had two other things on his mind. Exploiting his knowledge of aerodynamics, he pencilled a design that would send the bra into increased thrust. Prototypes were created and passed before the inventor's eyes. Satisfied at last, he went back to assisting in the air defences of the United States.

I had got to know Jane Russell some time before the premiere of *Underwater*, so I was aware how out of synch she was with the image Hughes's press agents had constructed for her. A part-time Sunday school teacher, she was either unaware or unconcerned about the explicit body language she inevitably transmitted. After a barbecue one evening she invited me to join her, her mother and her then husband Bob Waterfield for Sunday prayers. I retain a vision of her standing there in wincingly tight sweater and shorts, the long and magnificent legs bare and bronzed below. 'Lead us not into temptation,' she murmured beneath lowered eyelashes. 'Amen,' I said.

But now, on this junket in Florida, I was to witness her in a different dimension. The blandishments on offer at these junkets vary according to the film's budget, or the ingenuity of the spin doctors involved. Howard Hughes being very rich and powerful, RKO (the company involved) were given a blank cheque. As a consequence, the complimentary liquor on the flight to Florida had sluiced as generously into the passengers as had the fuel into the plane's four engines. Halfway towards our destination, those critics able to walk were invited forward to the cockpit in pairs to be initiated into the science of flying. Now and again the plane would gently dip or bank as the pilot demonstrated the Constellation's undoubted versatility. Publicity men wearing company smiles patrolled the aisles begging to be of assistance. My memory is naturally hazy – we are talking some forty years ago – but I recall one distant voice, insisting, 'You're gonna love this movie, believe me. Don't forget to name the producer. Believe me, this is the best thing Jane's ever done. Listen, would I bullshit you? Your glass is empty, for Chrissakes. It's a fantastic movie, honest. Would I bullshit you?'

On arrival at the airport a long procession of latest-model Cadillacs awaited us, chauffeured by men wearing red fezzes on their heads. These turned out to be members of a leading charitable organisation known as the 'Shriners'. (When you have a probable flop on your hands, the Rule Book says call in anybody who can help from the Salvation Army to the Marines.) Already installed in my hotel room was The Information Pack, a great wad of literature designed to con suckers into suspending disbelief.

There were also flippers, goggles, and wet suits for those hacks prepared to submerge for the occasion. Someone gave me a pen that could write rave notices underwater. Since I had no intention whatsoever of drowning for Hughes, RKO or Jane Russell, I joined a flotilla of glass-sided boats from which we could view the soggy epic just as effectively. A large screen had been lowered into the depths. Likewise, a waterproof projector and a waterproof projectionist. At the appointed hour, our boats proceeded to a compass bearing roughly equivalent to front-row circle.

At the same time, a shoal of snorkelling critics slid into the deep blue sea. Unfortunately, the combined disturbance created by the boats and the flippered critics shifted mud and silt off the sea bed. Moreover all the exotic marine life in the vicinity became visibly excited (we can assume they had never been to a movie before – not in Technicolor with Jane Russell, for sure). Meanwhile, the rising cloud of silt and mud had so darkened the screen it was difficult to see what was going on. This upset the underwater scribes, some of whom were having trouble with their breathing apparatus. A couple of them rose to the surface making frantic signals to be hauled ashore. One splattered onto the sand, eyes rolling, flippers in the vertical. I ordered our boat forward for a closer view of the proceedings. Catfish, flounder, sea urchins and some smaller fry in front-row stalls had got there before me. Some began nibbling at the screen. From my vantage point I had the uncanny impression that Jane Russell was breast-feeding a carp. Finally, the screen totally blacked out. It then slowly careened over on to its back. Fade out on Silver Springs, Florida. The publicity corps was puce with embarrassment. Hughes was never available for comment. Jane Russell returned home to California, tight-lipped. She was angry, but not merely because of the fiasco. While all this nonsense was going on, an even bigger bosom had brazenly barged in, to steal the limelight. Bursting fore and aft out of a vermilion swimsuit, a wet-lipped and eager creature named Jayne Mansfield had gate-crashed her way into the proceedings. She had no reason to be there. But her slick press agent, noting the size of the press contingent, had craftily fork-lifted his client onto the bandwagon. The ruse succeeded – for her, if not for the film. Any residual hopes of favourable publicity faded when the reviews appeared. They were universally damp. I didn't want to come down too hard on the film; Howard Hughes had gone to much expense and trouble; there were the Shriners with their Cadillacs; and Jane Russell looked just as great dunked as dry. Nevertheless, after much reflection, my review of the film concluded, 'Suffering catfish – it was awful!' Moral: you can lead critics to the water, but you cannot make them rave.

But it's an ill-wind... Jayne Mansfield's awesome dimensions – a forty-inch round trip – achieved far more press coverage than her elusive talents appeared to justify. She went on to better if not bigger things, but then faded just as swiftly. Legends are not measured in bra sizes. Those screen goddesses we most remember used their sexuality as backup to a unique and insouciant magic. A giggling Jean Harlow, spilled brazen and bra-less out of sheath-tight white satin; Marilyn Monroe, astride a subway ventilator in New York, her skirt billowing skywards – they played the scene more for laughs than titillation. The fun was in the element of self-parody. But all those famous beauties from Harlow through to Monroe and beyond owe much to that statuesque relic of the past, the incomparable Mae West. The archetypal sex symbol, she was the queen of the double entendres. And everybody liked her.

An outrageously camp platinum blonde with fraudulent eyelashes and an immortalised bosom, Mae West became a legend as much for what she said as the way she looked. Defiantly vulgar, she offset it by naming the dukes who dined her and reminding us that the Royal Air Force irresistibly named the world's best-known lifejacket after her – well, the most buoyant part of her. The Mae West lifejacket is as historic a fixture as the Plimsoll line (after Samuel Plimsoll), the Bunsen burner (after Robert Wilhelm Bunsen) and the Davy lamp (after Sir Humphry Davy). But, worthy though those learned gentry were, they did not scandalise a generation, nor bring out the riot squads. Mae West's mocking one-liners, often accompanied by a swivelling of the hips and an exaggerated kick back of a shimmering train, crackle through the Hollywood archives.

Samples: Mae West, on arriving at her office to be greeted by several lusty young males, says, 'I'm feeling a little tired today. One of those fellows'll have to go home.'

And, 'How tall are you son?'

'Ma'am, I'm six feet seven inches.'

'Let's forget about the six feet...'

And, 'Whenever I'm caught between two evils, I take the one I've never tried.'

Much smarter than her reputation suggested, her deftly calculated routines crashed through the taboos of the 1930s. The ten days she spent in jail for an over-suggestive belly dance was, she said, 'quite restful'. She was no Spice Girl or Madonna. She grabbed her audience by self-parody and delicious innuendo. In 1934, she was the highest-paid female star in Hollywood. That loaded invitation 'Come up and see me some time' became the catchphrase of successive generations. 'Unforgettable' is the one cliché that accurately defines her.

It was a taxi driver who pointed out her sumptuous Pacific beach house at Santa Monica. 'Know who lives there? Mae West. Just her, the housekeeper and her butler. What a woman!'

I phoned her. Maybe my accent reminded her of the time when English peers stood in line to entertain her or when Noël Coward bowed reverentially before serenading her at the piano. More likely it was because, forewarned, I addressed her as 'Miss West' and not the more familiar 'Mae'. When I said that I would very much like to meet her, her ladyship said she would be very happy to receive me. A grave, dark-suited retainer opened the door and steered me into a large ornate hall. He looked up expectantly to the top of a broad staircase. His faint smile as the Legend herself appeared was an uncanny reminder of Eric Von Stroheim and Gloria Swanson in *Sunset Boulevard*. I can see her now, sweeping down towards us, the satin-sleek blonde hair framing well-selected eyelashes, and a skittish smile. She was sixty-eight years old at the time, but she dared you to believe it.

The whole image, the flowing pink housecoat, lace handkerchief frothing from a ruffled wrist, was Barbara Cartland come to burlesque; though, on a straight carat count, Miss West was clips and pendants ahead of Britain's superannuated novelist. The glittering collection of jewels, which included gifts from sultans, viscounts and others, was kept in a bank vault. When the mood took her, she would visit them for the sheer thrill of slipping them through her fingers. As she showed me around the house, we paused before a mural on the first-floor landing. A fifteen-foot painting revealed Herculean giants in gold-leaf loin cloths adopting a variety of virile poses. In a nearby room, a nude figure of a much younger Mae West was sited beside the brandy decanter. It held my eyes longer than she thought strictly necessary. Making a rough guess at my thoughts she said, 'Where I was different from the others was because I projected sex with a soul. Mine was a body controlled by a brain.' Smiling wickedly, she tapped her temples, 'Here was GHQ. And here,' she added clicking her eyelashes southwards towards the treasured chest, 'was the battlefield.' It was a nostalgic afternoon for her. 'Dear Noël [Coward] sat just where you're sitting. I remember pouring tea for Viscount and Lady Byng. They were most charming and invited me to King George's Jubilee in London. So many other notabilities visited me on the set. That was how I met Sir Ibrahim, sultan of Johore, and his charming wife.' Thus spake the star of *The Constant Sinner*, *She Done Him Wrong* and *Klondike Annie*. Considering all the flak she had raised in her career, she seemed a shade over-sensitive. I had quoted a passage from a review of her autobiography, which suggested that she had declined that invitation to King George's Jubilee with a letter saying 'Sorry George – too busy'. She was adamant that she sent no such note. I said I thought the king would probably have laughed at it. But this imperious queen was not amused. Back in London I received a long letter from her (her name in gold on pale-blue paper) together with a copy of the relevant text in her autobiography. 'You will note,' she said, 'that the unfortunate phrase does not appear. Yours sincerely, Mae West.'

The initial capitals of her signature were written as two flourishing, perfectly symmetrical circles. Double entendres indeed.

Looking back over the last few pages, I am forced to admit that bosoms appear to overhang the narrative. It would be disingenuous to deny that, as far as tabloid journalism is concerned, the Bosom is a considerable money spinner. The term 'Page Three Girl' is universally identified as, in the words of the late, great S J Perelman, a 'zestful breastful'. That sex is good for the circulation holds true for mankind and the media alike. It has been the treasure chest of the tabloids from the *Mirror*'s cartoon heroine Jane in the 1940s, to the topless Titans of the *Sun* today. When Christabel Leighton-Porter posed nude in a life class at a Birmingham college, she could never have envisaged entering into the history books. But it was she who was the model for the artist William Pett's creation Jane. Her exploits, which played havoc with her flimsy underwear, drew a vast and appreciative audience in all the services. In my army years as a weapons instructor, I was asked more questions about Jane than I was about bombs, booby traps and Bren guns.

Whenever industrial crises and the like forced their stolid way into print it became crucial to sweeten the pill with some toothsome, wholesome sex. This device was memorably demonstrated one postwar morning in the *Daily Mirror* newsroom. The two characters in this instructive episode were the editor and the picture editor. The former, Jack Nener, had succeeded Sylvester Bolam as editor. They could not have been more different. Bolam was a soft-spoken aesthete who hummed madrigals on his tours of the newsroom. Nener, on the other hand, was decibels ahead of his predecessor, roaring chestily at long-suffering subordinates. Flamboyantly Welsh, snowy-haired and irascible, he wore polka-dot bow ties and suffered from gout.

Simon Clyne, the picture editor, was a cheerful, tubby character in spectacles who had acquired his considerable journalistic experience in the hard school of Manchester. He was one of the best picture editors in the Street, but a trifle intimidated by Nener at full throttle. It looked like being a lean day for news. The big story of the day was a rail dispute with truculent overtones as unions and management locked horns. It was dull, boring material, crying out for some pictorial light relief, preferably lightly clad. The gout-ridden Jack Nener plodded painfully in the direction of the picture desk. Simon Clyne was speaking to someone on the telephone; unless I misheard, it was to an important dignitary at a south London synagogue. Simon, it seems, was addressing the official on solemn matters concerning congregational affairs. It was an engrossing conversation. Clyne failed to notice Nener's broad shadow falling across his desk. The conversation continued at leisure with the participants discussing matters far removed from the brash imperatives of tabloid journalism. One eavesdropper had vague memories of references to the story of Jonah and the whale. Whatever it was, it did not inspire the editor. Jack Nener was shifting impatiently from one throbbing foot to the other. When you are editor of the (then) largest daily paper in the world, your picture editor's biblical preoccupations are not a primary concern. By now Clyne had sensed the editor's presence. He cupped his hand over the mouthpiece. 'Is there something you want, Jack?' he enquired mildly.

'Yes there is!' said the exasperated Welshman. 'I want some tits to go with the rail strike!'

Succinct and self-explanatory. The picture editor instantly obliged with some teasing pin-ups to render more palatable the dreary but essential coverage of the rail strike. That was many years ago. Today even our respected broadsheets indulge in the same tricks, softening those dull grey areas of solid text with sexy illustrations on the flimsiest of pretexts. Hollywood's obsession with the Sex Factor in its movie stars goes back to Clara Bow the 'It' girl, and Jean Harlow, the 'Blonde Bombshell'. The trouble is, the so-called 'vital statistics' have a limited shelf life. All's well when those enticing features are buoyantly self-supporting; but faking it when they're not imposes a considerable strain upon those who feel they have little else to offer. In an industry placing a sky-high premium on physical beauty, the lengths to which stars have gone in order to retain their looks – eyes, faces, necks, bosoms and buttocks – render the Bionic Man or Woman a far from fanciful notion. Some of my best friends in Hollywood have gone under the scalpel and been visibly rejuvenated by tucks and suction, and by blobs of silicone here and there. Some faces have been retouched to the point where I have asked old friends (to their considerable embarrassment), 'Haven't we met somewhere before?' At one time, this intricate art was one of Hollywood's best-kept secrets. No star wanted it to be known that he or she was a walking miracle of hemstitching or silicone substitutes. Today, actresses and famous socialites throw parties to show off their implants, raising the hand of the bashful surgeon like the referee announcing the winning prizefighter ('Ladies and gentlemen, this is Doctor Stitchenschreiber, and look at what he did for me!').

The late Betty Ford, once first lady, had a facelift following a nightmare episode of breast cancer and drug and alcohol addiction. She blithely told the world about the facial makeover declaring, 'I'm sixty years old and I wanted a nice new face to go with my beautiful new life.' Back in the 1970s, William Proxmire, senator for Wisconsin, actually put out a press release about his hair transplant. He made no mention of some additional refurbishment around his eyes, reportedly done at the same time. Jackie Gleason was publicly proud of his facelift, inviting friends and strangers to come up close to view the merchandise. Cher has never been exactly coy about her face-lift and other buoyant examples of a surgeon's ingenuity. Phyllis Diller's facelift and breast reduction figured in her comedy routines in addition to enlivening her dinner-party conversations. In fact what was once taboo now earns maximum Brownie points among the Beverly

Hills elite. Cosmetic surgery in the US is tax-deductible, and that covers all the procedures right down to the more recent advances, including penile reinforcement. In May 2003 in the *Independent*, Andrew Gumbel declared about Demi Moore,

> The tabloids have been working away at her overtime reporting in breathless tones how she has spent close to $400,000 on a full body makeover, including liposuction on her stomach, buttocks and thighs, collagen injections in her lips, porcelain caps on her teeth and an operation to replace her breast implants with smaller ones. Several... sightings of her over the last few months suggest that she looks a total knockout passing for as much as 20 years younger than her real age, 40 last November. [He adds cautiously about the alleged body work: 'all or none of it may be true'.]

In a Beverly Hills night club some time back, I dined with a plastic surgeon of skill and charm, named Rudi Unterthiner. Just as he pilots his own plane between Palm Springs and Los Angeles, he has reshaped many of Hollywood's most famous contours. (And quite a few unknown ones, for free.) As we looked down to the dance floor, he smiled. 'I've just noticed,' he said, 'there are four pairs of my breast implants dancing down there.' I wondered about that claim until I noticed one woman catch his eye with an appreciative wink. 'Satisfied customer?' I asked. 'Very much so', said he.

Only in America, Hollywood in particular, could someone like the darkly handsome Rudi, rise from being a fifty-dollar-a-week dishwasher to becoming a rich and much-sought-after practitioner in the noble art of self-pretence. Born in 1938 in the Italian Tyrol village of Sterzing (formerly part of Austria), he worked for a year in the coal mines north of Graz, on the nightshift so that he could study medicine at a college during the day. Unable to get a visa to America through the normal channels, the resourceful Rudi wrote directly to President Eisenhower, using an English dictionary and Tyrolean chutzpah. He landed an exchange visa, which gave him only temporary status in the US. Forced to exit the States periodically, he crossed the border into Canada. Shelving his long-held ambition to become a surgeon, he became a ski instructor. He was perfect in the role. Purveying bronzed

European charm and the sinewy masculinity of a Steve McQueen, he became the sultan of the slopes. Heiresses, film stars and other cover-girl skiers clamoured for his services. It enabled him to salt away the dollars needed for his medical education.

Rudi acquired his MD at Edmonton, Alberta, and started training as a neurosurgeon. But he soon discovered this was not his kind of surgery (an unsuccessful tracheotomy on a young child who'd been hit by a bus as he ran across the street with fifty cents clutched in his hand moved Rudi Unterthiner to tears and out of the department). 'I took leave of absence for a week and went to the mountains and thought for a while. Then I came back and on the first day they brought in a child who'd had both hands caught in a lawnmower. None of the doctors was enthused about the case because hand surgery is long, tedious work. Also this was a welfare situation, which attracted them even less. But I jumped in and said, "Let me try". I operated on this child and it was like a mosaic, putting everything together piece by piece. When, a few months later, the child had perfect function, I knew I had found my specialty.'

When I met him, Rudi ran three practices, in Lancaster, South California, in Los Angeles and in Palm Springs. He flew a Beachcraft Bonanza with which he commuted between his clinics. He also flew regularly down to Puerta Citas in Mexico, operating gratis on the poor and the maimed. Married to a lovely Shoshone wife, Linda, with two children, he has a ranch home that accommodates two goats, a mule and several horses. He once described himself as a 'human being, doctor and plastic surgeon – in that order'. The first of these enables him to empathise with the several stars who come to him with their problems. Considering the vast list of plastic surgeons practising in Los Angeles (2,700 on a recent count), the mind boggles at the reconditioned multitude bouncing and beaming along the sunlit sidewalks. Pert and proud above the waist, taut and pinch-proof below. Those who share my curiosity about the arcane world of plastic constructive surgery, may find Rudi's recital of his activities instructive. Like all serious practitioners he insists on laying out for his clients the advantages and the risks along the surgical route: the possible complications; the psychological effect the sudden transformation can have upon their personalities – or their friends; learning to live with a face you may not instantly recognise in the mirror.

Most of the doctor's clients know exactly what they want. They come bearing glossy magazines featuring their favourites. They point out examples, asking for Elizabeth Taylor noses, Raquel Welch breasts or maybe a half-portion of Ursula Andress. But, as the good doctor was quick to explain to me at the time, everything has to balance. 'It's no use looking like Raquel Welch around the bust if you're Mike Tyson around the thighs. Also, some doctors over-silicone the implants, which makes them far too firm, and anyone can see that the woman has had something done. The implant,' he declared, 'should look so natural that, if I were to line up several women and I sneaked an implant among them, you should be able to touch anywhere or anyone and not be able to tell the difference.' (As I reflected on that, a vision of a circus seal squeezing 'Rule Britannia' on a row of motor horns sprang instantly to mind.)

Plastic surgery being an expensive item, it follows that most of Dr Unterthiner's clients must be sufficiently well stashed not to enquire the cost of the operation. Their gratitude at emerging from the procedure is often on a scale of oil-sheikhdom generosity. One patient gave the doctor a watch worth $20,000. An offer of a yacht from one, a Cadillac from another were declined with thanks. A well-known actress, sobbing with delight at the Bardot bosoms she had acquired, kissed Rudi's hands as though she'd had an audience with the pope.

The element of vanity is common to all those who seek visible improvement under the surgeon's knife. But not all are driven by the same need. In films and television, where the camera close-up can be cruelly intrusive, plastic surgeons are as essential as the mechanics at motor racing pit stops. And they frequently have to work at the same frantic speed. The male star of a popular TV show, which had been running for five years, phoned the doctor one mid-week morning: 'The studio is deciding next week whether to go for a new series. Can you fix these bags under my eyes by Monday?' Request denied. Rudi Unterthiner makes no claims to being a miracle worker. Just occasionally, however, there are cases of a poignancy that he cannot refuse.

One morning, a youngish brunette with long hair and bright blue eyes called on the doctor's Beverly Hills clinic. She wanted a facelift. As he does with all his clients, Rudi carefully questioned her. A patient's motives and psychological profile are important factors in the decision whether to carry out the surgery. 'I gave her a lot of room to express why she wanted it. Was it for herself, her husband, her lover? I have to be keenly aware of whether there is total trust between the two of us.' Rudi was not totally convinced that the lady, in her early forties, was telling him the whole truth. He noticed some hesitation in her responses. Sufficient for him to ask her to go away and rethink the situation, then return for a further consultation, at which point he would take photographs. The second time he saw her he felt she was mature enough to undergo the surgery. But there was something about the expression in her eyes that made him hesitate. 'There was real passion in them,' he recalled. 'I wasn't sure whether it was fear or joy, or a mixture of both.' So he prolonged the consultation, feeling instinctively that she was holding back. His instinct was not wrong. 'I suppose I should tell you,' she said quietly, 'I have leukaemia.' The doctor shook his head. 'In that case,' he said, 'I have to advise you not to have this operation.' The patient's reaction was an explosion of anger then tears. 'You're just like the rest of them, sitting in judgement, deciding for other people and getting well paid for it!'

'But this may be dangerous,' the surgeon said quietly. 'I am no internal medicine specialist. But I do know leukaemia can be a problem. There could be dangerous consequences.'

'You think I don't know that?' she cried. 'Now just hear me. If I'm condemned to die, don't deny me the privilege of dying as beautiful as you can make me.' Rudi looked over her head at the diplomas on the wall. He wondered how her demand squared with the ethics of his profession. 'I was in this "skin" beauty business. But I was a physician first. I was also a human being.' He took her hands in his. 'I'd still like to give this a lot of thought.'

She said, 'I don't want you to give it a lot of thought. Look, if I am well, that is, in recession, would you do this for me?'

'That's not good enough,' Rudi Unterthiner said.

'What would be good enough?'

'I'd want a Board-trained haematologist, a specialist in blood diseases and leukaemia. If he gives you a complete check-up, with laboratory examination, physical examination, and sends me a written letter indicating the results of all these tests and states that he does not believe that surgery is contraindicated and there is no danger, I may consider it.'

That pacified her. They had this prolonged discussion about life and death. 'She was quite adamant about wanting me to beautify her.'

The woman was examined by the blood specialist. He confirmed that she was in remission and that there was no contraindication to the surgical procedure. Rudi carried out a facelift. The bandages removed, the patient viewed the face reflected in the mirror and was ecstatic. Her life expectancy, she well knew, was minimal. But now she no longer cared. She would go the way she wanted. Looking good into eternity.

CHAPTER SIX

Just Spell the Name Right

No traveller on safari in the Hollywood jungle can escape its most assiduous predator – the press agent. Publicity may be the oxygen of celebrity. The trick is how to get a whiff of it when you most need it. The multifaceted charmer created specifically for that purpose is the 'praiser', aka the 'mouthpiece', aka the press agent. Of all the disparate characters burrowing away in the City of the Angels, these verbosely articulate manipulators are by far the most intriguing. One of their primary functions is the window-dressing of second-rate talent. The worse the performance, the greater the need for their services. Many a dog of a picture has been rescued by the adroit manipulation of the press reviews. Let us assume a critic has written, 'No picture has amazed me more by the excess of its banalities or the dullness of the performances.' You may be sure that the quote outside the cinema will read,

'No picture has amazed me more...!'

A review that declares, 'This film will delight all those with a taste for the puerile and the mundane...' will resurface on the placards as

'This film will delight all...!'

These stratagems come second nature to publicity gurus hired to promote movies and their stars. But of course their primary function is to sell tickets. Press agents are as crucial to stars, producers and film distributors as oxygen is to a fading patient. If you are successful and therefore rich you can afford the services of the best. Of these, the legendary Rogers and Cowan have cornered the lucrative PR market in New York and Los Angeles for decades. Henry Rogers, immaculate in Brooks Brothers and Turnbull and Asser style, was the handsomer of the two and therefore the favourite of the screen goddesses among their clients. Warren Cowan eschewed his partner's English-gent persona, leaning more towards Rodeo Drive chic than Brooks Brothers elegance. Round faced and urbane, seeming always to be smiling even when he is not, he is underrated by stars and moguls at their peril. The muscle he exerts over even the most powerful movie stars – let alone over the major studios – can be awesome. Assisted by hand-picked clones of the sleekest and slickest operators, he brilliantly steers his clients through all the phases of the Fame Game. Should they become involved in scandal, then damage limitation becomes critical.

The press agent is the stars' shadow. He is concerned with what they do, what they say, whom they dine with; their faces, teeth, clothes, sexual preferences and – I almost forgot – their talent. All these elements combine to create The Image – the ultimate persona for which the character concerned will invest a large chunk of his present and future earnings. But sustaining an image, particularly one that is dramatically at odds with the client's true personality, is part of the fine madness that has afflicted several of Hollywood's most famous victims. Many of California's three thousand or so psychoanalysts are on round-the-clock call to those who find it all too much. It is hard enough to stand in front of the cameras and perform. Trying desperately to maintain a made-for-media personality has turned even the most resilient performers into basket cases. Thus the really effective press agent will be shrink, Svengali, minder and father-confessor as his client walks on eggshells towards stardom, or oblivion.

Of course, when you are that powerful, you take on only the most prestigious clients or those likely to end up that way. You do not need to subscribe to the 'just spell the name right' bromide by which the bogus and other no-hopers achieve their fifteen minutes of fame. That market is handled by the hustlers who 'plant' items in the gossip columns in the hope that a ripple might spread into recognition. It is a science of a kind and one should not underrate it. If you can lie disarmingly, exaggerate barefacedly, demonstrate the same chutzpah of the man who sold the Brooklyn Bridge, then there's a niche for you somewhere. But you will get nowhere unless you have some leverage with Hollywood's most influential trade papers, *Daily Variety* and the *Hollywood Reporter*. These two – called 'bathroom bibles' because they're mostly read on the toilet – exercise a power out of all proportion to their comparatively minuscule circulation. Stars, producers, directors and writers would sooner be an 'item in the trades' (and therefore read in influential quarters) than be mentioned in the *New York Times*, which scarcely anyone in the day-to-day hustle has time to read. 'Reading the trades' is an essential ritual for Hollywood's filmmakers. They slit the wrapping with trembling fingers well before the first coffee, jog or telephone call of the day. On seeing their names in print – whether the item is true or not – they experience that frisson of celebrity that sustains them for the day. It is a parasitical enterprise, leaving all participants content: the 'planter' who delivered the item; the paper who published it; above all, the central character in the conspiracy, the subject of the story. The archives of the business are stacked with examples of slick manipulators elbowing bogus situations into print. Some of the schemes are harmless and quite ingenious.

Hollywood's most relished fable on this subject concerned a publicist by the name of Stan Rosenfield. According to the well-informed David Shaw of the *LA Times*, he had a client, a former actress, who had decided she wanted to get back into the business. Rosenfield could have just put that story out in the hope that it would lead to offers. But he knew the result would be zilch or less. So he embellished the story by announcing that the actress concerned had already signed a contract for her comeback role. This was based on Rosenfield's maxim: 'The best way to get work in Hollywood is to make it look like you already have work.' (The euphemism 'resting' is poison in a town that equates the word with a terminal disease.) Mr Rosenfield put out a press release stating that his client had been signed up by a British producer named Roland Arch to star in a film called *Mother of Pearls*. He added the brief outline of the script, which concerned a nun who had escaped from Nazi Germany shepherding a dozen orphans.

What the inventive Mr Rosenfield did not say was that (a) there was no such producer; (b) there was no such film and therefore (c) no such nun or little orphaned children.

Nevertheless the *Hollywood Reporter* dutifully published the story and the signing of the contract. Unfortunately, the announcement did not immediately produce a rush of interested enquiries. Stan Rosenfield manned the fuel pumps. Two weeks on he put out another press release: 'The British producer Roland Arch has arrived in Los Angeles for discussions on *Mother of Pearls*.' As before, the 'trades' published the story again, plugging the name of Rosenfield's client as the star of the film. Nothing succeeds like excess. Mr Rosenfield felt he could now introduce a subplot – another client. He planted a follow-up item stating that his client, an unknown actress, would 'co-star' in *Mother of Pearls*. The *Hollywood Reporter* felt it could hardly ignore this development to its original story and published it.

Both actresses were ecstatic to see their names in print – and in the 'trades'! But then, having acquired the status of an 'item' in the *Reporter*, the 'star' received real offers from agents and producers who were interested in her. To Mr Rosenfield's astonishment, she was acutely embarrassed. 'You know, Stan, people are beginning to ask me about the movie, and the nun. And the orphans. So when do I start and who's gonna play the male lead? You gotta get me out of this!' The press agent was mortified. Such ingratitude! You get these chicks the kind of publicity to kill for and look how they repay you! But he now had to get the genie back into the lamp. So he put out another brief press release stating that 'because of delays in filming' the star of *Mother of Pearls* has requested and received her release from the picture. David Shaw writing in the *Los Angeles Times*, reported that at a party later, an actor friend came up to the actress and said, 'I hear you're not going to do the Roland Arch film after all. Good. I worked for him on a movie last year and he's a real sonofabitch!'

When all this is revealed for the fairly harmless chicanery it is, far from being aghast, the inhabitants burst into a round of applause.

Publicity is the name of the game. But there is one time of the year when the town's press agents have a billion-dollar field day: the run-up to Hollywood's spectacular exercise in self-love, the Oscars. Blast-off occurs immediately prior to the Academy nominations. It achieves optimum velocity on the eve of the Oscar ceremony itself. Projected on coast-to-coast TV, it attracts the largest audience of the year.

It is not without its critics: there are some – notably the late George C Scott, who refused to accept his Best Actor award – who consider the whole exercise demeaning, no more than a brazen exercise in full-frontal narcissism. Designed to influence those qualified to vote, whole-page advertisements (in black and white, around a thousand dollars a time; in colour, triple that) fulsomely extol the performances of their stars with all the superlatives in the press agents' canon. More than four thousand video cassettes of the nominees' films are sent out to Academy voters. The way the studios try to outdo each other in this annual stampede is close to indecent exposure. Everyone and anyone who could remotely be regarded as having some influence is importuned with the brazenness of a top-class call girl. I suppose it's difficult to fault the system when one realises how a nomination, let alone the Oscar itself, can send box-office receipts sky-high, create a star overnight or boost a fading career. Even those stars who claim to disdain the whole circus go along with it under pressure from their producers or the studios. As Roger Ebert, the well-known film critic, observed, 'For an actor, the idea that a studio will spend lots of money to help him or her win an Oscar is too hard to resist. If it means jumping through hoops in return, they'll do whatever it takes to get that nomination.'

So the whole charade becomes mutually parasitic. By publicly applauding their star, the studio guarantees his or her future loyalty and compliance. So everybody's happy. The press agents congratulate themselves on the 'socko coverage'. The 'trades' laugh all the way to the bank. It is estimated that the 'majors' spend upwards of half a million dollars each on page ads in the 'bathroom bibles'. I was in Hollywood when John Wayne's awesomely over-hyped epic *The Alamo* was launched upon the US and the world. Come nomination time, he plugged the film for 43 consecutive days in the trade papers. He also sent out a press release the length of an average novel in which he was depicted as 'the George Washington of films, storming the Celluloid heights for God and country'. (Reviewing the film back in October 1960, I noted that Wayne had put most of his personal fortune – and close relatives – in the picture, adding that in my view despite the massive hype and investment nothing could disguise the film's basic and sometimes boring imperfections.) Still the film earned seven nominations but only one Oscar, for the quality of its sound.

Some of the pre-nomination stunts can bring on the dry heaves. At a special screening for disabled viewers of *My Left Foot* each viewer was reportedly handed a chocolate foot. The film won Best Actor and Best Actress nominations for Daniel Day-Lewis and Brenda Fricker in addition to three other nominations. The point is, they almost certainly would have achieved their accolades *without* the hype. There are those in the trade who still blush at one particular ad plugging the performance of the actress Margaret Avery in *The Color Purple*. Some genius decided that the ad's message should be written in the primitive Afro-American dialect of the character she played: 'I knows dat I been blessed... Now I is up for one of de nominations for Best Supportin' Actress.' (And I writer would sho' like to have puked in de quietest corner of de plantation.)

But all the signs are that Academy voters have become increasingly put off by these tricks in the 'trades'. They know the nature of the beast. They can distinguish between hype and the real McCoy. They know, everybody knows, not everything in the 'bibles' can be taken as gospel truth. As George Schlatter, producer of the memorable hit TV show *Laugh In*, testified according to the *Los Angeles Times* in 1978, 'People lie to the trade papers as a matter of habit. They spend hundreds of thousands of dollars a year lying to the trades about the gross of a film, about the deals they made, and about the ratings of their TV shows.'

This view was confirmed by publicist David Steinberg, who observed wryly, 'The standing joke in the industry is that only fifty per cent of what you read in the "trades" is true, but the great fun is trying to figure out which fifty per cent.' To which we can add this colourful, if convoluted, judgement from the public relations guru

John Friedkin: 'What boggles my mind is not that everyone gives the trades bullshit or even that they print bullshit, but that some very sophisticated people who get their own bullshit printed every day are still willing to believe other people's bullshit when they read it.'

I think I know what he means.

For all that, I have a special regard for most Hollywood press agents, whose general demeanour depends largely upon the clients they have to handle. Success on the megaton scale can sometimes transform an otherwise amiable character into an enervating monster that makes Doctor Jekyll's alter ego seem positively affable. Prolonged exposure to the round-the-clock eccentricities of celebrities has forced many a press agent to make a bonfire of such vanities and go into a less humiliating occupation. Some are employed not to give information to reporters, but to keep all but the specially favoured at bay. These tight-lipped minders are paid handsomely for the many inspired ways they can say 'no comment'. Paradoxically, this arms-length policy works by conferring a scarcity value on the stars, which significantly enhances their status. Greta Garbo was the classic example. The billionaire eccentrics Howard Hughes and Paul Getty Sr shunned the press long ago, as Frank Sinatra was to do in later years. My own cordial relationship with this turbulent troubadour collapsed way back following a few critical comments I made on what seemed to me to be an over-sensitivity to public scrutiny on one of his visits to England. We will come to that minor outbreak of hostilities later on. But central to it was Frank's pathological distrust of the press. Even at his most charming – say over Bloody Marys in adoring company – there was always a palpable sense of an internal fuse slowly burning. Whenever we met I could never be sure whether I could get the 'Hey kid, how y'doin'?' routine or a stab of Sicilian disdain.

I met him several times afterwards. His genial but guarded affability suggested I may well have been paroled for good behaviour. But back in the Hollywood of the soaring fifties when Frank was young and Marilyn eclipsed the sun, press agents swarmed around gossip writers, editors and especially visiting columnists like arm-twisting beggars in the souks. 'Look, she's a good kid, all she needs is a break...' 'Listen there's a great talent in there somewhere – would I bullshit you?' 'I promise you this guy is the next James Dean. Kill me if I'm wrong.'

These barefaced exaggerations would usually take place in the seductive semi-darkness of the Polo Lounge at the Beverly Hills Hotel, over Polynesian cocktails at the Luau or other favoured haunts of rising stars and special pleaders. Fame is the spur. Success worshipped, failure despised, Kipling's twin impostors are not recognised in Hollywood, where triumph smells sweet and a loser is a loser is a loser. It is therefore the prime function of a press agent to spice up the package, or, as George Jean Nathan put it, 'ten million dollars' worth of intricate and ingenious machinery functioning elaborately to put skin on baloney'.

The most disappointed press agent I ever knew worked at the time for a leading American airline. I had met him at the *Underwater* fiasco starring Jane Russell. We sat in adjoining seats on a nonstop flight from Los Angeles to New York . At any rate no stop was intended.

Also on the plane were a dozen or so podiatrists on their way to a medical convention 'back east'. Among them sat an attractive television actress whose name, if I remember correctly, was Mary Castle. The PRO for the airline was keen to erase any memories of that junket to Florida. Loquacity being the nature of the beast, he kept up a nonstop monologue designed, subliminally, to enhance his company's aircraft in my eyes. I'm not sure I can remember his words precisely. But as I recall he said he was sure glad to have me aboard on account of he loved the Britishers who took all the flak in the Second World War and all that bombing in London to which his airline had three flights a day with great food and would I keep his card because if at any time he could be of help he would be glad to do so and that's my home phone but you can.

This verbal marathon was abruptly interrupted by a shrill ringing of a bell. Stewardesses began to run to and from the cockpit wearing those paralysed smiles that reassured no one, since in the darkness outside we could see a long tongue of flame streaking from number three engine. And very soon the pilot was announcing chattily that, as we were over Indianapolis, we might as well drop by and say hello.

By now engine number three had been cut off and we were descending at a no-nonsense speed. 'Aren't we making an emergency landing?' I asked the press agent.

He winced. 'How about calling it an unscheduled halt?'

'Nice try,' I said. 'But how about calling it a forced landing?'

The fact that Indianapolis was a 'dry' city would hardly have been critical under normal circumstances. But, at around two in the morning on a snowbound airfield and four hours to wait for a spare exhaust stack to be flown out from Kansas City, morale in the cabin hit zero. With no drinks being served on the plane a decision was made, the upshot of which was a pooling of passengers' personal liquor. There was plenty of it aboard. Passengers linked by a common emergency – and lashings of alcohol – tend to become very friendly indeed, notably in the euphoria of survival. Within two hours the cabin had taken on the raucous delirium of an office Christmas party. The actress, blissfully discovering she had twelve podiatrists literally at her feet (and a journalist and press agent for a bonus) kicked her shoes off and leaned back in ecstasy, a cross between Goya's clothed Maja and the barefoot Contessa. One of the medics, somewhat unsteadily, was examining her feet. He was swiftly elbowed aside by others eager to make their own hands-on diagnosis. 'Gee, you have a fascinating flexor longus digitorum,' one of them murmured, passing his hand over her ankle. The actress sighed contentedly. 'Tell me more,' she said. 'Just feel that tibialis osticus!' another doctor said (I cannot swear to the accuracy of the words, which were coming over loud but slurred).

Everybody seemed to be enjoying the situation, except of course the press agent. When you have been trumpeting the incomparable virtues of your company's airline it is mildly disheartening when, within an hour an engine catches fire, the plane is forced to make an emergency landing and happy podiatrists swarm around the unshod feet of a television star, her shapely limbs draped over the seat in front. Thoughts of what the media (I do not include the medical journals) might make of the situation drained all colour from his features. 'Don't worry,' I said, tapping my nose, 'I'll just forget the name of the airline – OK?' He put a grateful arm around my shoulder and said that he hoped next time I hit the coast I would bring my good woman and that we'd have ourselves a ball and that... But the rest was lost in the roar of the engines (four) as our plane soared up towards New York.

CHAPTER SEVEN

John Wayne

'Jeeze – don't tell me you're a friggin' pinko!'

Hollywood in the early 1950s showed journalists its pretty face but not its darkest corners. It offered you all its several pleasures virtually around the clock as long as you were not there to spoil the fun. You could explore the place at your will, but not hunt for skeletons in cupboards. There were plenty of these when I arrived there in June 1952. On the surface, 'Tinseltown' seemed exactly as I'd been led to expect. The red carpet was unrolled. Liquor, limousines and largesse cosseted the honoured guest. All the tacky and tactile delights of the greatest fun factory on earth were on offer. Lunches in the soft-leathered booths at the Brown Derby on Wilshire Boulevard with whoever needed a film to be plugged at the time. Dinners at Chasens with such A-class celebrities as Alfred Hitchcock, the actress Greer Garson, Mr and Mrs Henry Fonda, the Kirk Douglases and the Gregory Pecks. It was top-echelon bliss as long as you kept off politics, steered clear of religion, slavery and other conversational hot potatoes.

I discovered this soon enough when I met up with that great Western icon, John 'Duke' Wayne, the uncrowned king of Hollywood if not the universe. He was the biggest box-office draw in the Western world. He was revered and loved. Almost every role he played reflected the values he most admired: Patriotism, Freedom and the American Way of Life. None saluted the flag more fervently each day than did this drawling giant, born Marian Michael Morrison, 1907. This ritual, conducted every morning at his home near Newport Beach, Southern California, was in the spirit of many of the gung-ho films he made, such as *The Alamo*, *Operation Pacific*, *The Longest Day* and *The Green Berets*. Whoever the enemy, Wayne, seemingly sculpted out of Mount Rushmore, stood fought and died for the good old US of A. However, this side of him was only partially on offer when we met for our interview. It was Wayne the gruff, hard-drinking box-office idol on display, with a 'minder' eavesdropping in case I exceeded my brief. Wayne picked me up at my hotel in a Cadillac. This was some accolade, and the hotel manager stood back in awe. We drove up through the meandering Coldwater Canyon then down to the location in the San Fernando Valley. Wayne, a giant of a man with tanned, cracked-leather features and a bone-crushing handshake, was in rollicking form. A ritual initiation was called for. A huge grey cowboy hat was shoved down to my ears. I was then formally presented with a foot-long stick with a leather handle, autographed by the horse wranglers. This implement, they explained, was a horse persuader or 'Peter Beater'. A sharp tap with it on a stallion's genitals apparently worked miracles with an under-performing steed. I wondered, idly, whether the same trick would work with sluggish actors. Wayne rolled back with a roar of laughter, and the interview got off to a galloping start. The customary trivia out of the way, the subject turned to politics. In Britain, the Labour government had recently been replaced by the Conservatives, much to 'Big Duke's' delight. His right-wing credentials were legendary. I countered with a defence of Labour, citing the welfare state, full employment and the National Health Service (nothing so revolutionary as the 'common ownership of the means of production, distribution and exchange'). John Wayne recoiled as though jabbed by a cattle prod: 'Jeeze – don't tell me you're a friggin' pinko!' he growled. There was an uncomfortable silence. Out went the bonhomie. Down came the shutters. Anglo-American relations plummeted. The minder frowned at his watch. I was swiftly but courteously returned to my hotel – Stetson, Peter Beater and all.

'How d'you get on with Wayne?' a friend asked.

'OK, until I sang the praises of a free National Health Service.'

'Oh boy!' he laughed, 'that practically made you a card-carrying commie!'

This episode touched on the political undercurrents still swirling after the most agonised period of Hollywood's history. The early 1950s, as we have seen, were the latter end of the notorious anti-communist witch hunt, the 'Blacklist' and the humiliating inquisitions of the House Un-American Activities Committee (HUAC): the unpleasant handiwork of the late Senator Joe McCarthy (1905–57).

In an atmosphere of paranoia bordering on hysteria, careers were destroyed, lives were ruined and great writers and directors went to jail. Everyone was warned: pledge your loyalty or you're out of business. Film scripts were scrutinised by literary spies to ensure no subliminal left-wing messages hovered between the lines. Actors, writers and directors searched frantically through their press cuttings and CVs for any evidence of left-wing comments, or even the most obliquely liberal utterances in public. Inevitably, liberal-minded intellectuals were immediately suspect. One or two undoubtedly had been communists or at least left-wing activists. They were marked men. Studio bosses were warned not to hire them. Freedom of speech was an expendable luxury in the turbulence of the times. I remember asking a Hollywood aide if he could put me in touch with the film director Edward Dmytryk, a tough radical filmmaker with an impressive track record.

'Why would you want to talk to Dmytryk?' the aide asked.

'Why shouldn't I?'

'He's not the flavour of the month, believe me,' he warned.

Dmytryk was one of a band of martyrs known as the 'Hollywood Ten': Alvah Bessie, Herbert Biberman, Lester Cole, Edward Dmytryk, Ring Lardner Jr, John Howard Lawson, Albert Maltz, Sam Ornitz, Adrian Scott and Dalton Trumbo. Mostly writers, they had all refused to declare before the HUAC whether or not they were communists. All served prison sentences; some of Hollywood's greatest talents driven to scrubbing toilets, sweeping yards or working in the prison laundry. On release, many couldn't get work for years.

Another victim was the singer/actor Larry Parks, famous for his triumphant impersonation of Al Jolson of *Jazz Singer* legend. Forced to appear before a HUAC hearing, he confessed to having once been a communist. When he emerged from the committee room he said, 'I have just spoken ten words which have probably spelt my ruin: "I was a Communist Party member from 1941 to 1945".' He was not far wrong. He did not make a film for years. In spite of his confession, the studios were terrified to hire him. He and his wife Betty Garrett were driven to touring small-town theatres in the US and Canada. When I met him in London in the spring of 1954 he was still virtually a Hollywood exile. I asked him whether he thought the squeeze would last much longer. He chose his words with the caution of a frightened man: 'I think the average American is like the average Englishman – he recognises that all men make mistakes at times.' He never made another film of any substance.

Undoubtedly there were some in the Hollywood of that era who were or who had been communists. The anti-Soviet Cold War politics of the time had fuelled the Hollywood witch hunt. Many of the studio moguls became nervous. Influential right-wing columnists challenged them to hunt out and fire the alleged 'subversives'. (The columnist Hedda Hopper, the feared high priestess of malicious innuendo, targeted Dore Schary when he became head of production at MGM in 1948, dubbing the studio 'Metro-Goldwyn-Moscow'. Infuriated, Schary threatened to sue both her and her paper, the *Los Angeles Times*, for $5 million. The paper killed the item in its later editions and apologised.)

Nevertheless it became essential for the studio bosses to proclaim their patriotism. Until McCarthy, the powerful chieftains who ran the major studios had been free of any prejudice. Most of them, or their forbears, had come from Russia, Poland or Lithuania. But despite their immense studio power they felt threatened by the witch hunt's focus on Soviet communism and the alleged fellow travellers in the USA. For the first time since the immigrant former glove salesman Schmuel Gelbfisz (Sam Goldwyn) moved in to create the place half a century before, xenophobia and anti-Semitism surfaced in Hollywood. There was an exquisite example of this during a historic hearing in Washington of the House Un-American Activities Committee under the chairmanship of Congressman J Parnell Thomas. Nineteen witnesses were to appear. They called on leading Hollywood celebrities to fly to Washington to give them moral support. A planeload of stars led by the director John Huston, in a plane loaned by the billionaire Howard Hughes, flew to the capital in support. These included Humphrey Bogart, his wife Lauren Bacall, Ira Gershwin, Danny Kaye, Gene Kelly, John Garfield, June Havoc and others. They were a brave bunch of indignant stars fighting what they saw as a serious threat to Hollywood and the lives and livelihoods of many of its leading writers and directors.

But a certain Congressman, John Rankin, took an oblique view of the rallying celebrities. Holding up a list he declared: 'I want to read you some of their names. One of the names is June Havoc. We found out from the Motion Picture Almanac that her real name is June Hovick. Another is Danny Kaye, and we found out that his real name was David Daniel Kaminsky. Another one here is Eddie Cantor...whose real name is Eddie Iskowitz. There was one who calls himself Edward Robinson. His real name is Emmanuel Goldberg [in fact it was Goldenberg]. There is another one who calls himself Melvyn Douglas, whose real name is Melvyn Hesselberg. There are others too numerous to mention. They are attacking the committee for doing its duty to protect this country and save the American people from the horrible fate the communists have meted out to the unfortunate Christian people of Europe.'

Eddie Cantor, Danny Kaye, Edward G Robinson, Melvyn Douglas – just four of the biggest stars in Hollywood who brought considerable distinction to the industry. Congressman Rankin's rabid prejudice, however, discredited the man and any influence he might have had at the hearing.

All this happened long ago. In Hollywood terms it was practically prehistory. Coming back to the place in the late fifties, I noticed that almost all the blacklisted writers were back at their typewriters. Politics could be discussed without the fear that someone was listening with intent. Jane Fonda would speak out against the Vietnam War and be dubbed 'Hanoi Jane' by die-hard Republicans. Marlon Brando would face me cross-legged on the floor of his home on Mullholland

Drive and declare openly his views on capital punishment, the ill treatment of Native Americans, pollution and global capitalism. Frank Sinatra wooed President Kennedy, then, when that romance cooled, switched his invaluable support to Reagan. Barbra Streisand revealed a political conscience along with her superstardom, becoming a leading fund raiser for the Democrats.

Decades later, as the world moved into an uncertain 2003, a new class of celebrities joined the protest against the threatening war in Iraq. Signing the petition of a prominent anti-war group, Not In Our Name, were artists like Steve Earle, Bonnie Raitt, Yoko Ono and Hollywood figures Susan Sarandon, Danny Glover, Martin Sheen, Oliver Stone and Robert Altman. The protestors have been praised by some, considered unpatriotic by others, and possible targets of adverse publicity. On 21 April that year, the the *Independent* newspaper, under the headline, HOLLYWOOD REVIVES MCCARTHYIST CLIMATE, reported that Martin Sheen's anti-war views led to a credit card commercial of his being scrapped; Susan Sarandon was dropped as guest speaker for a Florida charity; the invitation to her husband Tim Robbins to a screening of his film *Bull Durham* at the National Baseball Hall of Fame was withdrawn because the organisers felt his presence might undermine the efforts of American troops in Iraq. Meanwhile, there were hate campaigns against certain well-known radio and TV performers because of their anti-war stance. As in Vietnam, the country was split on the issue. There were many who were convinced that getting rid of the Saddam regime was crucial to the fight against international terrorism.

But that old adage 'There's no such thing as bad publicity' applies as much today as it did when Errol Flynn was rampaging blithely and bisexually through the Hollywood boudoirs.

Scandal and hellraising have long been the raw material of fame. In the movie city the line between notoriety and celebrity is conveniently blurred. The lineage of hellraisers began with Robert Mitchum, continued through Lee Marvin, and was given leather-jacketed status by Marlon Brando. But for his violent death at an appallingly early age, James Dean would have been as good – or as bad – a hellraiser as all of them. He didn't quite have Brando's finesse. Within minutes of our first meeting in his studio dressing room he confided an urge to stand on a Hollywood rooftop and urinate upon the passing throng below. When I suggested that this was scarcely the conventional ambition of a promising young actor, he raised his eyebrows and said that he did not consider himself the conventional type. Some understatement considering his negative equity in manners, professional ethics and the treatment of his fellow actors. As I look back on our cheerless encounter at Warner Brothers years ago, the impression that lingered was of a moody but calculating opportunist driven by an urge to play Russian roulette with life. It was not merely because of his fatal recklessness behind the wheel of his Porsche, or his insane habit of riding his Harley-Davidson hands aloft at 120 mph. The tragedy of James Dean was that he deluded himself into believing that this rash flirtation with danger, like Richard Burton's notorious drinking, might elevate him from movie actor to megastar. Hellraisers make news make stars make money. Curiously, Dean had, for years, expressed a passion for bullfighting. The matador's narcissistic mirror vision in The Suit of Lights, he displayed a balletic artistry in the presence of death that sat well with the image he sought to create of a doomed hero. His friends would be dragged into simulating charging bulls while he made flourishing veronicas with his biker's jacket. The ultimate persona for James Dean would be a brooding composite of role models – Marlon Brando, Manolete and Billy the Kid.

Dean's truculent public persona was largely an act. It worked for him as it had paid off years before with more authentic hellraisers like Errol Flynn and Robert Mitchum. But myths have a limited shelf life. Moreover, his character weaknesses, not least a shameless tendency to exploit and sponge off others, would not, had he lived, have served him well as an actor. Only the finale, in that terrible car crash nearly fifty years or so ago, was real. And it was this reality, more than the myth, that fashioned him into the unfading icon of youth. I have written about the passing of famous movie stars, some who could legitimately be described as legends. But, as a million or more posthumous words have insisted, James Dean had some claim on immortality. Dean, like the Beatles, galvanised an entire generation. And, like that of John Lennon, his death was not the end. Merely a gear change from hero worship in life to cult hysteria in death. Dean's brutally foreshortened life – he was only 24 when he died – became a bandwagon on which mystics, life-after-death kooks and the generally rapacious have turned a useful dollar or two over the decades.

A British bank has used his enlarged photo to induce youngsters to open accounts on their expectation, one supposes, that their hero will keep a perpetual eye on their investments. Half a century on, the icon and the myth still draw tourists and the morbidly curious close to the spot in Cholame Valley where Dean died. At Blackwell's Corner, Lost Hills, a billboard announced, JAMES DEAN'S LAST STOP – 9.5 MILES. It was here that Dean stopped for a Coke before roaring off into that fatal crash. Glossy postcards of the actor do a fair trade all year round. You could browse through an even larger selection at Jack's Diner, half a mile along Highway 46 from the scene of the tragedy. A car park seems an odd place for a shrine, but there in the parking lot of Jack's Diner stood a silver sculpture with the legend, JAMES DEAN FEBRUARY 8 1931–SEPTEMBER 30 1955. Vandals have wreaked their mindless damage over the years. One used a shotgun to knock out the 'm' in 'James'. Meanwhile at the crash scene itself, fans from around the world stand in silence. Some are car fanatics driving up to the ill-fated spot in cars identical to the one in which Dean was killed. Thus the machine achieves equal billing with its owner. Some fans leave intimate notes at the site where Dean died, tender messages empathising with the hero who would have been 72 (as I write in July 2003) today.

The sad irony is that, though he died young after a lightning flash of a career, he can still earn big money – for shrewd entrepreneurs. For what it was worth, I was one of the few people to interview him before his life went up in flames. It was an awkward encounter. Taking his cue from his idol, Marlon Brando, Dean went through the ritual of playing hard to get. One impression I jotted down after that meeting at the studio was, 'This chap is fairly easy to dislike.' Arrogance and a monumental ego are not so hard to take if they're dished up with real awe-inspiring genius. But, when that arrogance and ego is an act, a piece of superficial role playing, then the received wisdom of the day – that he was a 'pain in the ass' may have had some credibility. It seemed to me that he was hell bent on making a bad impression, underscoring what he perceived to be the prime essential of a certain kind of celebrity. The distinguished director Elia Kazan had just completed *East of Eden*, in which Dean unquestionably was brilliant. But, though Kazan was justly enthusiastic of the actor's memorable performance, he did not rate him too highly as a human being. 'But you really should talk to him,' he said. Having had some highly rewarding sessions around that time with such talents as Clark Gable, Gary Cooper, Henry Fonda and Humphrey Bogart, I anticipated no coyness from the young actor whose Hollywood CV was still short on substance. I rang the studio and a press agent from Warner Brothers came to my hotel. I sensed a reluctance to get down to business.

'How's your good lady?' he enquired by way of a preamble.

'My good lady's fine,' I said. 'How's your good lady?'

He looked startled. 'Oh, great. You got everything you need?'

'Don't need a thing,' I assured him. 'Now, about Dean?'

Panic and perspiration showed on his face. 'Ah, that's what I wanna talk about. You know he...um...hates, well not exactly hates, but he doesn't really want to, know-what-I'm sayin'?'

'Fine,' I said. 'Let's forget it. Have a nice day and give my regards to your good lady.' This was in accordance with my standard practice: never try to talk to anyone who doesn't wish to talk to you.

Two hours later a phone call informed me that James Dean would like to meet me. We met in his studio dressing room, where he kept a .45 Colt revolver and a switchblade in his wardrobe. Even in a city that is paranoid about security, this personal weaponry seemed a little over the top. But I guessed they were more the accoutrements of the image than of the man. His general demeanour of cynicism beneath tortured eyebrows added to the pose. The consensus on the short and not noticeably happy life of James Dean was that he was a mixed-up genius whose anarchic persona reflected the frustrations and alienation of the youth of the fifties. I found a scruffy, disgruntled misfit, manifestly in need of a bath. Which of these assessments was the more accurate failed to emerge from our conversation. Having just seen his performance in *East of Eden* I didn't think it mattered. His portrayal of the emotionally confused farm boy Cal was compelling, with that thrill of pleasure that points to a superstar of the future.

(Kazan's immediate reaction on meeting Dean had by all accounts been positive: 'He did things that always attract me. He wasn't polite to me. He made me feel he wasn't straining to butter me up. He said, "I'll take you for a ride on my motorbike," which I did like a damn fool around the streets of New York. He was perfect for the part. I thought he was an extreme grotesque of a boy. A twisted boy.' Years later, Kazan offered a more definitive judgement: 'What I disliked was the Dean legend. He was the glorification of hatred and sickness. When he got success he was victimised by it. He was the hero to the people who saw him only as a little waif, when actually he was a pudding of hatred.')

Dean arrived late for the interview, roaring up on his motorcycle, which he parked alongside the rear wheel of a secretary's sleek convertible. Somebody told me that the security man on the gate asked him, 'You got a message to deliver, son?' but I suspect that was a 'plant' to feed the image. He entered the room, lit a cigarette, which drooped from his lips in the style of Humphrey Bogart (another Dean role model). He leaned against the wall eyeing me suspiciously, then glared at the press agent, who caught the signal and fled the room. When people eye me suspiciously I like to know why. 'What's on your mind?' I asked him. The response was the familiar tirade against the press; the 'cult of personality'; the conflict between the *actor* and the *celebrity* and all the familiar bellyaches of Stars Who Wish To Be Taken Seriously.

I told Dean that I'd heard the original version from Marlon Brando. This threw him into some confusion, since his reverence for the actor was well known, as was his blatant attempt to imitate him. Brando rode a motorbike with a racoon on his shoulder. Dean did the same with a cat. As Brando told Truman Capote, 'I hardly knew him. He had an *idée fixe* about me. Whatever I did, he did. He was always trying to get close to me. He used to call up and I'd listen to him talking on the answering service.' When the two finally met at a party, Dean, according to Brando, started throwing himself around. 'I took him aside and asked him, didn't he know he was sick? I finally gave him the name of an analyst.' Challenged on that, Dean sank down, hunched his shoulders and pleaded in his defence, 'It's just that I'm frightened. This success has all come too early for me. I've got to be given time to master the art of handling Hollywood.'

The press agent put his head round the door. 'Everything OK?' 'Fuck off!' said James Dean. 'Not the best way to handle Hollywood,' I laughed, 'like this urge of yours to pee down on the place from dizzy heights.' He acknowledged that compulsion but added in mitigation that it was only a sporadic obsession. He smiled at last, radiating the 'little-boy-lost' charm that the kids found irresistible. But this surfaced rarely. His face reflected the whole gamut of mood changes. He wanted to know what I thought of him. I said I wasn't sure. I said I'd heard he was a pain to work with and he smiled as though it were a minor compliment. 'Who says so?' he asked. 'Well, members of the cast [on *East of Eden*] to start with,' I suggested. 'You weren't exactly sweetness and light to Elia Kazan and your co-star Julie Harris either.' He shrugged and said, 'I'm an actor,' which in his book supposedly gave him a kind of *un*-diplomatic immunity.

In weighing up the good and the bad in James Dean, we cannot ignore the demons that fuelled his rage and ultimately his self-destruction. There was long, residual anger at his mother's death when he was a child, and what appears to have been a disastrous, alienating relationship with his father. There was, too, some confusion resulting from his sexual ambivalence. He had turbulent relationships with both men and women. Those were not happy days for 'deviants' in Hollywood, notably in the film studios ever nervous of the powerful puritan lobby. (Dean may or may not have known that gays dubbed him the 'Marshmallow Brando'. But it might not have bothered him that much.) He lived under the same roof for a while with the director Rogers Brackett who was gay and rich, and therefore able to lavish a small fortune on his beautiful though opportunistic companion. According to Val Holley in his biography *James Dean*, the actor's agent Isabel Draesemer said 'Jimmy came to me and asked whether marrying Beverly Wills, the young woman he was dating at the time, or moving in with Rogers Brackett, would be better for his career.' Dean grabbed the more promising option: Brackett had influence in

Hollywood and could make the introductions that counted. If it started rumours, it was more grist to the mill.

There is also evidence that Dean cited homosexuality – plus conscientious objection – as a means of avoiding the draft. But, though neither Kazan nor George Stevens (who directed him in *The Giant*) remembered their experiences with joy, there was a compassionate side to James Dean that deserves to be entered into the defence. One example of this was theatrical bordering on the bizarre. A singer, Toni Lee, who had lost a leg in a motorcycle accident recounts in her autobiography a strange episode with Dean. She and he were in a restaurant when they overheard some actors chatting. One of them was heard to make derogatory remarks about her disability. Deeply hurt, Lee fled from the restaurant. At four in the morning James Dean rang her doorbell. He asked her to undress completely. He then, according to Miss Lee, caressed the stump. 'It's beautiful,' he said. 'You're beautiful, and don't let anyone convince you otherwise. Now get dressed.' Why it was necessary for the whole of Miss Lee and not just the affected limb to be exposed is anybody's guess. But maybe Method actors demanded that kind of total commitment. In any event, the episode did wonders for the singer's confidence. It also revealed a rare tenderness in Dean's complex personality.

It is the measure of the man that, incredibly, he is still an icon to millions of young people around the world. Books, songs and films burnish the icon even further. Years after his death, Dean was sent more fan mail than was received by many living stars. The manner of his death, violently crashing his Porsche Spyder, was not totally unexpected. His closest friends persistently warned him he was taking one risk too many. But the wild, hundred-mile-an-hour escapades on twisting highways went with the image. The tragedy begs the question, would James Dean be alive today if he had never left his home town of Fairmont, Indiana, where folk were neighbourly and image counted for nothing? True, much of Dean's psyche can be attributed to the brutally early loss of his mother and his alienation from his father. But not all the victims of a dysfunctional childhood end up in the blazing interior of a mashed-up sports car. Cast in the role of 'rebel', James Dean added a few dangerous refinements of his own. His insane manoeuvres on his motorbike terrified his pillion passengers. He did tricks, rode with his hands in the air, slithered, grinning, in a cloud of dust on the edge of disaster.

Perhaps it was a compulsion whereby the almost effeminately beautiful youth felt he could become the macho Marlon Brando he secretly idolised. But, if subconsciously he was driven to believing that anything Marlon could do he could do better, it was self-delusion. Marlon was a wiser rebel. He dominated events. Made Hollywood dance to his tune. He was always in control except when, as in the case of his errant son, he was a helpless, and distressed, onlooker. But Dean envied, and foolishly imitated, his hero. There were plenty of wise heads on hand who warned him that he was chasing shadows. And there were signs that Dean was at last beginning to recognise this. His parting comment when I left him that day at the studio was the acknowledgement, 'I've still got lot of growing up to do.' Unfortunately this was denied him. Our loss was as immense as his.

CHAPTER EIGHT

Last Tangle in Paris

Film stars tend to behave in accordance with their public image. Olivier mocked. Sinatra intimidated. Streisand unsettled. Monroe teased. Burton outraged. Elizabeth Taylor scorned (as in 'You know you're a shit, Donald, dear'). There were some exceptions, however – Marlon Brando in particular. He employed none of those stratagems. With Brando you got what you saw. At most of our meetings, in London, Paris, Bangkok and Beverly Hills, he would take up a lotus position and stare expectantly, saying nothing for as long as it pleased him. This was invariably disconcerting, since getting him to talk was the name of the game. But the 'game' was precisely what Brando despised. He loathed that cynical concept we touched on earlier, 'I don't care what you say, just spell my name right', or its slick equivalent, 'there's no such thing as bad publicity'. He has consistently rejected all the trappings of publicity: the image making, the hype, the glossy-magazine route to alleged superstardom. This places him on the side of the angels, but not high on the list of enjoyable interviewees. I understood this and often told him I respected him for it. People who talk endlessly about themselves are not, by definition, the most entertaining conversationalists. In my experience, the greater the actors, the less they wanted to talk about themselves. They despised the gossip that is the lifeline for the second-rate or the freaky 'overnight sensation'. So, though 'drawing teeth' is a fair analogy, conversations with Marlon Brando are among the highlights of my forty years in the territory.

The late Elia Kazan, who directed three of Brando's finest films (*A Streetcar Named Desire*, *Viva Zapata* and *On the Waterfront*) reflected on the man twenty years later: 'He is full of deep hostilities, longings, feelings of distrust, but his out-front is gentle and nice.'

Bang on target. He could have added, 'easy to like but difficult to convince him of it'. Admiring him is the easy bit. He is unquestionably one of Hollywood's small bunch of acting geniuses. Even at a massively overweight 78 as I write this, he can still steal scenes from the best in the business. And, as with the rest in that tiny elite, it is performance he is concerned with, not personality. In the fame game that exists by making deals with the devil, Brando sells nothing of himself but his talent. Up there on his mountain-top eyrie on Mulholland Drive, he looks down on Hollywood with disdain, pity and only sporadically with gratitude. He has the supreme satisfaction of knowing that he has become rich and a living legend entirely on his own terms. In a profession whose generating current is the exercise of power, Brando is in awe of no one, fears nobody, and will submit to no judgements but his own. This kind of heresy does not endear him to the moguls and lesser tyrants who function best when acolytes all around obediently nod their heads on cue. There are many choice examples of Brando's well-articulated scorn at those who chase too eagerly after fame.

My favourite anecdote centred on a dinner party the distinguished author Norman Mailer gave to celebrate the deal he had just struck with the studio with his book, *The Naked and the Dead*. Naturally, all those invited were agog at being asked to the famous novelist's hilltop home. Except Marlon Brando, who was somewhat puzzled that Mailer, of all people, should require this overt nourishing of his ego. But everybody was there – John Ford, Cecil B De Mille, Adolphe Menjou, Charlie Chaplin, Bogart and almost every other dazzling star in the Hollywood firmament. According to on-the-spot witnesses it was not a happy occasion. Politically, many of the guests, like Menjou (right-wing reactionary) and Chaplin (left-wing radical) loved the food, hated the company. There were arguments and snide put-downs all round.

Brando, who had arrived in a borrowed tuxedo, avoided the guests, preferring conversation with the black bartender. But the pervasive bitchiness got to him. He decided to go home. Mailer saw him leaving and confronted him with, 'Where are you going? You didn't meet anybody.' Marlon Brando reportedly responded to his celebrated host as follows: 'What the fuck are *you* doing here, Mailer? You are not a screenwriter. Why aren't you in Vermont writing your next book?' No offence intended. Just Brando acquainting Mailer with the priorities as he saw them.

My respect for the man – though a decidedly disconcerting customer at times – is in no way diminished by his pathological dislike of the press. I remember his telling me years ago, 'I'm in the merchandising business selling dreams, emotions and illusions – that's all. Outside of that I am under no compulsion to sell myself as well. Sure, I don't like the press. What is there to like?' I allowed him his prejudices as long as he conceded that some actors too were hard to love. He conceded that with his slow wicked grin, enthusiastically including himself in that category.

Brando's genuine aversion to authority, and his uneasy relationships with women, can be attributed in part to his early childhood. His father by all accounts was a drunk and a verbal bully whom Brando both loved and hated. Brando Sr was a travelling salesman. The job gave him ample opportunity to pursue the two obsessions of his life, drink and a weakness for women, hookers in particular. Marlon, who was nicknamed 'Bud', would have liked a little encouragement from his father, some parental approval when he excelled at school or in sport. This was never forthcoming. The younger Brando grew up in an emotional limbo. Denied the one-to-one encouragement from his pa, bitter over the sufferings of his mother, who was also an alcoholic, Marlon virtually sleepwalked through his formal education. Everything he learned about life was a self-enriching exercise. He is immeasurably the better for it. His ultimate verdict on his father was 'a card-carrying prick'.

So Marlon and his two sisters more or less raised themselves. This clearly worked well for Brando. Despite being crudely and sarcastically put down by his father, achieving no empathy whatsoever with his mother, he mastered the art of acting, read almost everything worth reading, developing into one of Hollywood's most acute and uncompromising talents. He was great company, too, as well as being an ingenious practical joker. He achieved an admirable reputation as a lover – admirable in terms of the quality of his conquests (Marilyn Monroe included) – and for the discretion he exercised throughout the encounters.

Brando appears to have spent almost all his adult life in search of 'enlightenment' and of his 'essential nature'. He embraced Zen Buddhism, refining the art of meditation to the point where he believed he could endure extreme pain without wincing. (Deciding late on in life that he wanted to be circumcised – a fairly severe procedure for an adult male – he told the surgeon that he required no anaesthetic. Meditation, said Brando, would work just as painlessly. The doctor, while admiring Marlon's stoicism, advised his celebrated patient that meditation was, as yet, an untried antidote to the agony of foreskin removal. Marlon protested but finally relented, though he would have liked to have put his meditative powers to the test.)

While we're on this subject, perhaps I might offer the following snippet. Years ago the late Harry Saltzman, co-producer (with Cubby Broccoli) of the legendary James Bond films, invited a hundred or so guests to the circumcision ceremony of his baby son. The ritual would be performed in the orthodox manner, complete with the appropriate prayers. Those of us who do not flinch at the sight of a scalpel found ourselves in front-row stalls, so to speak. I was standing next to Danny Kaye. Once the cut had been made, the infant naturally yelled its displeasure at this unsolicited assault on his manhood. At that point, according to ancient custom, the *mohel* dipped his little finger in a glass of red wine (a vintage claret, you can bet your boots) and gently inserted it between the lips of the bawling infant. The effect was immediate. The wailing stopped. An appreciative gurgle followed. Danny Kaye sniffed. 'The lengths you have to go to get a drink around here!'

Back to Brando. The doctor's insistence in no way diminished Marlon's belief in meditation. But this 'inner searching' would never solve all of Brando's problems. There were too many demons to be overcome. To achieve this over the years, he has reclined on a daunting number of psychiatrists' couches. What emerged was a story of an emotional chaos originating in parental neglect, endured with some fortitude – and charity – by the celebrated victim. One can imagine the effect his recollections had on the expert analysts who questioned him. He would for sure have told them how he and his two sisters spent much of their young lives searching for their alcoholic mother in the darkened bars along Chicago's skid row. Growing up in the thrall of a domineering father, Brando developed a contempt for overbearing authority that has stayed with him all his life.

His rebelliousness at school and his dismissal from a military academy at sixteen were foregone conclusions. Yet there was never any attempt to blame behavioural excesses on a (to use today's jargon) dysfunctional family. Whether his children will blame his fame for their own personal dramas is another matter. Brando's impassioned plea on behalf of his accused son Christian, in a Los Angeles courtroom, was touching for the depth of its integrity. The young man was sentenced to ten years for killing the lover of his half-sister, Cheyenne. She was pregnant at the time. Her baby was born a drug addict. She killed herself three years later. Brando never speaks publicly about those appalling tragedies. But we can imagine what he feels, and thinks. Could his celebrity have been a factor in the catastrophes?

My first meeting with Marlon was aboard the *Ile de France* at Le Havre, in the autumn of 1954 (Cabin No. 122 as I recall). By then he had three films to his credit, which are still cinema classics today, *Viva Zapata*, *Julius Caesar* and *On the Waterfront*. All three roles – Mexican revolutionary, Shakespeare's Mark Antony and Budd Schulberg's punchy but heroic stevedore – demonstrated Brando's vast range and intensity of characterisation. (Years later, his performance as Don Corleone in *The Godfather* would dismiss any lingering doubts about his unique qualities as an actor. After seeing the film, the distinguished American film critic Pauline Kael declared, 'Marlon Brando is marvellous – but then he so often is.')

So I took a fair amount of hero worship up the gangplank to confront the famous passenger before he could disembark. My enthusiasm was not immediately reciprocated when I entered the cabin. I discovered then, and was reminded of it over the years, that Brando's response to journalists hangs crucially on the level of the relationship. By which I mean Brando does all the preliminary questioning to discover whether the two parties involved – he and I – have sufficient in common to sustain a reasonable conversation.

Years later, interviewers were required to pass an even more stringent test. As his collaborator Robert Lindsey recalls (*Brando: Songs My Mother Taught Me*),

> Within twenty minutes of our first meeting, he had my shoes off, my belt loosened and my fingers wired to an instrument that measured my galvanic skin response, all the while explaining that it was a technique he sometimes used to get a personality profile of people by asking questions and observing the reaction of the meter.

I must have passed the first hurdle with Brando that day, since he offered to share his poached eggs with me. During mouthfuls, he was prepared to concede that all in all he wasn't a bad actor and that while admitting he was not exactly beautiful he was not bad-looking either. The slow, mocking smile that hallmarks Brando's engaging persona acknowledged the minor conceit. Even then, before he would become a brooding Hollywood giant, Brando transmitted the kind of static one felt with men like Bogart and Sinatra. We met again later that month at Bandol in the South of France, where he created headlines everywhere by announcing his engagement to a fetching brunette, Josiane Mariani, daughter of a local fisherman. They had met the previous February in New York, where Josiane worked for Marlon's doctor. Riding pillion on Brando's hired motor scooter in Bandol, Mam'selle Mariani was blissfully unaware of the fault line beneath the tantalising Brando disposition: a chronic inability to hang around once conquest has been achieved. The so-called 'engagement' came to nothing. As Marlon would himself admit, 'I have had hundreds of women in my life and not spent more than two minutes with them. I am not constructed to be monogamous. Neither are gorillas or baboons.' When I pointed out that gorillas and baboons don't have a problem with gossip columns he said, 'Nor with inquisitive journalists.'

Brando has been married twice, to Anna Kashfi (1957–9) and Movita (1960–1). His love affairs span more than fifty years and cover a variety of nationalities and skin hues: the Latin, the Gallic, Polynesian – and lusty, home-grown white Caucasian. Of the last of these, Marilyn Monroe was his most famous liaison. It happened in 1955 and was a secret well kept by both parties. The fact that she called him two days before she died suggests a deeper significance to their relationship. It is ironic that in her despair she should call a man who himself had been in psychological turmoil for years. But knowing them both I was not surprised that *in extremis* she would have found him, like Arthur Miller, a gentle and reassuring influence. Unfortunately, that lifeline came too late. Brando could easily have made a fistful of dollars disclosing the verbal intimacies he and Marilyn exchanged in the twilight hours of her life. The fact that he (like Joe di Maggio) has declined to do so is much to his credit. (Responding to a request by the author Anthony Summers for a comment on the affair, Brando said, 'I did know her, and out of sentiment for her I could never talk about her for publication. I think you can understand that.'). Nevertheless, despite a respect for all the decencies, women appear to have been Brando's one blind spot, wayward wives included. He can state the following without batting an eyelid: 'At home one night, before leaving to visit a woman in Beverly Hills whose husband was spending the night in hospital for some tests, I ate a quart of ice cream.'

That must be the ultimate in *sang-froid*. He had designs on the actress Jean Peters, his co-star in *Viva Zapata*. Other actors, aware of her closeness to the all-powerful billionaire Howard Hughes (they eventually married), might have walked backwards in her direction. Not Brando. Access through the front door denied, he climbed onto the roof of her house in the early hours, intending to rope himself down to the bedroom window. The attempt failed. He was spotted by Jean's chaperone and gave up. Which was just as well. The records reveal no successful breaches of the security surrounding Hughes's favoured protégée. But his failure with Jean Peters only underscores his successes elsewhere, which in numbers alone would not have shamed Casanova. Unlike that Italian eighteenth-century adventurer, Brando has always been resolutely, and chivalrously, tight-lipped about his sexual conquests.

But he was always ready to talk about the infinity of causes that have taken his time, his money and his controversial stances over the years. The humiliation and privation of the Native American; the environmental threat to the planet; capital punishment; racial conflicts in the US – on all these issues, and more, Brando has been up at the barricades, using his celebrity for all it was worth: the only excuse, as far as he was concerned, for exploiting his worldwide reputation. Much of this emerged when I joined him in Thailand, where he was filming *The Ugly American*. If I recall that episode more vividly than others, it is because it barely escaped developing into a diplomatic incident at the time. We assembled, the night before the premiere, for a formal dinner among mangoes and palms in a secluded setting outside Bangkok. Moonlight and flickering candles illuminated the shimmering silverware on the twenty-foot-long table. The soundtrack was a medley of twanging strings, the croaking of mating frogs and the occasional screech from the tall trees. Marlon Brando was flanked by George Englund, the film's director, and the host, a former government minister, Kukrit Pramoj, who also played a part in the film. A handsome, cultivated man, he spoke impeccable English, and was splendidly turned out with the gleaming insignia of his rank. Exotic Thai maidens floated around us serving several delicacies, each one being elegantly described by our host seated immediately opposite me. He smiled expansively. I beamed back likewise. His conversation reflected a cultured and philosophical mind. My responses reflected a jet-lagged correspondent whose tired, Western-oriented wit bombed spectacularly on that fateful, moonlit night. I have forgotten what I had said that apparently offended him. But whatever it was he turned and said something to George Englund. The gist of it, I gathered, was that he considered he had been insulted. By me. George Englund leaped up to reassure him. Unsuccessfully. Kukrit Pramoj decided he would exit immediately. His entourage decided likewise. In the darkness the birds seemed to be shrieking louder than ever.

Now, suddenly, other guests were leaving in a hurry. Despite everything, the diplomat bowed courteously in my direction. Protocol, and fears about the film's premiere on the following evening, required that the film executives immediately chase after him, placating him all the way to his limousine. Since the film touched on sensitive political issues, the company chiefs were understandably nervous. Brando, meanwhile, smiling his inscrutable smile, was relishing the situation. An enthusiast for any kind of mischief – notably where he is not the victim – he consoled me. 'I know what you meant, but I have a feeling you blew it,' he said not unkindly. Then he left too. The publicity man who arranged my visit was palpably in shock. He dashed off on an urgent errand of damage limitation. I was suddenly alone, marooned at midnight in a steamy jungle setting outside Bangkok, deserted and disconsolate at a fully laden twenty-foot table miles from my hotel and the rescue of a night's sleep. Silently, the exotically clad Thai servants glided away with trays of untouched food. A magnificent banquet was suddenly bereft of happy eaters. I started talking to myself: 'What did I say? I mean I was only trying to be...surely he must have realised...' But, discounting the creatures in the river and the trees, I was addressing an audience of one. I had flown halfway across the world to cover Brando's *The Ugly American*. And with one incautious quip I had become 'The Ugly Englishman'.

The torment did not end there. The following morning it was clear that Marlon Brando and George Englund had managed to pacify Mr Pramoj. Quite apart from his role in the picture, he had played an influential role as a liaison between the company and the Thai authorities. Nevertheless, I hardly expected to find slipped under my door a gilt-edged invitation to an after-premiere dinner signed by none other than the offended Mr Pramoj himself. The guests included the most distinguished figures in Bangkok, members of the diplomatic corps, bemedalled and bejewelled celebrities from Thailand and its neighbours. They filed majestically along an infinity of red carpeting greeted by a master of ceremony with a microphone in his hand. His voice as he announced the guests' names boomed out from loud-speakers deployed in the giant trees that dominated the glittering scene. I drew up alongside the welcoming party, which included the dignitary whom I had apparently insulted only hours before. I gave my name and heard it reverberate back to me at full decibels from the four corners of Asia: 'Ah, yes, Donald Zec'. I'm sure I heard him say, 'A nut I intend to crack!'

The message was ominous enough. To hear it thundering from loudspeakers in the tallest branches of the moonlit trees was positively scary. I had plenty of time to ponder that remark when the night's entertainment began featuring the singers and dancers of the Thai opera. Barefoot and exotically costumed, they snaked slowly down from the hills in two lines of descending light to a Kleig-lit stage. For several hours, a whole story was enacted in the Thai style. Exquisite hands with elongated fingernails were passed coyly in front of darting eyes accompanied by meaningful movements in double-slow time. I noted that Marlon Brando's head nodded occasionally, which may well have been in appreciation. My own descending eyelids were kept aloft by direct glances from Mr Pramoj's observant eyes. I had not slept in 28 hours. But there was no way he was going to catch me sleeping. I discovered that supporting your chin on the prongs of a fish fork is as good a head-lifter as any. The following day I went to Mr Pramoj's home to offer my apologies. His servant asked me to wait momentarily as his master was engaged in prayers and meditation. He had felt aggrieved but was too kindly and civilised for the situation to remain that way. He emerged serene, and we shook hands. On reflection he realised that my remarks – we both couldn't remember exactly what I had said – had simply caused a misunderstanding. The incident could safely be buried in Bangkok. On that happy note I returned to Britain, discovered I had contracted a virulent gastric illness, lost fourteen pounds and was hospitalised for two weeks. Which gave me ample time to meditate: wise Englishman does not try to be witty in Bangkok.

Brando, on the other hand, emerged triumphantly from the premiere. His role in the film was of a US ambassador in a fictional country in Southeast Asia. The story, based on the novel by William J Lederer, was an anti-communist tract and sought to dramatise the clash between the American diplomat and the culturally sensitive country to which he is posted. Brando's acceptance of the role reflected his own beliefs. To him, the film was a metaphor for policies that in some measure led to Vietnam and the carnage that followed. Born a generation or so later, he would have *paid* Steven Spielberg to play the Anthony Hopkins role as the white radical in *Amistad*. (Well, maybe not. The story goes that, on one particular film, Brando was so distrustful of the producers he demanded to be paid in *cash*, in *sacks*, each *day* of the production. He just liked the tactile delight of manhandling a sackful of greenbacks into his car each night.)

He would not have needed that facility filming *The Nightcomers* for Michael Winner. Britain's colourful film-director-turned-man-about-town enjoyed a lively friendship with Brando, both men masters of the art of making waves. A sadistic hero in Winner's raw and explicit film, Brando's character is brilliantly drawn. The location was in Paris. I went there to talk to him. Marlon sat on the floor of his vast apartment as though in meditation, legs crossed, hands clasped, eyes half closed. But he was not meditating. I figured that the posture he had adopted was consistent with some fairly boisterous activities the night before. He certainly winced at any jarring sound. It was mid-morning and the traffic noises outside furrowed his Caesar-like brow. His voice rarely rose above a whisper. I recall congratulating him on his performance in *The Godfather*. Sometimes when you compliment a movie actor you get the coy, foot-shuffling response. Not with Brando. There was a long silence while he sifted the compliment through the fine gauze of his mind. A clock ticked away. The traffic outside rumbled on. Those strange eyes closed momentarily. And then the words uncoiled:

'I have no disproportionate reactions to success. I've often chuckled softly to myself at the idiot workings of success and failure in our business. Anybody can become famous for almost anything. If you could contrive a way of enlarging your earlobes to a length of four feet, making baroque designs to go under your armpits then wind them round your kneecaps, you'd be famous overnight. People in our business are oriented only to winning. Failure disgusts them. Or what they think is failure. They love the aura of success. It warms them like a bonfire on a bitter day. This poisonous concept that if you are not successful you are automatically a failure is spreading more and more. Kipling said it all, defining triumph and disaster as those "twin impostors".' He closed his eyes again then smiled on a thought.

'In Hollywood, the number of teeth revealed in everybody's "Good morning" smile to me was in direct ratio to the money I was earning. I'd get the two-teeth "Good morning" or the three-toothed job, or the full upper and lower ivories, depending entirely upon the size of my salary. All in deference to the Eleventh Commandment of our trade – "Thou Shalt Be A Success".' This was the Gospel According To Marlon Brando.

Now, in the last third of his life, Brando has raised the drawbridge. The rebel has mellowed. He has fought his battles, is a shade less driven to save the world. Still in demand, though, with scripts arriving almost daily offering million-dollar sweeteners for his consideration. We may wonder whether the same will happen to Tom Cruise, Bruce Willis, Kevin Costner, Leonardo diCaprio and their like when they are in their seventies. For, despite his Falstaffian bulk and life-battered features, Brando remains at 79 an actor to be reckoned with. And a much finer American than Hollywood has judged him.

But I believe he was wrong about Charlie Chaplin. His condemnation of one of history's most widely loved geniuses was brutal, the more so because it was Marlon Brando, a champion of the underdog himself, who launched the tirade. Recalling his experiences on that ill-fated film *A Countess from Hong Kong*, he describes Chaplin as 'fearsomely cruel', 'sadistic' and 'an egotistical tyrant and penny pincher'.

What infuriated Brando, apparently, was Chaplin's treatment of his son Sydney, whom, Marlon alleged, Charlie humiliated constantly. (Was this a subconscious flashback to Brando's own battles with his father, a likelier candidate perhaps for those 'cruel' or 'sadistic' labels?) The atmosphere on the set grew more tense by the minute. The explosion came when Brando arrived fifteen minutes late. According to Brando, Charlie lambasted him in front of the whole cast, 'telling me that I had no sense of professional ethics and that I was a disgrace to my profession'. Brando demanded an apology, threatening to take the next plane back to the United States. Shortly afterwards, Chaplin knocked on the door and apologised. Ironically, his son Sydney, the catalyst for Brando's anger, shrugged off the notion of 'standing up to' his father. (I remember his telling me once, 'I really love the old guy.') 'He's getting old,' he said to Brando. 'He's had the flu, there are problems on the picture, he's a worried man.' It was generous of this talented young Chaplin, burdened if not overshadowed by his famous father. The whole prodigious Chaplin brood – eight children by his wife Oona – would have the same problem. But I recall Charlie sighing in his own defence, 'Blame the Tramp, not me.'

Marlon Brando, who has been comprehensively psychoanalysed by the best in the business, almost certainly made some handsome allowances for the man he concedes was a genius. Admittedly, *A Countess from Hong Kong* bombed as a movie and was savaged by the critics. It was self-evidently a 'bridge too far' for Chaplin, and begged the question, 'Why did he do it?' The answer was painfully obvious: making motion pictures was Chaplin's life-support system. Anything else spelled oblivion. Unfortunately, the genius that had moved the world was no longer there. The public 'thumbs-down' was hard for him to take. None of this 'growing old gracefully' for the stubborn little legend. It was the world that was out of step. Nothing would persuade him that his kind of movie making was past its sell-by date. When great men lose their power base, then hit out in all directions, onlookers run short of things to say.

I found myself in that situation some years ago, when Chaplin invited me to attend the wedding of his daughter Josephine to Nicholas Sistovaris. His attitude to the press – the American press in particular – was as cynical as Brando's. But he correctly identified me as a well-wisher, based on my coverage of his disgraceful treatment by newspapers and politicians in America, leading to his ultimate expulsion from the country. I had headlined my last piece on him, THE BIGGEST LITTLE MAN IN THE WORLD, and was prepared to take on anybody who disagreed.

What his detractors in the US resented most was the way he was worshipped around the globe. It rankled heavily with them that the Chinese leader Chou En-lai was proud to call Charlie his friend. It infuriated them that leading statesmen throughout the world were proud to shake the impish genius's hand (and prudently count their fingers afterwards). They could never understand why Einstein, Stravinsky, George Bernard Shaw, H G Wells, Churchill – let alone the fearsome giants of Hollywood – leaped to kiss the cuffs of those famous baggy trousers. The truth is that Chaplin was hated because he was rich, reviled because he declined to become an American citizen, feared because his films dared to champion the underdog, a subversive activity in an era when 'liberal' was a dirty word.

City Lights, *The Kid*, *Shoulder Arms*, *The Great Dictator* and *Modern Times* – through these classics Charlie Chaplin expressed the miseries of poverty, the tenderness of love, the human suffering in war, the poison of Nazism and the finer idiocies of a machine-dominated world. He was the guru of the world's greatest comics. No need for words. I remember his saying, 'I walk on the stage, serious, dignified, solemn; pause before an easy chair, spread my coat-tails, and with a most elegant gesture sit...on the cat.'

So I pleaded guilty to irreversible hero worship – and was flattered to receive the invitation to his daughter Josephine's wedding. He and his wife Oona, daughter of the playwright Eugene O'Neill, lived in an eighteenth-century farmhouse in the tiny village of Corsier, above Vevey, Switzerland. He welcomed me with that broad-toothed smile, a dapper, white-haired figure who resembled your friendly local bank manager. He loved his house and showed me where he worked, looking across five acres of lawn, and beyond the lake to the snow-capped mountains in the distance. Oona served us tea. When she left the room Charlie described her as 'a present that came to me, beautifully gift-wrapped by the Almighty'. They had been married then for more than thirty years. Oona, a handsomely elegant woman, matched her husband's accolade with, 'I was a mere child when we met. I have been in love with him ever since. He is my world. He protected me when I was young. Now I protect him.'

But she could not protect him from himself. That night, while Noël Coward held court to a glitterati of celebrated admirers, Chaplin beckoned me upstairs to his study. It was almost in total darkness apart from a small lamp over his desk. The anger had been building up inside him following the bad notices he had received on *A Countess from Hong Kong*.

'The British press were brutal to me,' he said bitterly. 'What do they want from me? The sexy, violent muck which fouls up the screen today? I saw a film privately the other night which reduced human love to the level of the farmyard. There was one close-up where the man was actually kissing a woman's breast! Don't people believe in tenderness any more? Has everyone forgotten the magic that comes with the mere squeezing of a hand?'

I felt sorry for the old man. Here was the great Chaplin, reluctant to step out of his own limelight. Out of joint with his time, frantically trying to revive the magic that died with the arrival of talking pictures. Come bad reviews, hell and high water, nothing was going to stop Charlie Chaplin making the cameras roll. He believed his kind of filmmaking was timeless and would always find an audience. He was wrong. He also talked about writing a play, an opera, more film scripts. In the end, he did none of those things. The spirit was more than willing. The flesh visibly less so. I couldn't tell him this. He was too warm and friendly, like a favourite uncle. Moreover, I hadn't flown to Switzerland to tell this genius he was over the hill. You do not tell one of the tiny number of true screen immortals that his time is up. I did say, though, that I felt honoured that he had invited me to his home; that he must feel chuffed at the notion that billions have worshipped him for generations and would continue to do so as long as images could flicker on screens large and small. He weighed the compliment in Buddha-like concentration. 'I made movies,' he said finally.

We went downstairs and the crowd of guests – dukes and duchesses, the queen of Spain and the Count and Countess Chevreau d'Antraigues, along with Noël Coward, Truman Capote and David Niven – stood up and cheered. Chaplin smiled. Born in a slum, raised in the workhouse, while his mother was in an asylum – he had come a long way for this ovation that night in Vevey. He was touched and the tears were visible. All this, and Oona too. It was a night to remember – which I suspect helped him finally to come to terms with reality. As he would write not long after in his memoirs, '...And so the world grows young. And youth takes over. And we who have lived a little longer become a little more estranged as we journey on our way.'

CHAPTER NINE

Bewitched and Bewildered

Movie-making is a very serious business and Hollywood has unimpeachable credentials as the best in the trade. But, life being a cabaret, there are on the fringes of Tinseltown a vast assortment of cult merchants, fetishists, voodooists and other wonder-workers who turn a quick dollar at the expense of their superstitious or plain nutty customers. Situations that, elsewhere, might require instant intervention by men in white coats leave LA's case-hardened inhabitants totally unfazed. One Hallowe'en night in Hollywood, I witnessed a TV debate between two rival witches whom I rated as only a broomstick ride from the nearest funny farm. One was an exotic brunette named Louise Huebner, a sixth-generation witch whose forbears shrieked through the dark forests of Yugoslavia. The other was a sensuous hellcat bearing the unconvincing name 'Zsuasanna Budapest'. A militant Hungarian-born feminist, she was – probably still is – dedicated to this credo of her 'Matriarchal Spiritual Centre' or witches' coven: 'We believe that wimmin' [witch word for women] lost supremacy through the aggressions of males who...formed the patriarchal hordes responsible for the invention of rape and the subjugation of wimmin.'

Naturally (I use that word loosely) each of these two spell-casters believed herself to be infinitely superior to the other in the sorcery business. And pretty early on in the debate they were hissing and evil-eyeing each other with a vengeance, much to the delight of the audience, including this observer, who couldn't wait to make their acquaintance. Status-wise as they say, Miss Huebner seemed to have the edge on Miss Budapest. She was, after all, the then Official Witch of Los Angeles County and had the citation to prove it. (Just why Los Angeles should need an Official Witch has never been seriously challenged. Too risky I suppose. 'I had to open my big mouth,' croaked an Armani-clad frog at Universal.) Miss Huebner received her citation at a public ceremony at the famous Hollywood Bowl one moonlit night some years ago. She expressed her gratitude by casting a spell for 'increased sexual activity' upon every male in the huge audience. This was much appreciated by the recipients, who couldn't wait to test-run the magic before it wore off. There was only one dissenting voice. It belonged to an uptight councillor who considered that the magic spell was an abuse of Miss Huebner's official title. So, in her vine-entangled hideaway on a mountain top (where else?) in Pasadena, the snubbed witch lit a few candles, murmured a few significant words to her pet rat, then announced her terrible retribution.

She would now put into reverse her libidinous spell of the night before. Henceforth the sexuality of all the menfolk would be reduced, starting with the aforementioned disgruntled official. When the telegrams and phone calls of protest zoomed into his office he hastily withdrew his objection. Miss Huebner's title, 'Official Witch of Los Angeles County', remained intact. The eight hundred other witches of LA County rattled their chicken bones with delight. As well they might. The witch business is big business in America.

The trade, worldwide, in, say, Bat's Blood (for breaking spells), Lovers' Oil (for rejuvenating affairs), War Water (attack the enemy, like the 'other woman') and Double-crossing Oil (for revenge) is matched by huge sales of assorted candles, which, together with prescribed incantations, open up a vast area of seductive and mischievous possibilities. So, disbelief temporarily suspended, I drove to Pasadena. Here, against a necromantic background of stuffed bats, dark tapestries, an iron cauldron and mystical figurines, Miss Huebner was an engaging and most hospitable witch. Her black cat, Ivan the Terrible, who normally sits atop the grand piano, remained outside keeping company with a white-bearded goat, who may not always have been a goat. Miss Huebner made no bones about her exploitation of the witch business. 'But I do have these psychic powers,' she claimed, 'and I've proved it. My grandmother practised witchcraft in Yugoslavia and my mother is into it too.' How did she feel about Zsuasanna the rival witch's accusation that she was 'a has-been who is jealous because I have this big movement and she cannot relate to it? 'Big movement?' cackled the Official Witch of LA County derisively. 'I am jealous of no one, least of all of a disciple of "The Virgin Huntress of the Night"!' At which point, Ivan the Terrible jumped unexpectedly onto my lap and I nearly jumped on-to Miss Huebner's.

'She', alleged the Yugoslav witch, referring to Miss Budapest, 'is involved in some kind of fantasy trying to revive an old religion having to do with mythology, gods and goddesses. I understand she was arrested once,' Miss Huebner glittered, 'for tarot-card reading' (then illegal in the United States). Miss Budapest later confirmed this but claimed it was just a plain piece of spite by the LA police department, because she had predicted that a policewoman would be divorced – and she was.

Louise Huebner demonstrated similar prescience, forecasting among other events the late Jackie Kennedy's second marriage eleven months in advance and President Johnson's retirement without standing for re-election. But that's not the profitable end of the witch trade. This comes from the hocus-pocus marketing (do I mean gibberish?), like Miss Huebner's candlelit ritual for getting rid of an 'Unwanted Lover':

Midnight...nude...enter a quiet place, light the wick of a large black candle, ring a clear bell three times. On a parchment, write the name of the unwanted lover, draw the symbols for the Sun and the Moon. With the juice from eight pomegranate seeds, stain the paper. Burn the paper in the flame of the candle. With the ashes...touch your forehead three times, gaze into the flames for three minutes. Whirl to the left (three times). Raise your arms high over your head. Cry out to Nai No Kami (the earthquake god) 'Once is enough!'

It was enough for me. I thought it was time to meet her rival, Zsuasanna, from the Dracula country whose goulash I'd pass on any day. Miss Budapest operated from a weird emporium near the Pacific beach twenty miles from Los Angeles. She claimed thousands of customers, or followers, throughout America and just as many overseas. Her book, *The Feminist Book of Lights and Shadows*, was 'lovingly dedicated', as Louise Huebner asserted, 'to our Gracious Lady, Diana, Virgin Huntress of the Night.' This confirmed my suspicion that women – sorry, *wimmin* – figure more prominently in Miss Budapest's voodoo-oriented world than men. All the rituals she espouses – the feasting, the dancing, the nude self-blessing and other moonlit pranks – don't have a single male to curse themselves with. I found Zsuasanna sitting on a high stool dressed unseductively in a roughly woven muu-muu. Shop girls darted around her selling books, oils, candles, and I HELPED A WITCH T-shirts. There appeared to be a run on Oil of Cleopatra ('Heavy love vibration with control' said the catalogue).

All this activity, I suggested, seemed at odds with Zsuasanna's put-down of her rival: 'She represents the old-fashioned Hollywood-style commercial exploitation of witchcraft. Ours is a religious movement,' she insisted, as a bottle of bat's blood was wrapped and wafted away by a staring-eyed customer. She did confess, however, that sex and its aphrodisiacal spin-offs were a briskly profitable part of the organisation. 'Sure, we worship sex,' she agreed, adding tartly, 'but it is never abused and *we* don't put spells on people to make them better at it!'

'But you do have nude ceremonies on a hilltop at full moon,' I said.

'Weather permitting,' conceded the witch. 'But we are nude because the human body represents truth. Once we have no clothes on then there is no separation, no class. Our bodies are the temple and we worship them accordingly.'

'What about sacrificial rites?'

'Bullshit,' snapped the high priestess.

On which appropriate note, I left for the happier screwballs of Beverly Hills.

All things considered, it was more a change of location than a jump into sanity. My date, the following day, was with the actress Dyan Cannon in her Spanish-style home on Malibu beach. During the ritual tour of the place we stopped at a small door hidden under the stairs. 'That', declared Miss Cannon, 'is my padded cell.' There are, of course, several possible responses to such a statement, including a swift glance at one's watch, a leap into the car, and away. But the tawny-haired Miss Cannon, recognising my dilemma, explained, 'This is where I practise primal screaming. It saved my life. It stopped me from killing myself, doping, drinking, destroying my body and my mind.'

What is it about Hollywood in general and celebrity in particular that, apart from anything else, makes its victims such a poor insurance risk? Why should a profession whose rewards are mind-boggling, where the work isn't exactly slave labour, require an army of shrinks, soothsayers, hocus-pocus merchants and assorted medics to keep its performers on the road?

It may be true that, when it comes to drink, drugs, hazardous sex and all the other life-threatening indulgences of the age, Hollywood is no worse than anywhere else. But the City of the Angels isn't 'anywhere else'. Here, its leading players are in the 24-hour glare of the public eye. The world's media, relentlessly and profitably, keep them under round-the-clock scrutiny. The sudden and often premature death of a superstar is high drama, each and every lurid detail of the victim's life and death reverberating electronically around the globe. For there is a vested interest here. The public perceives itself to be part owner of celebrities. It buys the tickets that pack the cinemas that enrich the studios that create the stars who are driven to live the kind of distorted lives celebrity demands. And it sometimes kills them.

Some have been luckier than others. An eleventh-hour rescue via the Betty Ford Clinic, Palm Springs, kept Liza Minnelli and Elizabeth Taylor from a self-inflicted oblivion. But others are nameplates at Forest Lawn and Hollywood Memorial Parks, their birth and death dates confirming their tragically foreshortened lives. Their common denominator was an alarming capacity for self-destruction. And most of them died at an appallingly early age. Judy Garland at 47, Mario Lanza 38, Jean Harlow 26, Errol Flynn 50, Marilyn Monroe 36, Montgomery Clift 46, James Dean 24; Peter Sellers, Tony Hancock, Lee Marvin... Born into any other profession, they might all be alive today. Sorting through the many film-star obituaries I've been required to write over the years is a melancholy exercise. Lives splendidly enriched and enriching, then prematurely, needlessly wasted. And, if they sometimes cannot handle the poisoned chalice of celebrity, how much harder it seems to be for their offspring.

Having megastar parents can sometimes be more of a curse than a blessing. While the actor Dustin Hoffman attended the Oscar ceremonies in March 1988, his 32-year-old stepdaughter Karina faced charges in a British court of stealing cheques to the value of £5,358 from the company where she worked. As we have seen, in 1990 Marlon Brando's son Christian was sentenced to ten years for killing the lover of his half-sister Cheyenne, who was pregnant at the time and subsequently killed herself. Paul Newman's son Allan also took his own life. Victoria Sellers, daughter of Peter Sellers and Britt Ekland, famously flirted with drugs. Judy Garland's daughter Liza Minnelli was caught in the slipstream of her mother's squally life of drugs, drink and broken marriages. She survived that and her own addictions with a little help from the Betty Ford Clinic in California. Christina, daughter of the Hollywood legend Joan Crawford, was almost traumatised by the tyranny of her upbringing. Her book *Mommy Dearest* was a devastating portrait of the dark inheritance of fame.

Celebrity, especially in Hollywood, is a demanding intruder on a marriage. The huge number of psychoanalysts on round-the-clock call in this relatively tiny community is in direct ratio to the vast array of neuroses on offer. I can scarcely count the number of hours I've spent in darkened bars listening to the tormented soul-bearing of distraught idols. Peter Sellers was a classic example. He was a near-sighted genius with a thousand faces, yet desperately short of an authentic identity. Pathologically insecure, he took refuge in his characters, from Goon to Clouseau. But, when these had run their course, their audiences slipping, he was emotionally marooned and hard to console. In a pathetically short life he made more than fifty films, many of them classics like *I'm All Right Jack*, *Dr Strangelove*, *The Millionairess*, *The Pink Panther* and *Being There*. He was without question one of the finest comic actors of his time. But he was also a self-styled manic depressive, swinging from inspired comedy to outbursts of almost uncontrollable fury. With all his fame, several homes, his cars and public and adulation, his self-doubt nagged at him constantly. He never stopped working, plunging from one film to another with barely a pause for breath. He was driven by panic, not greed, a pathological urge to confirm what the world had long recognised – that at his best there was nobody funnier.

So the camera was his Svengali, enticing him on a relentless treadmill with disastrous results. In April 1964 he had a massive heart attack in Hollywood. Fortunately for Sellers, the distinguished Beverly Hills physician Dr Rex Kennamar was able to arrange emergency admission to the world-renowned Cedars-Sinai Hospital, the most exclusive medical centre in Los Angeles. At around 2.30 on the morning of the 7 April, Sellers's heart stopped beating. There was frenzied activity by a large team of doctors. Sellers's medical notes show he was pronounced clinically dead, then revived eight times. He survived. God and his newly acquired wife Britt Ekland were given the main credit for the miracle. 'Both were in my corner that night,' he said to me on his recovery. But the demons remained. After a long session with him in Beverly Hills in February 1968, I returned later that evening to find a scroll waiting for me in the hotel mail box. Sellers had sent it to me urging me to read it. The hand-scripted message on parchment read: Slow me down Lord. Ease the pounding of my heart by the quieting of my mind...Break the tensions of my nerves...Give me amid the confusions of the day, the calmness of everlasting hills...'

Quite an entreaty from a tormented genius. Sellers died 24 July 1980. He was 54. He had been married four times: to Anne Hayes with whom he had a son Michael and daughter Sarah; Britt Ekland, who bore him a daughter Victoria, then Miranda Quarry, and finally the actress Lynn Frederick. In between there had been some brief interludes with Mia Farrow and Liza Minnelli. All these women regarded their relationship with Peter Sellers as an exercise in walking on eggshells. Clairvoyance, spiritualism and the supernatural were his psychological crutches. The famous clairvoyant Maurice Woodruff was as crucial to Sellers as Lee Strasberg the drama coach was to Marilyn Monroe. At one point, Sellers believed his career was being personally protected by famous comics of the past – in particular Dan Leno, the legendary comedian of the late nineteenth century. At one long melancholy dinner in London he gave me the whole scenario: the mysticism, the unseen influences, plus a few tears as he reflected upon the misery of genius. His life ended on a cliché: the tragedy of a clown. On the night before she flew to the US to marry Sellers, Britt Ekland said, 'I am worried about Peter. I don't really know what man he is.'

Sadly, neither did he.

There was one resource that did not appear in the Sellers Case Book: primal therapy, as prescribed by a Mr Arthur Janov (author of The Primal Scream and The Primal Revolution) had not apparently been recommended. This is a very serious therapy. Some swear by it. Others favour the couch, the bromides, a brief traipse through their childhood fantasies followed by tennis, daiquiris and dinner with their like-minded shrinks.

But clearly Dyan Cannon's 'primal screaming cell' worked wonders, for her. Measuring five feet square with kick-resistant foam-padded walls, and a thirty-watt lamp on a dimmer, the cell could just about accommodate the two of us crouched in foetal positions. Admittedly if you were going to find yourself in such enforced intimacy, Dyan Cannon was as pleasing a companion as you could hope for. It is only when you saw the marks she had clawed and scuffed in her frenzied attacks on the foam rubber that you realised this lady took her bunker very seriously indeed. Nevertheless, accustomed though we are to the traumas and tribulations of movie stars, I found the claustrophobic gloom of the cell decidedly spooky. The cell was totally soundproofed – a necessary precaution, for when the 'pain' welled up within her Miss Cannon locked herself inside the chamber and 'I scream, kick the wall, punch it, letting out all my aggressions. The tears begin to flow, the pain is unblocked, and all the boxed-in defences explode, releasing the things that made me so crazy I couldn't stand it any more. I hear myself say things that shock me, but when I come out I've purged myself of the pressures which were destroying me.'

'Nice room,' I said. But I wondered why this zesty beauty with a laugh that echoed through the canyons should end up kicking the stuffing out of foam-rubber walls. Well the circumstances of her birth give us some clues: certainly having a Baptist deacon father and an archetypal Jewish mother might just get an analyst off first base. She was born Samille Diane Friesen in Seattle. She discovered early on that pleasing her Baptist deacon father and her schmaltzy Jewish mother involved some very delicate footwork.

To please Dad she sang 'Jesus Loves Me, Yes I Know'; to reassure Momma she read the Talmud and collected for Israel, while her Christian boyfriend Joe Green obligingly called himself Greenbaum, which brought him more helpings of chicken soup than he could handle.

But the dichotomy was too much of a strain for the Friesens' darling daughter. She went to the University of Washington and read anthropology just to get away. She never wanted for any material things. 'Both my parents were generous. But they were fanatical about their different faiths. I was', she added grimly, 'split right down the middle and as uneasy as all hell about it.' After university she shuffled a pack of jobs, which included typing for the Boeing Aircraft Company and acting as a masseuse at a reducing clinic in Los Angeles. She had no notion of becoming an actress. This happened in the best traditions of 'she-was-an-unknown-when-this-stranger-came-along' cliché on which the Hollywood myth was founded.

She *was* unknown. A stranger *did* approach her in a Beverly Hills restaurant. He *did* ask her if she was an actress. And, in strict accordance with the rules, Diane lied and said, 'Yes'.

Of course the man turned out to be a talent scout and introduced her to the producer Jerry Wald, who flipped and said, 'Jeeze you're just like a cannon!' And, before cynics could say 'yee-uck', Dyan Cannon was thus launched on her merry way. Well, it was merry at first. She played the comic-erotic wife in *Bob & Carol & Ted & Alice*, for which she won the New York Film Critics Award and a Best Actress nomination for an Oscar. If you are curious to know what goes on inside the mind of an actress on such a night listen to this:

'I sat there in my Indian costume watching the man on the stage fumble with the envelope. I was hoping to win but I knew that somebody else's name would be called, that the cameras would swing onto me so that millions could see me destroyed. I told myself, "Right,

Dyan, get the good sport act ready." But inside I was dying. "Me, me" a voice screamed inside me, I should have won!'

'Dying', 'destroyed', 'a voice screaming' – all over the wrong name on a slip of paper in an envelope. It was then she began to understand the madness. 'I said to myself, "Dyan, this is a murderous mistake. You feel like crying, letting it out in one big disappointed shriek, why shouldn't you? Better than screwing down into the arteries of your heart."' (Better still, treat the Oscar for what it frequently is, a triumph of hype over substance.) Which eventually she did. Starring in *The Last of Sheila*, a gutsy film in which she played a bitchy agent, Dyan Cannon convinced the film men that here was a fresh contemporary female with all the lush voluptuousness of the old-style Hollywood. *The Last of Sheila*, followed by a Broadway debut with Jane Fonda in *The Fun Couple*, then touring with *How to Succeed in Business Without Really Trying*, brought her to the attention of Cary Grant. She met him to discuss work but stayed to talk about marriage. They were wed in Las Vegas in 1965. The last time I met them both together was at a film luncheon for the press in London. Cary was a reluctant guest. Pathologically distrustful of journalists, he had the bad luck to find the assembled scribes in a particularly boorish mood.

I remember the occasion well because it annoyed me to see one of Hollywood's most enduring stars at the receiving end of some particularly bone-headed behaviour. Their questions to him displayed an ignorance of the man and even less knowledge of his massive screen achievements. Sycophancy is not part of a journalist's kit. But showing respect where it is due seemed to me to be an inescapable courtesy. Cary's credits alone, *The Philadelphia Story*, *Arsenic and Old Lace*, *Notorious*, *To Catch a Thief*, *Night and Day* (as Cole Porter), *Indiscreet*, *North by Northwest* etc. called for a little admiration if not awe. Not that Grant wanted – or needed – it. But he certainly had not anticipated that the occasion would develop into an unusually abrasive interrogation. I've asked a few awkward questions in my time but this was just plain rude. Grant was too decent a guy to be the target of it. A little fair play seemed to be called for. I stood up and told my colleagues that I thought their questions were out of line and apologised to Cary for their discourtesies. The following day the couple wired me their appreciation in a telegram signed Cary and Dyan Grant. They did not remain that way for long. Less than two years later they were divorced.

And it is when one probes the alleged causes of the breakdown that the lady's primal screaming may not have been such an overreaction. According to her evidence in the divorce court, as a husband Cary Grant was moody, obsessive and hypercritical. She claimed he saved the string from parcels and the buttons from worn-out shirts, and marked the wine bottle. He put her over his knee and spanked her if she wore too much makeup or too short a skirt. Dyan Cannon's ultimate verdict on the breakdown of the marriage? She said at the time, 'I was probably looking for a father figure and maybe he was looking for a momma. Who knows? People thought I was a tough broad, but I was more child than woman at the time.'

The union brought a daughter, Jennifer, whom both doted on. Cary bought a house on Malibu so that he could be near her. But the revelations in court knocked the spirit out of him. He never made another picture. I had much sympathy for both parties. Dyan Cannon emerged as the stronger survivor. But then she appeared to carry a far lighter burden of emotional and psychological baggage. Cary Grant's five marriages to as disparate a handful of wives as you could find suggests all kinds of problems behind the dimpled charm millions of women adored if not lusted over. But these were minor issues compared with the emotional turmoil that would take him into psychotherapy, hypnotherapy and well-publicised trips with LSD. Clearly there was a monumental contrast between Cary's smiling, Boston gentleman image and his looming alter ego, which shadowed him throughout his life. He was born Archibald Alexander Leach, Bristol, England, 18 January 1904. Cary Grant was the shining idol, jointly constructed in the Dream Factory by astute press agents and the chuckling acquiescence of the star himself. Leach represented the uncomfortable reality of a singularly agonised childhood. Cary would talk at length to me about Grant. He was infinitely – and understandably – more reticent about this mysterious chap named Archie. Jekyll and Hyde may not be a too-fanciful analogy for this dichotomy in the life of Cary Grant.

He was barely ten years old when, on returning home from school outside Bristol, he found the house deserted, his mother gone. No word, no note of explanation. His father Elias said merely, 'She's gone away, lad.' Kindlier relatives told the boy that his mother had died suddenly of a heart attack. It was years later before Archie Leach discovered the truth: that his father had had her committed to what was then called the local lunatic asylum, the Country Home for Mental Defectives a mile or two away. Several reasons were given. There was no doubt that she had suffered depression after the death of her first child, John, just two days before his first birthday. It was known that in her worst moments she drank excessively. But there were also rumours that her husband, Elias, had acquired a mistress.

The totality of these revelations gnawed at the emotions of the young Archie Leach. And they carried over into the life of Cary Grant, an uncomfortable throwback to an insistent ghost. A more benign echo of the past centred on the possibility that he was Jewish, stemming from his father Elias's supposedly Jewish ancestry. No evidence has been produced to suggest that Elias and Elsie were other than good Christians who attended the local Episcopalian church. More persuasive, perhaps, was the fact that the young baby Leach had been circumcised. Not conclusive of course. Marlon Brando, as we know, had also been circumcised – his reasons medical rather than ethnic. Nevertheless, Cary Grant's alleged Jewish background was freely discussed in Hollywood, not least by his several wives. Cary Grant himself smiled at all the talk, but characteristically offered no answers either way. However, he gave generously to Jewish causes, attended fundraising dinners for Israel, including a huge event in Madison Square Garden, where he wore the traditional skull cap in deference to his Jewish hosts. Certainly one famous writer, the critic Paulene Kael, suggested that his father Elias probably came from a Jewish background. The enigma becomes more intriguing when we see Cary's entry in the 1962 edition of *Who's Who In America*, in which Cary gives his mother's name as Lillian, a much-favoured name in Jewish families.

Cary and I first met in London. He was staying at the Connaught Hotel, a select hideaway for the reclusively minded rich. Celebrities like Cary Grant in fact. What amused me, as it would certainly have intrigued the hotel, was to find him washing his 'smalls', ladies' panties to be precise, in the bathroom. 'I wear these for comfort and economy,' he said, anticipating an enquiry. 'And they dry in minutes.' If he seemed a shade emphatic on the subject, I assumed it was because of another persistent Hollywood rumour that he was, if not gay, then at least ambivalent in his sexual preferences. I never saw any evidence of it. The rumour was based on the fact that for a period he and the actor Randolph Scott shared a house together. Five marriages – let alone his hopeless infatuation with Sophia Loren – ought to have silenced the rumour mongers.

Back at the Connaught Hotel, his 'smalls' having been draped over a rail, Cary Grant and I strolled out into the twilight of London's Park Lane. Suddenly, he took a flying leap in the air and hung from the bar of a hotel awning. He swung gently in the gathering darkness as the liveried hall porter emerged. 'Can I be of any assistance, sir?' the man enquired. 'No, thank you, my good man,' boomed my healthy companion. 'I'm just taking care of the old vertebrae. Do that regularly and they'll never bite back at you!'

'Aren't you Cary Grant, sir?' the porter asked.

'You know, I often wonder,' Grant responded with some truth.

Sometimes, when we walked on the beach at Malibu or sat over drinks in Beverly Hills, Cary would talk with obvious pleasure about his early beginnings. He was proud to tell me that his father had been a presser in the rag trade; how he had started out in show business, as a member of Bob Pender's Troupe of Knockabout Comedians, a group of slapstick acrobats he had watched as a boy at the Bristol Hippodrome; and how he had sailed with them aboard the SS *Olympic* to the United States while overhead in first class the legendary Douglas Fairbanks and Mary Pickford were celebrating their honeymoon. Punctuating his speech with low-register chuckles, he talked about his years as a tumbler, straight man and juvenile lead. A health freak who knew the calorie count on every morsel he ate, he was a Coney Island lifeguard for a while. His six foot four of tanned, lithe and dimpled manhood drew an excited audience of admiring females. And led of course to Hollywood and his triumph as the best

light-comedy star in the business. Alfred Hitchcock would build on
the unique material, creating that deceptively casual style that many
stars imitated but none mastered. He made 72 films, which brought
him a vast private fortune.

Yet his lifestyle and his home in California scarcely reflected it.
Metro producer Dory Schary, arriving at Grant's home in Beverly Hills
one day, was astonished at the Spartan interior. 'Not a paper, cigarette,
flower or picture – nothing in the living room except two chairs and a
sofa.' To some, this reluctance to live on the grand scale of a Hollywood
'great' suggested tight-fistedness. 'He still has the first dollar he ever
earned' was the gibe. Not the actor I knew. Others hit on the more
likely reason, a massive insecurity. 'Sure, I earn all this money,' he once
said to me. 'But it's fantasy money. One lousy run of pictures and
they'll be taking the furniture and cutting off the phone.' Haunted by
his alter ego, Archibald Leach, the tailor's presser's son, he bore a
subconscious sense of guilt, shame almost, at being Cary Grant.

A scrutiny of the valuables he kept locked in the fireproof wall safe
of his home revealed the intensity of Grant's obsession with his past.
No silver trophies, awards, fancy baubles or other glittering testimony
to his truly remarkable career. Instead, there was his school blazer, a
box of scout cap badges, his father's pocket watch and his mother's
rings. The inescapable 'markers' of Archibald Alexander Leach.

'What do these mean to you?' I once asked him.

'Agony, actually, old chum,' he replied with a fair imitation of a
Cary Grant smile.

'Care to talk about it?'

'Nope.'

If he found living with the two contrasting images, Cary Grant and
Archie Leach, an unending torment, it was no less so for at least four
of the women he married. They could never be sure which part of their
husband's dual personality they might have to cope with at any given
hour or day. Would it be Grant or Leach? Jekyll or Hyde? His first wife,
Virginia Merrill, told a divorce judge that he drank excessively, and
choked and beat her, even threatened to kill her. The Woolworth
heiress Barbara Hutton, ten years later, told another court how he
would cower in his bedroom and refuse to attend the dinners she gave

because he complained he felt like 'an ignorant guest in his own house'. He had a better life with Betsy Drake, a very civilised and cultivated actress. But that marriage failed, too, his wife pleading 'grievous mental suffering'. And as we've seen, there was Dyan Cannon, wife number four, alleging spanking amid other more bizarre behaviour.

But then along came Barbara Harris, a former London public relations executive nearly fifty years younger than he. She was vivacious, undemanding, uncompetitive and British – Cary could settle happily for that. And so too could Archibald Leach. Then a still virile, carrot-nibbling 82-year-old Cary was clearly enjoying the best years of his life. Young Leach no longer figured in the life of the happy octogenarian. Well, almost not. One aspect of the little boy in Grant was always there, an essential part of the chuckling, suntanned Cary Grant. One afternoon in my home in London, I discovered that he collected car numbers. Not ordinary car numbers of course. The rarer, single-figure kind. He leaped to the window. 'Just saw a seven go past! I've got every number now from one to fourteen, except the thirteen. Badly need a thirteen,' he said. He was 61 at the time.

Cary Grant, even in his darker moments, was wonderful company. He was made for the cinema screen and, though he would never claim it, achieved an unmatched excellence in that medium. Every major actor in Hollywood, and Olivier and Noël Coward over here, marvelled at his skill in making the most difficult scenes appear so easy. His reactions – the sudden turn of the head, the unsettling stare, the impeccable timing of his responses – stole the show and reduced the much-vaunted Method School of Acting to mumbling absurdity.

Cary Grant had a much sharper brain than he cared to reveal. He knew a great deal about the world beyond movies, but reserved his concerns, his thoughts and his lightly expressed cynicism for the handful of intimates he hung on to. He had a more versatile talent than Hollywood ever seriously recognised. And, when finally he emerged successfully from LSD and protracted sessions of psychotherapy, he became the complete individual he had striven so long to be. He never whinged when his personal life struck a reef. In therapy he reprised the traumas of his life from the day his mother disappeared through to the harsh and shaming accusations of four disillusioned wives. For the first time in his life he could see himself starkly in focus. Accused of behaving badly to women, wives in particular, he pleaded guilty to all charges. His long, hallucinatory trip to self-awareness drew this candid admission: 'It was horrendous. I had to face things about myself I didn't know were there. Now I know I hurt every woman I ever loved.' The realisation was cathartic. At last he could bury Archie Leach and enjoy being Cary Grant. And, speaking as one who was delighted to share his company, I can say that there was much in the man to enjoy.

CHAPTER TEN

Dangerous Capers

In April 1998 the chic and influential denizens of New York's art world streamed into a famous studio on the corner of Broadway and East Houston Street. Here, in the workplace of the important pop artist Jeff Koons, they had gathered to launch the biography of an obscure painter, Nat Tate, who committed suicide at the age of 31. Written by the best-selling British author, William Boyd, the life story of the painter was tragic indeed. An apparently undiscovered genius, a great lover in the class of Samuel Beckett, Tate boarded the Staten Island ferry off New York one afternoon, threw off his coat, hat and scarf and jumped overboard. His body was never found.

When the rock star David Bowie, whose publishing company was launching the book, read this extract, the assembled throng of critics, art gurus, dealers, media personalities and a chattering of Beautiful People were visibly moved. As well they might be. Little, if any, of Tate's work survived. Nothing to confirm the apparent importance of his work. This was not an insignificant element in the drama. For those in the buzzing crowd who sought to ask the question, '*Who* is Nat Tate?' received far from satisfactory responses. Art critics who did not know the answer either pretended not to hear or gobbledegooked their way out of trouble.

The *Independent*'s arts news editor David Lister, who confessed to never having heard of Tate, dared to ask a 'folly of art critics' at the party, 'Is he very well known?' (an innocent enough question). The replies were not convincing. 'The critics nodded their heads sagely and murmured, "Not terribly well known...not hugely...didn't have much of a reputation outside of New York..." Very odd, thought Lister. He decided to research the short and tragic life of the doomed abstract expressionist. This was much to the discomfort of the publishers, the aforementioned art critics and others. For the entire enterprise was an elaborate hoax dreamed up by the author, Will Boyd, with the tongue-in-cheek endorsements of Picasso's biographer, John Richardson, and that literary gadfly GoreVidal. But once David Lister began gnawing away at the subject, the ruse collapsed within hours.

The blushing perpetrators admitted that things had got a bit out of hand; that they never intended the stunt to be more than a 24-hour caper. But of course the book acquired huge chunks of free publicity, which undoubtedly was the object of the exercise. And within a week or two Nat Tate was properly and unceremoniously buried by his creator. All in all not a bad hoax as hoaxes go. But it was minor-league duplicity compared with the sensational Clifford Irving/Howard Hughes Affair. I had a peripheral involvement in the whole extraordinary business, which eventually took me to a federal prison in Connecticut and into a lively correspondence with one of its most celebrated inmates.

It was 7 December 1971, when the well-respected publishers McGraw-Hill Inc. announced the publishing coup of the century. They had acquired world publishing rights to a 230,000-word transcript of taped reminiscences of Howard R Hughes. The announcement, by the company's vice-president Albert R Leventhal, declared that the autobiography – based on almost one hundred taping sessions – would be published on 27 March 1972 and that *Life* magazine would serialise an abridged version of the book in three instalments of ten thousand words each, beginning 10 March. Hughes, Leventhal said, had spent the last year working on his memoirs with the American novelist Clifford Michael Irving on the Spanish island of Ibiza.

Predictably, the announcement created headlines around the world. For years every newspaper, television network and book publisher had been offering lottery-prize inducements for almost any material that lifted veils from the bizarre life and times of Howard Hughes. And here at last was the real McCoy. The world's most secret and elusive tycoon talking publicly for the first time. The authentic story of Hughes – the spectacular womaniser who dated and discarded legends; the man who bought and manipulated politicians; the record-breaking aviator and courageous test pilot; the strange, some said mad, recluse whose grotesque physical appearance at his death shocked the world – all this and more seemed about to emerge. It would be the publishing sensation of the age. If it was true.

It was not. I suspected it from the start. Not that I was in possession of privileged information. But I knew enough about Howard Hughes to dismiss as fanciful the whole enterprise. Any questions I ever wanted to raise about him in his lifetime I had to channel through his personal attorney, Greg Bautzer. No answers were ever forthcoming, though the affable Mr Bautzer occasionally dined me at the famous Bistro in Beverly Hills to soften my disappointment. A big, powerful man, Bautzer was fiercely loyal to the reclusive billionaire, as were Hughes's two other close friends, the late Cubby Broccoli, and the actor Cary Grant. All three confirmed Hughes's pathological concern for his privacy and honoured it up to, and even after, his death. Hughes detested the media. He had not the slightest interest in novels or their authors. Everything he was engaged in, his massive commercial manipulations, political manoeuvring and nocturnal trysts with Hollywood goddesses, was as securely hidden from the public gaze as the Dead Sea Scrolls. So the notion that Hughes of all people might suddenly decide to publish his life story, and even worse, find the time to tape a hundred interview sessions with a lesser-known expatriate author based on Ibiza, was a joke – a painfully costly one, as the two leading perpetrators would soon discover.

Clifford Irving, author of eight novels, had long been obsessed by Howard Hughes and the ruthless battle for control of his multibillion-dollar empire. A gifted writer with an irresistible attraction towards danger if not disaster, he hit on the idea of writing the blockbuster of the decade: *The Official Howard Hughes' Autobiography: As told to Clifford Irving*. The manuscript was completed. A fake. For the insane idea to succeed Irving was gambling on two crucial imperatives: (1) that the frail and isolated magnate was either dead or, if alive, his phobia about appearing in public would deter him from publicly nailing the author; and (2) that the author's comprehensive knowledge of Hughes, and the byzantine empire he presided over, would guarantee the book's authenticity. It was a daring and hazardous enterprise, requiring the instincts of a gambler, the audacity of a buccaneer and maybe just a touch of blind stupidity. So, having tossed the grenade, Irving took cover and awaited events.

He had not long to wait. Within hours, the Hughes Organization issued a terse denial. In a few derisory words they rubbished Irving and the book. Irving was quick to react. He shrugged off their denial by asserting that the project was so secret 'they didn't know a damn thing about it'. Ordinarily, the company's disclaimer should have strangled the scam at birth. But, apart from Irving, there were other 'interested parties' – creating a dark subplot to the affair, which significantly raised the stakes.

Some five months earlier, the influential American columnist Jack Anderson had written an item in which he stated that Howard Hughes had given $100,000 to 'help Richard Nixon win the presidency'. According to Anderson, the money had been siphoned from takings at the Silver Slipper, a Hughes gambling emporium in Las Vegas, and used for the Nixon campaign. Apparently masterminded by Robert Maheu, a senior associate of Hughes's, the $100,000 was delivered by Richard Danner, a Hughes executive, to Bebe Robozo, a Nixon confidante. The report was political dynamite, and the immediate target was president Nixon. Characteristically, Nixon had thought he had distanced himself from the payout by having Bebe Rebozo as the shadowy intermediary. Instead, the Hughes $100,000 handout was in the open. Nixon lambasted Rebozo, who deflected the heat onto Richard Danner, demanding to know how Anderson had discovered the deal.

The answer was conclusive and damning: Anderson had seen the memo outlining details of the Hughes handout. A presidential denial was therefore inconceivable There was a hiatus of several weeks during which Nixon nervously trod water, hoping that the story would expire through lack of hard evidence. His barefaced alibi was that (a) he never knew that the $100,000 had come from Hughes, and that (b) in fact the money had been borrowed by his mother from an accountant. And after a month or so it seemed that Nixon's adroit capacity for deflecting embarrassing accusations had paid off yet again. Then came the announcement about the Clifford Irving book. It raised some questions. What did Irving know about the Hughes contribution to Nixon? How much did he know about the principal characters in the arrangement? And, crucially, did he know that Nixon had been directly involved in the transaction? It was now no longer relevant whether the book was a hoax or not. If McGraw-Hill published it, their imprimatur would be a sufficient endorsement – and indictment.

As with the Watergate tapes, the White House feverishly embarked on a damage-limitation exercise, simultaneously ordering two of its leading Watergate conspirators, Charles Colson and John W Dean, to get a sight of the Irving manuscript. A White House 'operative' was instructed to ferret through Irving's garbage at his Westport, Connecticut, home. They imagined there'd be rich pickings from screwed-up pages, familiar debris from writers' preliminary drafts. It wasn't so much the book they were worried about. Their main concern was that Robert Maheu, who had an outstanding lawsuit against Hughes, might be behind the whole scam. They were dismayed to find nothing incriminating in Irving's garbage. But eventually they secured a copy of the manuscript. Which was bad news. Clifford Irving knew plenty. Dates, times, places, figures and the people involved. Understandably so, since for a hoax on this scale to succeed the words had to read as though based upon an unimpeachable source. This had been well achieved. Irving had done his homework.

If the revelation of the $100,000 payout was dynamite, Irving's further allegations threatened political mayhem. Irving fished back through murkier waters to matters even before Nixon became president. He claimed that Hughes had paid the then Vice-President Nixon $400,000 for favours involving litigation over TransWorld Airlines. And more. And more. All of which stirred the pot and had the publishers licking their lips in anticipation. There was only one way now that the Hughes Organization could publicly expose the book as fraudulent: Howard Hughes would have to come out from the shadows and tell the world the truth. In effect, the mountain would have to come to Mohammed. Well, not exactly. There was no way Howard Hughes would ever emerge from the hermetically sealed, germ-free, burglar-alarmed and heavily guarded seclusion that passed for his then existence at Nassau in the Bahamas. But he would be prepared to be interviewed by telephone hook-up to a carefully selected group of seven American reporters – James Bacon of Hearst newspapers, Gene Handsaker of the Associated Press, Gladwin Hill of the *New York Times*, Marvin Miles of the *Los Angeles Times*, Roy Neal of NBC (the moderator), Vernon Scott of United Press International and Wayne Thomas of the *Chicago Tribune*. All of them had known Hughes in his less reclusive years. They would recognise his voice, ask the sorts of questions that could expose an impostor.

They were flown in to the Sheraton-Universal Hotel in Hollywood. Three thousand miles away, Hughes put on earphones at the Britannia Beach Hotel in Nassau. It was the first time Hughes had talked to the press in fifteen years. It was Friday, 7 January 1972. According to Donald J Barlett and James B Steele's definitive biography of Hughes, he prepared himself that day by counting out eight codeine tablets, dissolving them in water in a syringe, then injecting himself. A few hours later he picked up the telephone and the interview began.

'Good afternoon, Mr Hughes,' said Roy Neal.

'Good afternoon to you,' Hughes answered.

According to Neal, there was no mistaking that voice. As each reporter introduced himself, the verdict was the same. Each confirmed unequivocally that this was the voice of Howard Hughes. A whole variety of subjects were covered. There was particular interest in the several aircraft with which Hughes had been famously associated – the Constellation, the ill-fated 'Spruce Goose' (the gigantic flying boat that never flew more than a couple of feet off the water), and the secret warplane in which he suffered his appalling accident after insisting upon test-flying it himself. Then finally the sixty-four thousand dollar question: what did he have to say about the so-called Hughes autobiography by Clifford Irving?

His answer was short and explicit: 'I don't know him. I never saw him. I had never heard of him until a matter of days ago when this thing first came to my attention.'

At this point, the $750,000 advance reportedly paid to Clifford Irving by the publishers seemed a decidedly shaky investment. Which was the least of Irving's worries. When the case came to court, Hughes's 28-word disclaimer was sufficient for Irving to be sentenced to two and a half years' imprisonment. It was a savage comeuppance for this handsome, lithe adventurer who enjoyed the good life and everything under the hot sun of Ibiza. His wife Edith, who went along with the ruse, was jailed for two years by a Swiss court for using false identity papers to deposit money in a Zürich Bank. The sentence was received with some glee in the Hughes Organization, though I doubt that Irving's prime accuser Howard Hughes derived any personal satisfaction. The whole episode had been an irritant – no more. When I phoned Hughes's lawyer Greg Bautzer, who had now become a good friend, to ask whether his famous client had been embarrassed by the whole affair, he laughed, 'You must be joking. Hughes is about as easy to embarrass as a cobra!'

Clifford Irving, on the other hand (now Inmate Number 00040 at the Federal Correctional Institution at Danbury, Connecticut), was incandescent with anger. Sure, he'd lived dangerously, scheming up the wrong hoax, involving the wrong man, at the wrong time. But whom had he hurt? Certainly not Hughes, whose several massive lawsuits involving major corporate figures made the Irving Affair pretty small beer. The publishers, too, though left with egg on their face, would get their money back. The only real casualties, apart from Irving himself, was his wife Edith, now herself in jail, and their children.

I felt sorry for him, which does not mean I support the trade in fake autobiographies. I shared the oblique admiration of many other writers who marvelled at his ability to turn out a highly persuasive book of memoirs and reminiscences that could dupe one of the most important publishing houses in America and the prestigious Time-Life Magazines. Now all that labour was for nothing. Nearly a quarter of a million words of research and hard graft, which would now not earn him a cent. His wife's loyalty had landed her in prison, too. Their marriage had already taken a knock owing to a brief liaison between Irving and a Danish beauty called Nina (of the then famous singing duo, Nina and Frederick). Trouble all round. Yes, I felt sorry for

Irving and wrote to him at the prison to tell him so. He was pleased to get the letter. He sensed, correctly, some empathy from a journalist and a well-wisher. I asked if I could fly over and interview him. He wrote back and said he'd be delighted.

It might have helped if I had checked out the invitation with the prison governor beforehand. I did not, and one bright morning in July 1973 I dropped by the gates of the prison to see if my newly acquired pen pal was receiving callers. The sun was shining. The giant trees and rich flora of Connecticut were breathtaking, enabling this visitor to approach the fortress-like establishment in fairly buoyant spirits. The euphoria did not last long. Prisons, federal correctional institutions if you will, are rigidly impervious to smiling newspapermen, let alone the changing seasons. They inflict their own bleak mood, which erases all smiles at the steely entrance gates. I arrived with a bottle of Jack Daniel's and a written invitation from Inmate Number 00040. Both made no impression whatsoever on the expressionless officer who received me. Apparently, in inviting me, Clifford Irving had overlooked an important proviso. If he saw me, that would automatically reduce by one other visits planned for that month, notably by his children. This was too precious a sacrifice for the devoted father.

'He knows the score,' the officer said, 'and the choice is his.' Then, with a marked softening of tone he added, 'I realise you've come a long way. But those are the rules. You can of course submit some questions to this person, which I will make sure he receives.'

The Jack Daniel's also being disallowed, I drove it back to my hotel. It's an ill wind... But what questions should I put to Clifford Irving? History would clearly rate him a better author than he was a hoaxer. But how did he now rate himself? What kind of self-assessment had taken place since the electric gates had clanked shut on him?

To that question and several others, Irving responded with a writer's candour and a total absence of self-pity. He must have been aware that the parole board would fine-tooth-comb his statements in assessing his profile for early release. But there was no evidence of subliminal self-pleading. No attempt to say things they might want to hear. All in all, rich material, I thought, for a great book – by a genuine autobiographer.

It's a long time ago. But Irving's answers cast a fascinating slant on how one mad, bad idea can sweep several lives into a whirlwind. Imagine yourself the jury, and read on:

What will you do once you are released?

'First of all to get my children back into decent emotional shape. They have had – and are having – a godawful experience because they are parentless and being shuttled and shepherded back and forth across the Atlantic, finding it very difficult to understand and cope. They need a lot of devotion and guidance, stability and a parent. I mean to give it to them once I am out of this wasteland.

'And then, catch up on a potpourri of missed joys: cold white wine, claret, rare roast beef; sailing my boat on the Med on a summer day; playing with my kids at the beach; seeing my wife smile one day [*in abeyance over the Nina affair*]; sex (although here in prison one sublimates that lack in order to stay relatively sane); and loving in all its forms.

'And privacy! Well, the list could almost be endless. Admittedly mundane objectives. I don't like to be pompous and set grand goals. They will become clearer when I am freed.'

What are your professional aims and private resolutions?

'My plans are to teach for a while at Cornell University while I am writing my next book. I've been asked to do a lecture tour, act in Hollywood etc., and before the trouble started I was planning with some friends a diamond-hunting expedition in Surinam. I want to get back to Europe which is my home. When I get out of prison I'll take stock. Now it's premature.

'Personal resolutions: to rehabilitate my children and my marriage. To avoid Danish blondes.'

What went wrong with Clifford Irving?

'What went wrong with Clifford Irving? I'm not sure I can use those words without winking. I went to the edge of my personality, my possibilities, took a leap and got lost for a while. It was a thoroughly exhilarating experience.'

You once used the phrase 'the devil got into me' in a BBC interview. Have you got rid of him?

'The devil is in all of us or we would be insufferable. Not just pious bores, but incomplete. I should have said [in that interview] "The devil in me got the upper hand for too long a time." The devil is not only the prankster in us, the child; he is also the challenger who says to the complacent God, the parent-induced conscience or the superego, or what you will: "Look here, there's another way to do things! Let's go that dark, untravelled route this time." That's how we learn, expand our consciousness – by penetrating the unknown. It's risky, and moral law – as in all uncharted frontier lands – can be shadowy.

'A man must learn to use and control his devil, not exorcise him. Mine is still there. I expect in the future we'll have some good debates and make some interesting journeys together.'

To whom do you feel you have to make amends?

'To my children. They who are the innocents have suffered the most – although they are beautiful and fine spirits and I believe in the long run will come out whole and strong. To Edith, my wife: I never should have allowed her to become culpably involved. If I'd had my head squarely on my shoulders I would have sent a friend, not her, to the Swiss banks in Zürich.

'The publishers? For the most part they were thrilled by the sequence of events which broke the tedium of their lives; moreover they've recouped their money and had more than their pound of flesh from me.

'Howard Hughes? You can't apologise to a phantom.'

There's a convention in Hollywood whereby people take out ads in the trade papers to make public amends. If you were to do the same, to whom would it be addressed and what would you say?

'You may be sure I would take out no such ad. If I had to, however, it might read:

APOLOGIES FROM CLIFFORD IRVING TO:

the Swiss banks for forcing them to reveal they are...the repositories for illegal and funny money from all over the world;

the Zürich judges for forcing them to sentence my wife to prison and thus reveal that they are more responsible to the Swiss banks than to the spirit of justice and compassion;

McGraw-Hill for deluding them into publication of a book that would have enriched them by some two million dollars;

Hollywood . . . to be embalmed in its seductive maw was no particular hardship.

LEFT: Busking in Wardour Street. The idea was to see whether show biz's famed generosity actually extended to film moguls delving into their pockets on the street.

ABOVE: 'The price of petrol has been increased by one penny – official.' The famous Philip Zec cartoon of the Second World War infuriated the government.

LEFT: John George Haigh, choirboy-turned-serial-killer. This portrait (framed) was a parting gift to Donald Zec.

ABOVE: Humphrey Bogart (seen here with Ingrid Bergman), the supreme tough guy of the cinema.

RIGHT: Ingrid Bergman, a strong companionable and most courageous beauty, at home in Rome with Donald Zec.

ABOVE: From my vantage point I had the uncanny impression that Jane Russell was breast-feeding a carp.

RIGHT: The incomparable Mae West, queen of the double entendres.

ABOVE: John 'Duke' Wayne, Hollywood's greatest action hero. None saluted the flag more fervently.

LEFT: The late James Dean, a tragically wasted talent but an unfading icon of the young.

BELOW: Marlon Brando: a superb actor, but at interviews he could out-silence the Sphinx.

ABOVE: Laurel and Hardy, the greatest comedy duo ever, who stumbled and tripped their way into immortality.

RIGHT: Port and pheasant . . . a bizarre banquet at the Savoy.

RIGHT: Sophia Loren, a fine actress and friend. Richard Burton described her as 'beautiful as an erotic dream'.

RIGHT: Happy newlyweds Elizabeth Taylor and Mike Todd. Donald Zec views the 'merchandise'; Elizabeth loves anything that sparkles.

LEFT: Elizabeth Taylor and Richard Burton; the most sensational and defiant love affair of the decade.

BELOW: In more blissful times.

ABOVE: Peter Sellers, a troubled genius.

ABOVE RIGHT: Cary Grant, a much underrated legend, and wonderful company.

RIGHT: A hoax too far: the author Clifford Irving.

LEFT: Mr and Mrs Arthur Miller had a genuine love, which was touching to witness.

ABOVE: Marilyn, perilously irresistible, with Donald Zec in London.

LEFT: A phone call from Marilyn in New York – posed specially to record the occasion.

ABOVE: A conjugal absurdity in Amsterdam: honeymooners John and Yoko share their 'bed for peace' with the author.

BELOW: The Maharishi Mahesh Yogi.

ABOVE: The late producer Cubby Broccoli, of 007 fame; the friendly legend and the legendary friend.

ABOVE: Frank Sinatra was the greatest but he engendered a palpable sense of a burning fuse.

RIGHT: Sammy Davis Jr, who was warned off the new Columbia star Kim Novak.

To my good friend Donald Zec — May I wish you the very best of everything in life. Always from Mario Lanza. Rome 25/10/57

Dear Donald — These foolish things remind me of you — Love Mario 22/6/59

ABOVE: Mario Lanza – a magnificent voice, but Puccini with pizza was the maestro's downfall.

LEFT: A smiling Brigitte Bardot, once the flower of French sexuality, with Donald Zec in London.

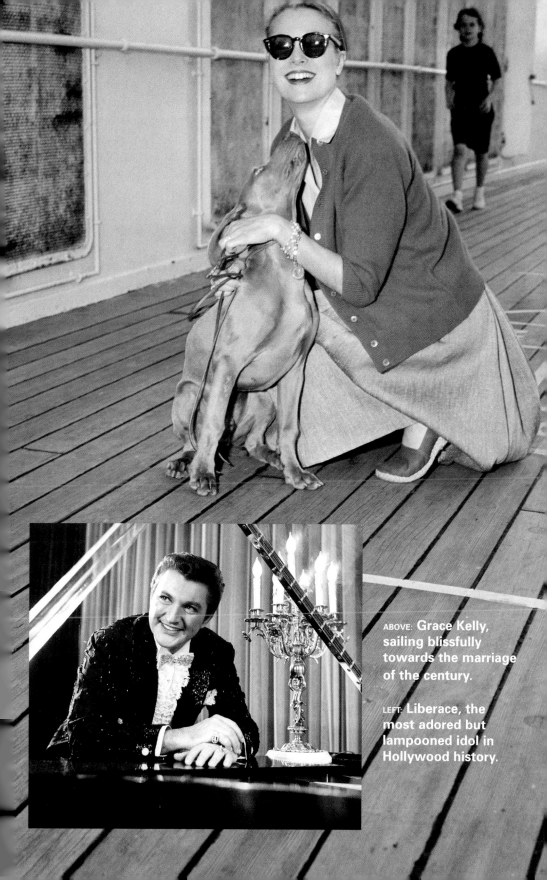

ABOVE: **Grace Kelly, sailing blissfully towards the marriage of the century.**

LEFT: **Liberace, the most adored but lampooned idol in Hollywood history.**

ABOVE: The late and likeable Rock Hudson; huge torment behind the boyish smile.

ABOVE RIGHT: The great Nureyev, a defiant Tartar who hated all convention – the sexual, the moral and the political.

RIGHT: The hugely talented Barbra Streisand, a class act with all the qualities required to make a legend.

LEFT: Lee Marvin: a memorable encounter at 21404 Pacific Coast Highway, California.

BELOW: The boxing legend Muhammad Ali – world statesmen are proud to shake his hand.

ABOVE: Laurence Olivier with Marilyn Monroe in London, during filming of *The Prince and the Showgirl*. Her performance delighted Britain's greatest actor.

RIGHT: Laurence Olivier, the ultimate legend. He could hold an audience with the tenacity of a pit-bull terrier.

Time-Life for showing their expertise for what it is;

Howard Hughes, wherever, whoever and if he may be, for failing to immortalise him by pushing the book through to publication.'

'Privately however, I would apologise to a few friends whom, for obvious reasons of security, I had to delude. Robert Kirsch of the *L.A. Times* and Dwye Evans of Heinemann are two of them.'

How much of yourself can be profitably exploited when once you are back in business . . . and what do you feel might be better suppressed?

'I have never consciously exploited any part of myself, except perhaps when the going got tough in the winter of '72 and I had to be super-cool in the face of adversity. I don't analyse myself – at least not comfortably. I think my nature is that of a doer rather than an intellectual because I trust my instincts. Obviously that trust is occasionally – perhaps often – misplaced. I am usually willing and able to pay the price of such mistakes, although I don't like it when others are forced to pay as well.

'I suppose I will have to learn to suppress my easy ability to take a risk. But if you do that altogether, then you might as well be dead.'

As a talented author how do you see your skill being more usefully applied in the future?

'In writing of course. I'm a novelist, a teller of tales (short ones, tall ones), and that means working towards telling truths about human lives. I will certainly write a novel using this prison experience; that's almost an obligation. I will also at some point attempt to resurrect the autobiography of Howard Hughes and get it published in some form, perhaps fiction. After all, it may be the most famous unpublished book in history; deservedly so I believe. It's a superb work of the imagination and it would be a pity if people never found out what the fuss had really been all about.'

Who has helped you most – if you were in a mood to hand out bouquets, to whom would you give them?

'I'm always in the mood to hand out bouquets. Almost all of our friends have helped me actively or by a simple affirmation of loyalty. In England I have an eleven-year-old son Joshua by a former marriage; he's written me many letters and come across the Atlantic to visit me in prison, and he's made me more than proud of him. A great many people I've never met have written to me, and still do, offering help and good wishes – including an anonymous lady from Baltimore who writes cheerily once a month and signs her letters "Grandma". My attorneys are beautiful people too and have become good friends – Maurice Nessen, Philip Lorber and Harold Weinberger.

'And there are men with whom I've done time who have been faithful comrades; you will find more consistent brotherhood in prisons than in most jungle territories outside the walls. Most of all I have to thank Kay Peters, a dear friend of ours, who has been caring for our children while my wife and I are locked away. She is a large-hearted human being.

'I always knew that loyalty to individuals was perhaps the most precious and valuable trait you could breed into a person and this entire experience has confirmed it for me.

'Best wishes, Clifford.'

The interview was published in London and immediately reproduced in America. I wondered what its effect might be on the parole board. Their arcane deliberations are rarely, if ever, disclosed. But a month or so later Clifford Irving wrote to me from the jail.

Danbury, 15th Sept. 1973.

Dear Donald,

Thanks, this time I did receive the clips. Of course I approve the result – it's a good picture of my wife too, but I can't send it to her because of the company she keeps.

I was denied parole late July – no reason given. This despite the fact that Danbury Federal Correctional Institution recommended release and a children's psychiatrist submitted a report stating that it was essential for at least one of the parents to return to the kids. At the moment I'm appealing for a rehearing via a lawyer in Washington. If that fails I'll go to court against the Parole Board. They are obviously cold-blooded bastards. The only thing to do is fight. My children are here now, visiting. They are a delight. And they are really angry about my not being with them, so I can't take the line of least resistance and let the Board have its way unchallenged.

Thanks again, and I too look forward to that drink,

Best wishes, Clifford.

CHAPTER ELEVEN

The Many Lives of Marilyn Monroe

To be telephoned at half past three in the morning would normally have been a thumping assault on the nervous system. But, as the caller happened to be Marilyn Monroe, there was a rapid readjustment of the reflexes. ('Of course you haven't disturbed me!' seemed a minor deceit under the circumstances.) For on the night that she called from New York – 23 January 1960 to be precise – Marilyn was just about the most famous and most exciting female on earth. She was the ultimate star who, on the face of it, was at the height of her achievements both as an actress and a woman. She was then married to Arthur Miller, America's most distinguished playwright. She had starred memorably opposite Britain's theatrical genius Sir Laurence Olivier, creating media frenzy across the land. The impact of her arrival in London dominated the newspapers and brought the crowds out in their thousands, prompting this comment from Arthur Miller: 'The country could have been towed into the Indian Ocean without anyone noticing.' Famous men, from Joe DiMaggio and Frank Sinatra to President John F Kennedy and his younger brother Robert, found her perilously irresistible. Her screen magic had a resonance that extended far beyond the darkness of the cinema. Hers was a love affair with the planet and she relished it as she delighted in the cornucopia of a body that was at the basis of it all.

At the time she phoned, everything in her turbulent life had seemed at last to come together. When in those early hours I mumbled, 'Who's calling?' she replied gleefully, 'This is Marilyn

Monroe Miller.' One did not need to be an analyst to get the message: incarcerated in an orphanage, not because of the loss of parents but through their absence; her mother institutionalised as a paranoid schizophrenic following an attempt to smother the infant in her cot; exploited early on by a succession of disreputable lovers – to be seen now as 'Mrs Arthur Miller' was the ultimate achievement. A quantum leap from humiliation to ecstasy. What I remember most about our conversation was not the teasing banter for which this delicious creature was famous (though there was some of that, particularly in reference to the French idol Yves Montand, with whom she would go on to have an affair). Instead, she defended herself against allegations that she was a pain and a penance to work with; that she was often late, demanded too many retakes, and was occasionally too emotionally frazzled to give a performance. The director who took most of the stick was the brilliant filmmaker, the late Billy Wilder, who made the Monroe classic *Some Like It Hot*. When I asked him why he put up with it, he responded with his writer's flair, 'Look, I have an Aunt Bessie who I guarantee would be on the set an hour ahead of time; dressed, made up, word-perfect, ready to go, as co-operative as a geisha girl. But who the hell would pay a dime to see my Aunt Bessie on the screen?'

Marilyn's defence of her position was expressed in the middle of my night, not hers: 'They complain because I'm supposed to be a tough negotiator about scripts, choosing my fellow actors, my costumes and so on. I certainly am tough when my work is at stake. It was because of certain problems with my work that I checked out of Hollywood five years ago. There are some things that one just does sell down the river.'

Around this time (January 1960) there had been some sporadic outbursts of neo-Nazism in Europe. It distressed her, she said, to see it happening. Assuming the Jewish faith on her marriage to Miller, she could declare with some passion, 'It is very sad and very alarming. I am so glad that the British people are condemning it.'

Not the expected response from the rinky-dink heroine famous for her teasing one-liners and sexy repartee. But the fact is Monroe was a much smarter person than Hollywood allowed. She had an intuitive intelligence, with a shrewd instinct about how to play a role. When she was making *The Prince and the Showgirl* with Laurence Oliver, the distinguished actress Dame Sybil Thorndyke said, 'That little girl is the only one here who knows how to act before a camera.'

Marilyn Monroe was not a great actress. Nor was she a particularly elevated human being. But, in her appallingly short life, she lit up the universe like a supernova, which in a flash becomes one hundred million times brighter than the sun before exploding into oblivion. But it brought her more misery than happiness. As Joshua Logan, director of her film *Bus Stop*, commented, 'I almost choke up when I think of her. I don't think she ever had two days of happiness or contentment in her life unless it was when she was working.' There was little joy in her first marriage, at sixteen, to the LA cop James Dougherty in 1942. Marriage to the baseball star Joe DiMaggio in 1954 was a squally affair and lasted only ten months. Far more damaging to her self-esteem were the casual affairs with a string of assorted lovers. They regarded her as fair game; passed her between friends the way people swap the names of newly favoured restaurants. Certainly she was scarcely an unwilling partner. She was a sexual spendthrift who lavished what she had with a passion, real or simulated. As Arthur Miller observes perceptively in his magnificent autobiography *Timebends – A Life*, 'She seemed to see all men as boys, children with immediate needs that it was her place in nature to fulfill.'

Thus Marilyn, the woman, pleasured great men and humble lovers with equal generosity and tenderness. But, on the set, the film star was a far less pliant and accommodating creature. No 'born trouper', she drove directors far beyond the limits of ordinary patience. Frustrated studio chiefs, worried about soaring budgets, bellowed all the way to their lawyers. Alcohol gave her no respite. Tranquillisers brought no tranquillity. I'm glad that I knew her in the glowing era of her life.

It is more than forty years since her gruesome and untimely end. But the questions persist as to what, or perhaps who, caused her death. The indictment of collective guilt still tugs at the conscience of Hollywood. I met her several times over the years, in Los Angeles, New York, Arizona and London, and we talked occasionally on the transatlantic phone. Part of her magic was this ability to convince us deluded interviewers that ours was an intimacy matched by none other. My recollections are not merely of an unfathomable talent abruptly and needlessly extinguished. They are also of a gorgeous, giving creature who ironically had an intrinsic decency that put her lofty detractors to shame.

I have written the obituaries of several of Hollywood's 'legends'. We mourned their passing and admired their achievements. But Monroe's death evoked anger, too. The sheer scale of the exploitation, despite the impeccable credentials of the principals involved, still troubles the mind. The assorted politicians and other celebrities who achieved the prevailing objective of 'getting Marilyn in the sack' scarcely paused in their heavy breathing to consider the victim. Their needs were the priority. Hers scarcely entered the equation. 'A parasite', says one dictionary, 'is an animal, which lives in or on another from which it obtains nourishment. The host does not benefit from the association and is often harmed by it.' There is much anecdotal evidence in Monroe's life to confirm that definition. Few would dispute her right to be up there with the other screen immortals. But she never believed herself to be the megastar she was. For as long as I knew her she was too pathologically insecure to enjoy her triumphs. There was no palpable sense of the fact that the world adored her. Men and women alike. Despite all the adulation, she never saw herself as a legend in the making.

The more insecure she became, the more the ghost of her mother intruded and made her doubt her own sanity. As Arthur Miller wrote, 'Beneath her insouciance and wit, death was her companion everywhere.' Her single resource, other than her talent, was her sexuality. Hers was the most delicious arrangement of living flesh on the planet. If she was too profligate with it – well, during the early struggles of her life it was the only game in town. Perhaps the most telling comment among the millions of posthumous essays on her life and times was from the photographer Philippe Halsman: 'With a stranger [male] she only felt safe when she knew he desired her.' Perversely, having been raped and abused in her childhood, she feared honest sex least of all. On this territory at least she was in control.

So she had become adept at gratifying the urges of assorted lovers. If, as has been said, Marilyn only sporadically achieved total satisfaction, faking ecstasy was well within her compass as an actress. And in any event these encounters – Marlon Brando aside – were minor-league affairs, holding-pattern liaisons between marriages. A born giver, Marilyn displayed a special tenderness to older men. She became a ministering angel, stirring their memories if nothing else. The most prestigious of these was the powerful studio chief, Joseph Schenck.

The story goes that when the film producer George Seaton wanted to talk to Marilyn about a possible film, and asked her to come and see him at three o'clock, she is quoted as replying, 'I can't come to your office at three o'clock because every day at three o'clock I go to Mr Schenck's office. But don't worry, I'm always done with Mr Schenck by three fifteen; I'll be at your office at three twenty.'

But, for reasons known only to the parties concerned, the sessions ended abruptly. Now Mr Schenck had a problem: how to get Marilyn off his hands – tactfully. He called a Mr Joni Taps, a senior aide to Harry Cohn, head of Columbia Studios. Mr Taps recalls, 'I received a telephone call from Joe Schenck who was the head of Twentieth Century-Fox. He said to me, "I've a girl on the lot that I want to get off the lot. I've been going with her and I don't want her around any more. Give her twenty out of twenty-six weeks at minimum salary." I said, "I'll have to ask Harry Cohn. Why don't *you* ask Harry, Joe?"

'"I don't want to ask that sonofabitch for anything."

'So I went up to Harry Cohn and I said, "Joe Schenck called. He's got a girl over on the lot that he wants off the lot but he's gotta send her someplace. He wants her to get twenty out of twenty-six weeks at 175 dollars a week. And he thinks you're a sonofabitch and he doesn't want to ask you. But what do you wanna do about it?"

'"Well, if he wants to get rid of her that badly, sign her up."'

Long after, when Schenck became seriously ill, he asked his secretary to send for Monroe. Marilyn dismissed the nurses and comforted the aged mogul in ways not listed in the *Nurses' Journal*. The medicos subsequently recorded a considerable boost of the spirits in their otherwise stricken patient.

I first met Marilyn after the release of *Niagara*, the film that launched her career. It was a perfect Californian day. The sun shone. We were outside some studio lot and she was brought over to me the way a prize thoroughbred might be paraded for appraisal. The sweating publicity man's sales talk was heavy with fact-sheet superlatives. Short on inspiration myself at the time, I settled for a dictionary definition of a star: 'a heavenly body radiating flashes of light'. But, as the world and her multitude of intimates well knew, there was infinitely more to Monroe than that. There was a boldness to her sexuality, yet an innocence too. She was a highly tactile female, and the most fleeting physical contact, like a simple hand squeeze, was high on the generating current of intimacy. The casual gesture of linking arms achieved high-voltage intensity when it was Marilyn's arm that was making the contact.

Since experience had taught her to regard all men as potential seducers – married Englishmen not excluded – she had the most adroit strategy for controlling the situation. The linked-arms gesture and the spontaneous laughter set the tone and the limits of the moment. Those who equated that nude calendar with a somewhat brash and brazen personality misread Marilyn by miles. It is true that she delighted in her nudity, regarding clothes as a bit of a nuisance. But it was more a celebration than a tease. Sure, there was a touch of 'If you've got it, baby, flaunt it' – at least while her mirror still confirmed that she was delectable fore and aft. Yet she hated vulgarity and craved respectability and status. (It was a craving she shared with Sophia Loren. Born illegitimate and in poverty, Sophia achieved the status of an Oscar-winning star, plus the ultimate accolade of being appointed a roving ambassador for the United Nations.) Told by Hollywood's (then) most famous astrologer, Carol Richter, that her star sign, Gemini, was shared by such stars as Rosalind Russell, Rosemary Clooney and Judy Garland, Marilyn brought the stargazer down to earth with the stern, 'I was born under the same sign as Ralph Waldo Emerson, Queen Victoria and Walt Whitman.' So there!

Carol Richter was just one of the many soothsayers Marilyn turned to in her confused uncertain hours. A New York psychiatrist was also on 24-hour alert to cope with the many emotional crises that plagued her burgeoning career. But in her rare moments of peace of mind, there was a lot of kindness in Marilyn. Because of her own stricken childhood, she empathised with the derelicts and deprived in society. She would sooner have hugged an orphan than a producer.

We do not know how her second husband, Joe DiMaggio, reacted on their first meeting. He kept those and all subsequent feelings about Marilyn to himself. But Arthur Miller, describing the woman he would later marry, soared into epic prose: 'Her radiance was surrounded by a perplexing darkness and I knew that I must flee or walk into a doom beyond all knowing.'

In short, the distinguished playwright was knocked out like others who had keeled over at the first glance.

Once – well, 4.30 p.m., 10 April 1958 to be precise – she invited me to her apartment on E57th Street New York. She and Miller were married then, and the tall bespectacled genius was in another room clacking away at his typewriter. The spring sunshine illuminated those radiant Monroe features. Golden hair fell around the sweetest smile in Manhattan. The decor was cool, clinical, wall-to-wall whiteness. The curtains, the carpet, the walls and the piano all white, the sofa alone beige. In a corner, a marble table bore a variety of tributes all dedicated to the lady who was now pouring the tea. A silver-framed illuminated address was inscribed, 'To Marilyn, the wonder of the age'. Beside it stood a headless torso in black marble of Aphrodite. Other pictures of Marilyn were deployed elsewhere in the room. They provided glowing reassurance, if not authentic self-esteem. This heady mix of sunshine, Marilyn and Chanel No. 5 inhibited serious conversation.

That may well have been the lady's intention. Other screen goddesses in my experience have not been slow to recount harrowing tales of tormented childhood. But Marilyn Monroe rarely unlocked the secrets of her appalling upbringing. She did not want to recall her ten years in foster homes, the bleak incarceration in orphanages and her life with a state-appointed guardian while her mother was in an asylum. She dreaded any reference to her mother's schizophrenia for fear of its being linked to her own neuroses. And in the serenity of that afternoon it was no time to hark back to the abuse and degradation of her infancy. She said how much she loved her husband and the softness in her voice confirmed it. She said she was frighteningly happy, a phrase more revealing in hindsight than at the time. She said also that despite previous miscarriages she longed for a baby. She would not know that in a comparatively short time not having a child would be the least of her disappointments. But, at the time, the euphoria of her marriage to the genius in the adjoining room shone in her eyes. It was tempting at the time to regard this marriage as the fascination of an untutored innocent for an intellectual heavyweight. This was a simplistic judgement and, from my knowledge of Marilyn, far from the truth. She herself declared spiritedly, 'It was the man I married, not the mind.'

Out of respect for Miller's parents, Isadore and Augusta, both Jews though not strictly orthodox, Marilyn had insisted upon a typically Jewish marriage. She had privately received coaching in Jewish customs and traditions from Rabbi Robert Goldburg in New York. She made the essential commitment that any child of the marriage would be brought up in the Jewish faith. But Marilyn's most adroit move was to learn a few basic recipes – like chicken soup, gefilte fish and potato latkes from Arthur Miller's mother. This was the ultimate initiation and convinced the delighted Augusta that far from losing a son she was gaining a Jewish daughter. There would never be a critical shortage of chicken soup in the Arthur Miller household, *Gott sie Danke!*

Eventually the tapping typewriter in the study stopped and Arthur Miller appeared, polishing his spectacles. A gentle giant of a man, he was clearly relieved to break away from his work. Politely, he apologised for disturbing us. He did not want tea. Nor did he wish to engage in conversation. Instead he sat down on the sofa beside his wife and just looked at her. Correction: he feasted on her. He took in the tangle of golden curls falling around those famous features; the afternoon sunlight lingering on the blueness of her eyes and on the soft panel of bare midriff beneath the carefully unbuttoned shirt. There was a long silence while Miller scrutinised her, pleasure and pride of ownership in his eyes. I didn't utter a word, not wanting to shatter the fine intimacy of the moment. Marilyn blushed, wriggling with delight. This wordless coalescence between the unlikeliest partners of the age was touching to witness. Built on genuine love, but fraught with Marilyn's tragic neuroses, it would be obliterated by events. But at that moment Mr and Mrs Arthur Miller were mutually ecstatic, making this observer feel, as the army says, 'surplus to establishment'. Finally Miller stood up and walked back to his typewriter. He had enjoyed his creative 'fix' for the day and was ready to write another scene. As an antidote to writer's block it might as well be Marilyn Monroe as anyone else.

The more I met with her the more I was struck by Monroe's total lack of guile. She was a singularly honest creature in a profession where truth is an optional accessory. She rejected all the coy artifices that come with the persona of the average sex goddess. No tricks or Princess Di bashfulness beneath lowered eyelashes. She knew her strength lay in her desirability and there were no half-measures in that area. But, as her nude-calendar image faded into a recognition of her genuine talent, she began to hate the very publicity that had created her. All the hype, the phoney blurbs, the gossip items and the slick one-liners that supposedly sell movies began to pall. Many of her famous off-the-cuff remarks were dreamed up by press agents. Though she smiled and giggled on cue, she inwardly detested the whole routine. The only way out, as she saw it, was to be taken seriously as an actress, to get the critics, not merely the gossip writers, on her side. She was getting close to achieving that with *The Seven Year Itch*. But it was *Bus Stop* that drew this from Bosley Crowther, the distinguished critic of the *New York Times*:

> Marilyn Monroe has finally proved herself as an actress. Fortunately for her and for the tradition of diligence leading to success, she gives a performance in this picture that marks her as a genuine acting star, not just a plushy personality and a sex symbol...

Criticised by directors for holding up production, Marilyn could have cited that accolade in mitigation. The way she disrupted productions, specifically Billy Wilder's *Some Like It Hot*, is writ large in the Hollywood archives. But so are her credits; and, as we've seen, Wilder conceded that Monroe's quirkiness was a trivial price to pay for the incomparable – and bankable – magic that came with it.

I flew with Marilyn from Los Angeles to Arizona for the location shooting on *Bus Stop*. An incident on the flight made the trip memorable: midway over the desert there was a slight flurry among the cabin crew. One of the plane's four engines had overheated. The pilot shut it down and the aircraft wobbled slightly. It may have taken me longer than others to be aware of the fact. Strapped in beside the most desirable creature on the planet, I found an engine malfunction to be a minor distraction. But it gave the two of us something else to talk about. I suggested that, if by some mischance the plane were to crash, the event would sweep wars, revolutions and other trivia off the front pages of the world. The entire globe would be talking about Marilyn Monroe. The thought didn't appear to delight her. I wondered aloud (admittedly with a reporter's cunning) how she thought she would be remembered. Typically, she did not answer at once. The question required serious thought. Twenty miles of Arizona desert slid away beneath us. Then with not much of a smile she murmured, 'Marilyn Monroe, 37, 22, 38.'

I may have got the dimensions wrong, since those 'vital statistics' changed marginally over the years. Perhaps her comment might have recalled a press agent's invention; maybe it was just a tease. But, even as irony, the comment is revealing. It indicated that Marilyn, despite the accolades and the public adoration, was still painfully short on self-esteem. Bereft of any emotional resources of her own, she turned in panic to whoever or whatever would see her through the night. She had psychiatrists in New York and Los Angeles who compared notes on a whole casebook of hang-ups. Both were on a 24-hour hook-up with plausible answers for her troubled mind. She insisted that one of them join her on the Arizona location.

She drew less clinical support from an odd-looking Paula Strasberg, dubbed 'The Lady In Black' (the colour of her voluminous black cloak, which, in addition to a giant handbag, became her trademark). Married to Lee Strasberg, exponent of the Method School of Acting, she was Marilyn's closest confidante. A dramatic coach turned Jewish mother, she fussed, lectured, cajoled and mothered Monroe while film crews kicked their heels and waited and waited. Josh Logan, the kindliest of directors, could never be certain that he would have a functioning actress on his hands. The production was on a knife edge. As he soothed, encouraged and just occasionally bawled out this fragile goddess, he could scarcely believe what it took to bring Marilyn Monroe in front of the cameras as she paced around in her trailer in search of 'motivation'.

The press was kept well away from witnessing these dramas (though one cameraman reported seeing Marilyn throwing up behind the scenes). Just the same, most observers were aware of the ominous undercurrents. The relationship between Marilyn and her co-star Don Murray was noticeably cool. Murray was cast as the gullible cowboy in love with a steamy café singer played by Marilyn. But there was little sexual chemistry between them, which increased Monroe's sense of unease. She needed to have her leading man aroused if not smitten. Don Murray neither felt that nor could he simulate it. In the scene where she has to slap him across the face, Marilyn did so with such ferocity that it produced an instant crisis. The incident was seen by some as Monroe's response to Murray's apparent indifference. More likely it was just another expression of the fears and frustrations that were on the flip side of Monroe's angel-of-sex persona. Despite all this, the vomiting and the tranquillisers, she still managed to give one of her best portrayals ever. Hindsight suggests that much credit for this is due to Arthur Miller.

Looking back over her life, it's sad to realise how little she received despite all that she gave. Most of the men who enjoyed her sexual generosity expressed their gratitude and departed. They were not unduly concerned about the emotional disarray they left behind. The analysts could pick up the pieces. But there were a few who recognised the battles Marilyn was having with herself and were deeply concerned about their outcome, notably her second husband, Joe DiMaggio and, years later, Arthur Miller – the two most devoted men in her life. The grim case histories she toted with her into these marriages demanded the love, the patience and the compassion of saints. Both husbands in their different ways gave Marilyn all that and more. All through the years, long after their marriage had crashed, Joe DiMaggio behaved with extraordinary forbearance. He took her tormented phone calls in the small hours of the night. He listened patiently to her tirades of anger against the studio executives she saw as persecutors. He conferred with doctors and analysts in those dark periods when his ex-wife teetered towards the abyss. He claimed no medals for doing so. He loved her and continued to do so even when living with her became a nightmare.

And, when it was over, that tired cliché of celebrity divorce, 'we remain good friends' meant exactly what it said. But DiMaggio was more fortunate than Miller. The Marilyn he knew suffered chronic insecurities to be sure. But she had not had to face the idiot's delight of superstardom. That was to be Arthur Miller's bed of nails.

Arriving in Phoenix and transferring to the location, Marilyn seemed happy enough. Meanwhile, her husband-to-be was sweating out the mandatory six weeks' residency in Nevada necessary for his divorce. I remember watching Marilyn preparing for a scene standing in the semi-darkness behind the cameras. She flapped her hands in the standard ritual of relaxation. She murmured her lines. She pressed a hand against her forehead and then leaned up against a wall. She called for 'makeup' and urgently demanded a verdict on her hair. Now and again as some inner thought troubled her she involuntarily shook her head in response. (Long after, on the set of *The Prince and the Showgirl*, Laurence Olivier would try to reassure her. He would tell her how he himself was so nervous he would frequently throw up before going on stage.) But Larry's performances were underpinned by years of training, the technique honed to perfection. Monroe's magic was intuitive, as perilous as thin ice. In the short time I was with her in Arizona she showed no signs of the depression, the anger and the indignation simmering behind the sugary-sweet exterior. But, at night, Miller would hear it all in a lone phone booth on a Nevada highway. As he listened to her tremulous complaints, her railing against Logan, her yearning to throw it all in and settle for just being 'Mrs Arthur Miller', he must have sensed turbulence ahead. But out there in the desert only tenderness and reassurance was called for. Thinking back over our conversations, I marvel at her total absence of self-pity. Ten foster homes; two years in an orphanage; a mother out of reach in an asylum – Marilyn Monroe deserved more than ordinary compassion.

She learned early on of her mother's attempt to smother her at birth. There is some doubt as to who her father was. Official forms asking her father's name she simply marked 'Unknown'. The records show that her maternal great-grandfather hanged himself. Her maternal grandfather died young in an asylum. If she revealed all this – and more – to Arthur Miller it was because he had the love and the wisdom of years to heal the pain. She apparently recounted to him a strangely affecting tale about the woman she called 'Aunt Ana', who in fact was a kind of guardian. On the day after Ana's death, Marilyn, deeply shocked, went and lay down in her bed, her head buried in the pillow. She then went to the cemetery, lay down in the newly dug grave and looked up at the sky...

We met again in London, where she was to make her film with Larry Olivier. Again Marilyn Monroe in public was the sweet, ring-a-ding star, stunning as ever in front of an army of cameramen. She reiterated how happy she was with Miller. And, though he would have pointed her towards good reading, she insisted, 'He never tried to change me.' And so on. These were holding-pattern utterances for public consumption. Privately it was the internal agony as before, compounded by the challenge of performing opposite the world's finest actor. The familiar problems of her awkwardness and late arrivals surfaced again. Increasing insomnia and cocktails of drugs added to her problems.

It has been said that Miller and Olivier commiserated with each other about their volatile wives. Vivien Leigh was by far the heavier cross to bear. This exquisite beauty and Olivier had enjoyed a theatrical courtship of extraordinary incandescence. Their marriage was the stuff of romantic novels. But, while Marilyn's demons were born of insecurity, Vivien's were darker and more dangerous. She became a demanding flirtatious imp, thrown grotesquely off balance by hard liquor. The Oliviers' 21 years together may have captivated the world. But they foundered on her near hysteria, violence and sexual fantasies. The marriage said to have been 'made in heaven' ended in hell.

Marilyn's divorce from Arthur Miller suffered no such histrionics. None of the couple's intimates doubted that Miller had made titanic efforts to sustain his wife and therefore his marriage. It was never going to be easy for this sane, supremely gifted dramatist to move easily in the raucously superficial world of show business. Although that was not the real problem, Miller well understood the nature of that beast. But Marilyn couldn't handle the twin stresses of the movies and her marriage. It could not work, and eventually did not.

There was the Yves Montand affair, on which the saddest comment came from the Frenchman's distinguished actress wife, Simone Signoret: 'I am the most famous cuckold in the world.' She and her husband had moved into the Beverly Hills Hotel for his film with Marilyn, appropriately titled *Let's Make Love*. Which of the two co-stars proffered that invitation is academic. The affair was as inevitable as was its abrupt and virtually painless termination. What pain there was, was born with remarkable dignity by Montand's wife. She had seen how unbalanced Marilyn had become and with Gallic magnanimity tried to help her. The situation was not helped by the studio cynically planting rumours of the affair to bolster the film. Pursued by reporters, Signoret parried their questions with, 'Do you know many men who would stay detached if they had Marilyn Monroe in their arms?' It was a good try, but few were deceived. When the two faces were held up to the light, Marilyn's and hers, one was radiant, the other ravaged. But when Monroe died, this fine French actress wrote with epic generosity, 'She never knew how much I did not detest her.'

The assessment of the life and times of Marilyn Monroe is a never-ending exercise. Her relationships with the Kennedys lack both documentary evidence and crucial testimony from Marilyn herself. Moreover, America's constitutional 'Right To Know' does not apparently extend to presidents or their brothers. And in any event it scarcely matters. The violent tragedy of the Kennedy deaths vastly overshadows Marilyn's own passing. Yet she is no less mourned by millions. She died long before her time, and we will probably never know the truth about those terrible final hours. But she left us much to marvel at. Miller, who knows all about greatness, would certainly accord her more than a footnote in history. A simpler test, of course, is whether anyone could ever replace her. By that criterion Marilyn Monroe need have no fears at all.

CHAPTER TWELVE

Port and Pheasant in the
Farcical Fifties

The 1950s was a decade of frivolities. But these were upstaged as 1960 dawned when Elizabeth Taylor and Richard Burton steamed into the headlines. They met in Rome; the earth moved; and from then on their every sensual tremor was broadcast worldwide with everything one needed to know between the covers. The couple occupied a great deal of my professional time and credulity. (One of my most vivid memories is watching Burton honk Elizabeth's breasts like an old-time London cabbie squeezing the hooter.) But bear with me. They will strut their stuff later. Meanwhile, as a curtain-raiser to their conjugal antics, we had the arrival on these shores of history's supreme comedy duo, Laurel and Hardy. Just as Rudolph Nureyev hero-worshipped Fred Astaire, and Yehudi Menuhin revered the great jazz violinist Stéphane Grappelli, so that theatrical giant Laurence Olivier idolised the incomparable Oliver Hardy.

If *re*-acting is the essence of performance then the Fat One, 'Ollie', was the master. His long-suffering stare into the camera amid the mayhem created by his lugubrious partner, Stan Laurel, transmitted more messages than Western Union. Hardy's exasperated 'that's another fine mess you've gotten me into!' is the longest-running punchline in screen comedy. Hardy was always the gentleman despite the Bunter-tight jacket and too-short baggy trousers. The courtly sweep of the bowler hat and the beaming smile under the spit-curled fringe was the benign antidote to Stan Laurel's dimwit catastrophes.

But the *pièce de résistance*, the sublime 'bit of business' that only the great Chaplin could have matched, was Hardy's disarming fluttering of his tie. This was an inspired piece of comedy, which explained why the great mime artist Marcel Marceau put Ollie and Stan high on his list of role models. Admittedly, these geniuses go way back in cinema history, before Morecambe and Wise arrived to deliver variations on the theme. But real legends, by definition, have an infinite lifespan. Every day of the week a Laurel and Hardy film is being shown *somewhere*. One of their greatest classics, *Way Out West*, in which they memorably sing and dance, is reissued in cinemas and on TV as frequently as *Casablanca* plays again and again. (Film critic David Robinson chuckled away from *Way Out West* declaring, 'Not only is this one of their most perfect films, it ranks with the best screen comedy anywhere.')

As they tripped, skidded and stumbled towards immortality, the duo made more than a hundred films – silents, shorts, two-reelers and full-length features. So an invitation to meet them for a drink at London's Washington Hotel in January 1952 was something only a fatal accident would prevent. We are accustomed to film stars looking nothing like their screen images. But this pair, both in style and demeanour, looked as though they'd just ambled down from the screen. Ollie beaming over a mini-moustache, two chins and a plunging waistline, flourished me into an armchair. The Thin One (the creative thrust of the partnership) scratched his head on cue and threw in a forlorn, 'You're most welcome.' A waiter bowed in with a tray of drinks. Hardy bowed in return, an apple-cheeked smile framing those innocent rosebud lips. They had come to England for a nine-month tour with the famous railroad-station sketch featured in their film *Night Owls*. 'House full' notices were a foregone conclusion. Like all great clowns, they knew they made millions laugh but couldn't begin to explain it.

Much of what they did, said Hardy, happened by accident: his twiddling of the tie, Laurel's scratching of the head, the 'Cuckoo Song' signature tune all 'just sort of happened. They were funny so they stayed.' Comics as a rule do not draw the crowds the way today's pop idols do. But there were historic exceptions. Charlie Chaplin was one. Laurel and Hardy another. There were real tears in Stan Laurel's eyes as he and Hardy spoke of their reception in Europe. On their first trip to Paris in the thirties the president of France sent his personal car to parade them along the jam-packed Champs-Elysées. 'Remember China?' mused Laurel. 'Indeed I do,' said his devoted friend. They had apparently taken a rare vacation, ending up touring China, a far more enigmatic location than it is today. Curiosity took them to a remote spot in the interior. They visited a Buddhist temple. News of their presence in China had preceded them. They entered the temple. Officials gently steered them towards the altar. There before them, grinning cheekily amid the burnished gold, was a gigantic photographic blow-up of Ollie and Stan. (Above them, the expression on the face of 'The Enlightened One' was maybe a shade less inscrutable than before.)

Before arriving in England, their ship had docked at Cobh in Ireland. Word had got around that Laurel and Hardy were on board. A huge flotilla of boats moved in around their ship blowing sirens and whistles and exploding fireworks. 'But then something happened that we'll never forget,' said Stan. 'All the church bells in Cobh started to ring out our theme song. Babe [Hardy's life-long nickname] looked at me and we cried. Maybe people liked our pictures because we put so much love into them. Who knows?' Well, history for sure. Their appeal covered all ages, classes and genders and still goes on and on. Just in case their genius has eluded you, get hold of a video of *Way Out West*. If you do not find this an absolute scream check for possible malfunction that little nerve at the tip of your elbow.

Humour has a thousand faces. Sometimes newspapers add to the fun like the *Sun*'s FREDDIE STARR ATE MY HAMSTER. Way back in time, the *Daily Mirror*, with a flash of foolishness, placed a woman astride an egg to see if she could in the fullness of time hatch a chick. The experiment failed, with much squawking disapproval across the nation and with heaven knows what confusion inside the egg. That stunt was soon forgotten. But accidental humour can be just as hilarious. Politicians frequently oblige with their own unscripted idiocies. Now and again, an MP will drop a brick of such magnitude that the embarrassment can last a political lifetime. There was one such piece of unintended farce back in October 1955, which caused much glee across the nation and just happened to involve me at the time. The clanger concerned was dropped by the then chancellor of the Exchequer, the late Lord R A Butler (Marlborough, Pembroke College Cambridge). A brilliant academic who nearly became prime minister, 'Rab' Butler was nevertheless somewhat short on political savvy. He made a speech in which he sought to alert the British people against needless extravagance in hard times. But these were not the words he used. With that genial tactlessness for which die-hard Tories were famous at the time, he warned, 'We must not drop back into easy evenings with port wine and over-ripe pheasant...'

This vision of millions of Britons gorging themselves on well-ripened pheasant, warming the backsides of their jodhpurs in front of crackling log fires while slurping on the vintage port, was too delicious for ordinary media comment. Well so it was to my late friend and boss, Lord Hugh Cudlipp, then editorial director of Mirror Group Newspapers. Never one to disdain so promising a gift to a vigilant tabloid, he was on the phone to me in a flash: 'Why don't you give a port-and-pheasant party to a dozen ordinary people, maybe a charlady or two, somewhere private, just to test out the average Briton's reaction to the chancellor's warning?'

The stunt promised the exquisite mischief for which the *Mirror* and the ebullient Hugh Cudlipp were famous. I was equally intrigued, both by the challenge and possibly the vintage port. I alerted the banqueting manager at London's Savoy Hotel to reserve a private room. (My request for a set menu of twelve portions of over-ripe pheasant and a half a dozen bottles of the finest vintage port, plus smoked-salmon sandwiches for a photographer, was noted without comment.)

You may imagine, as I did, that it would be relatively simple to go out into the streets of London and persuade a dozen or so ordinary folk into having dinner with you – *and* at the Savoy. But it was not until I actually tried it that the absurdity of it began to dawn. On the corner of Baker Street and Marylebone Road, I approached a figure in overalls who I assumed met the 'average-working-man' criterion. Adopting a cheerful demeanour – not easy in the pouring rain – I said,

'I don't suppose you'd care to have dinner with me tonight. Just a handful...'

He recoiled as though struck.

'Gitt-aht-ovit!'

I got-aht-ovit.

Outside the church at St John's Wood roundabout – I reasoned that the saintly location would confirm my best intentions – I latched onto a 'typical housewife'.

'Good day,' I breezed. 'I'm from the *Mirror*. We're having a little dinner...'

'*Bitte? Sprechen Sie Deutsch?*' queried the alarmed stranger.

'*Nein.*'

'*Ach!* No spik Engleesch.'

'Dinner. Hotel Savoy,' I faltered in pidgin English.

'*Ich kann nicht verstehen!*' she shouted over the chimes of the church clock.

'That's fine,' I reassured her. '*Auf Weidersehen guten tag, danke* just the same.'

It was now 3 p.m., time enough, I hoped, to steer a handful of guests in the direction of the Savoy Hotel. Some 'typical secretaries' in Abbey Road retreated from my invitation with suspicion. I was, after all, wearing what now looked like a dirty raincoat. By 4 p.m. I was seriously worried. Twelve portions of over-ripe pheasant lay bleakly in waiting at the Savoy. Bela Zola, one of the most gifted photographers of the day, was setting up his equipment and polishing his lenses. A beautifully candlelit banquet was going begging. I was racked by such thoughts as: (1) What am I going to do with the grub if nobody shows? (2) What item will fill the large space earmarked for Monday's paper?

It was now raining hard. Surfing along the Finchley Road, I fetched up in front of a barricaded crater at the bottom of which four men were digging deep to repair a water main. I leaned over as they heaved chunks of clay and rubble up onto the surface. Wet muck sloshed over my far from watertight brogues. Then I actually heard myself ask: 'Excuse me, gentlemen, I don't suppose you'd all care to have dinner with me at the Savoy Hotel tonight. Quite informal. We're having pheasant...'

That madness caused the men to pause in their labours. 'You feeling all right, mate?' one of them asked.

'Yes, fine,' I replied, burbling something about 'Rab' Butler's warning to the nation. This merely compounded the drivel. Somehow port and pheasant did not go well with sand and cement. One of the men beckoned me to lean a shade closer over the parapet.

'Can you take advice?'

'Of course,' I said.

'Well I advise you to piss off,' he said not unkindly

Advice taken.

We can fast-forward to the *dénouement* of this episode. An eleventh-hour rescue came in the form of a friend named Dolly, who lived in north London. A popular hostess with an irresistible attraction to wacky situations, she leaped to my rescue like John Wayne with the US Cavalry. It took me thirty seconds to explain the crisis. It took her fifteen minutes to round up a gaggle of guests, which included a bus driver, a porter, a canteen assistant and other friends of her local greengrocer. An hour or so later this disparate bunch filed into the Princess Ida suite at the Savoy wearing their Sunday best and a variety of bemused expressions. My memory is somewhat hazy as to how the evening progressed, except to say that I hated every embarrassing moment of it. As an exercise to prove that Mr and Mrs Average Briton generally preferred fish and chips to port and pheasant, the affair was an unqualified success.

But it was no night for gourmets. 'Blimey, it don' arf pong' fairly summarised the reaction to Mr Butler's *plat du jour*. This did not go down well with the waiter driven to pouring lashings of vintage port like cheap plonk. One woman reeled off, pale and queasy, to the ladies' room. Her partner complained his pheasant tasted like bad pork. Another guest pushed his plate away in revulsion and asked if stew was on the menu. A giggling female announced by way of conversation that she was six months pregnant. This called for another litre of vintage port. The dinner ended in rollicking disorder, with some fairly explicit suggestions as to what the chancellor could do with his port and pheasant. The story filled the middle pages of the *Mirror* in the following Monday's edition. Any notion that this lofty academic might feel somewhat chastened by what he read was instantly dispelled by his phone call to Hugh Cudlipp some days later. His response was entirely in character: 'How droll,' the minister drawled.

It may be that chancellors of the Exchequer are structured to be less vulnerable to gentle mockery than other politicians. Almost ten years later I featured another chancellor, Selwyn Lloyd MP QC, in a series called 'Men of Power'. He was a great gift to the media and the mischievous cartoonist. The gales of derision that blew up after 'Rab' Butler's port-and-pheasant gaffe was a breeze compared with the withering scorn heaped on Selwyn Lloyd. (As foreign secretary during the Suez Crisis, he took most of the flak for that catastrophic episode.) He was no less unpopular as chancellor. As I wrote at the time,

> In the raking crossfire of politics few men have been more jeered, scoffed at, blown up or shouted down than the precise, immaculate Mr. Selwyn Lloyd MP. 'Poor bumbling braggart...this tortured misfit...a stranded whale...portfolio without a Minister...' These are just a few lively selections from the records.
>
> Cartoonists like to portray him as a kind of baffled parrot, blinking, beaky and bewildered. All of which might have shaken even the most case-hardened politicians. But not John Selwyn Brooke Lloyd. He has displayed...an infinite capacity for taking pain.

But, on meeting the man and the irresistible charm and courtesy he transmitted at the time, I was forced to concede what a nice bloke he was. I hoped this and other felicities in my profile of him would take the curse off this comment on our interview: 'The carefully-weighed words emerged like the slow deliberation of a leaking tap – intermittent pearls of predictability.'

I did not anticipate a response. Politicians, like actors, are accustomed to taking the rough with the smooth. But a day or two later I received a handwritten note under the red-sealed insignia of the chancellor of the exchequer:

> Dear Mr Zec – I hope it will not ruin your reputation if I write to say how much I enjoyed the profile. You were in most ways

much too kind about me (although I'm not sure about the 'leaking tap'.) With many thanks and every good wish. Yours sincerely, Selwyn Lloyd.

They were real diplomats in those days.

The moral of the port-and-pheasant fiasco was that on balance it is best for newspapers to maintain an arm's-length relationship with their readers. Stunts that require the random participation of readers often misfire. But columnists, when desperate for an idea, occasionally turn to their readers for help. In a moment of journalistic whimsy I hit on that old standby – a competition. I issued an invitation to readers (around 15 million at the time) to write in a few sentences why they would like to have dinner with Sophia Loren and William Holden and what they would say to them. (In the easygoing Britain of the time one could engage in sprees of this sort without blushing.) Fortunately, Sophia and Bill Holden were close enough friends to submit to the nonsense. Neither superstar was exactly short of publicity. Nor was a private dinner in the company of awe-struck fans a dazzling prospect. But they came along with the sort of curiosity one has for traffic accidents.

Selecting two of the most promising letters from the thousands of replies, I arranged for the winners to be brought to the hotel. Mr Holden had 'won' a Mrs Patricia Dyer from Frinton in Essex. Sophia acquired Denis Doyle of Bilston, Staffordshire. Over the oysters, the turtle soup, the chicken and the chilled Niersteiner I sensed growing unease. Clearly Bill Holden had had a hard day. A dark frown clouded his handsome features. Mrs Dyer was nervous and stared mutely at him from her position on his left. Bill stared back over his Scotch on the rocks, his eyes glittering into an unmistakable 'what the hell am I doing here?' There were long silences. Finally Mrs Dyer, drawing on the inspiration of the sages, asked Holden, 'What is your favourite film?'

Holden stared back in disbelief.

'It hasn't been made yet,' he said.

Mrs Dyer clutched another straw: 'If you quit show business altogether,' she faltered, 'what would you do?'

'Die,' growled Bill.

The good lady geared herself for the final question that had won her this scintillating, forthcoming and informative superstar for the evening: 'With what five people have you most enjoyed working?'

'None.'

Rigor mortis. Mrs Dyer took refuge in her chicken. The occasion was disintegrating into nightmare. I glanced over at Sophia, who looked delicious in a lace-topped dress with a tantalising see-through neckline. She was having her problems too. Her male escort, Mr Doyle, was as mute as a sphinx. Not a murmur escaped from him. He peered at her through his spectacles as though merely checking to see if she was still there. The occasion was sinking into the numbness of a house of mourning. I made signs to Mr Doyle, urging him to ask Sophia his winning question, or at least show some awareness of the rare creature aglow beside him. He responded with a bashful grin and still said nothing. Sophia's dark eyes widened. Here she was, giving this character the full 'Mama Mia!' treatment – perfumed by Givenchy, dressed by Schubert, the neckline a plunging revelation – and this guy was virtually ignoring her. It was too much.

'Lissen Mr Dial,' she hissed, 'you won me, why don' you spik to me?' (The Honourable Roving Ambassador for the United Nations now speaks English without a trace of an accent. But at the time (1957) the words were still sprinkled with parmesan.) Mr Doyle reacted with a nervous falsetto giggle. 'Go on,' I coaxed him, trying to kick-start conversation. At last the words came via a palsied epiglottis: 'You have wealth and success, but you still work without a stop. What drives you on and on?'

'Luffoffart,' replied the Neapolitan goddess, delighted that the ice had finally been broken. Her words stopped the evening in its tracks. Holden looked at her enquiringly. So too did Mr Doyle, Mrs Dyer, and a waiter hovering within earshot.

'Luffoffart,' Sophia repeated, frowning at our foolishness.

'Say it slowly, dear,' I said.

She glanced disdainfully around the table. 'Love...of...art,' she pronounced with cool deliberation. 'Don' you spik English?'

That Mr Doyle was tongue-tied in the lady's presence did not surprise me, nor should it have worried him. Over the years some very famous men were also rendered speechless in her company. They discovered that close proximity to this voluptuous beauty was palpably unsettling. The late Peter Sellers and Cary Grant were two prime examples of the hopelessly smitten. Had she been free – instead of being contentedly married to the devoted Carlo Ponti – both would have competed to replace him. Their passion for her was not merely because she was a sublimely attractive female. There were other qualities that made her an irresistible companion. Elizabeth Taylor in an inspired moment – she had just bitten Richard Burton – described Sophia as a miraculous woman. To Burton, she was 'as beautiful as an erotic dream and as sane as bootlaces'. Within that sanity was the shrewd wisdom born of a punishing childhood, vulnerable adolescence and the perilous ascent from film extra to megastardom. We can understand why Sellers and Grant found comfort in her gentle Earth Mother insight. By the time they had become fatally – but futilely – attracted to her, Sophia Loren had met Jean Cocteau and Picasso; she had dined with the Queen; she had cooked spaghetti for the Yugoslav leader Marshal Tito at his private villa on the island of Brioni, inviting the supreme commander to pronounce upon the sauce. And she had acquired a chic sophistication uncommon in the superstar business.

I thought Sophia was pretty sensational when I first encountered her in London more than forty years ago. She was a raw, untutored starlet then who spoke little English, hiding her insecurities under a camera-teasing smile. But the poise, the potent chemistry and that incredible face and figure pointed unmistakably to a sex goddess of the future. With it came the instinct and intuition of a born actress. Her intensely moving performance in Vittorio de Sico's masterpiece *Two Women*, for which she won an Oscar, brought her international stature. I placed her high on my list of all-time favourites. I did so not merely because she was a gorgeous creature magnificently endowed in all the essential areas, but also because of the way in which she refashioned herself from being a Neapolitan sex symbol to being a cultivated lady of some importance. Famous film beauties from Marilyn to Madonna have long teased the public on the basis of 'if you've got it, baby, flaunt it'. But Sophia had long given up that game. It was too vulgar. When Brando playfully slapped her bottom on the set of *Countess from Hong Kong* she swung round with murderous disapproval in her eyes.

While we are on the intriguing subject of Sophia's posterior, both she and I relished this incident at the Edgwarebury Country Club, Herts. This was where she and Ponti stayed during the controversy in Italy over the legitimacy of their marriage. When Sophia swept into the dining room, she had to weave her way between elderly apple-cheeked retired admirals and wealthy widows to get to her table. At one point a whiskery gent approached her, cleared his throat and said, 'Um...er...excuse me, madam, I fear you are sitting on my *Times*.' She rose and handed it to him. If a resident could be more concerned with his paper than with the goddess unknowingly seated upon it, then clearly, Sophia reasoned, this was the place to be.

Sophia, of course, was well aware of the impact of her sexuality. But there were limits to how far she would go in putting herself on public display. She hated being visually appraised the way thoroughbreds are at bloodstock auctions. Driving away from that 'Win a Movie Star' dinner I recall her saying, 'I know everything I have done so far has been more body work than acting. But you will see. I will prove myself one day and win an Oscar.' Smart forecasting. This certainty of focus and serene self-confidence were bound to appeal to Sellers and Grant, who were pathologically short on both. But they fell into the trap of mistaking an affectionate Neapolitan hug for the passionate real McCoy. We can sympathise with them. To rest their buzzing heads on the most accommodating shoulder in movies was more therapeutic than a couch-load of shrinks.

But tea and sympathy was the most they could hope for from Sophia. There had already been too many complications in her life. Her childhood was densely populated with unwelcome ghosts. She could scarcely forget scavenging for survival with the rest of the hungry *scugnizzi* in a drab suburb of wartime Naples. She had shrugged off the humiliation of being born illegitimate – a *figlia naturale* – in a ward for unmarried mothers. In fact, Sophia considers herself enriched by the wartime poverty, and the so-called stigma of her birth. The tears she shed as a roving UN ambassador in Somalia holding a starving child in her arms was an echo of her life. She could

instantly empathise with those emaciated victims. In the months I
spent with her preparing her biography – there are worse chores a man
can have – it was her gutsy handle on life that impressed me most.

There can be no doubt that Sophia's fierce ambitions were driven
by the frustrated dreams of her mother Romilda. A formidable beauty
herself, she secretly yearned to be 'discovered', inspired by the
Hollywood stars of the twenties and thirties. She believed she had the
same magic and that destiny would prove it. Destiny obliged in the
powerful shape of Metro-Goldwyn-Mayer. The great Swedish actress
Greta Garbo was then the jewel in the company's crown. They
decided to exploit their investment by organising with splendid
unoriginality a contest to find 'Garbo's Double'. The first prize was a
trip to Hollywood, a screen test, and a possible leap into fame.
Romilda's heart missed a beat as she read the posters. She had been
told many times that she was the image of Garbo. She had the same
finely chiselled nose, the huge eyes and the long hair falling around
the lovely oval face. She surveyed herself in the mirror – and saw
Garbo. So, of course, did many others. Soon the amused populace of
Naples and Rome were treated to a bizarre procession of tall, floppy-
hatted, limpid-eyed Garbos, their faces all flour-white with pencilled
eyebrows flocking to the halls where the entrants were being judged.
Romilda Villani also pulled on a large hat, slid into flat-heeled shoes
and promptly seeded herself Numero Uno. And she was right. She
won the contest (Pirandello, Italy's revered dramatist, was chairman of
the judges).

But Romilda was never allowed to claim the coveted prize that
would take her to Hollywood. Strong objections came from her
parents, Domenico and Luisa Villani, reinforced by veiled threats by
the Black Hand, a secret Sicilian society fiercely opposed to Italian
women being enticed into the 'sinful' embrace of the movies. But
Romilda remained undaunted. With a thousand lire in her purse, then
aged eighteen, she took the train to Rome, installed herself in a box-
sized room near the Trevi Fountain and sauntered out into the city.
What happened afterwards was scarcely in accordance with the
Barbara Cartland School of Romance. *Brief Encounter* is a more
appropriate analogy.

When I raised the sensitive aspect of her birth with Sophia, she smiled and said, 'I think my mother can tell you more about how I was born than I can.' Her telephoned request to Romilda to put herself at my disposal was a sugar-sweet ultimatum. Signora Villani and I had met on a couple of occasions before in London and Paris. But here in Italy she was on home ground. If this was going to be her 'fifteen minutes of fame' she intended to make the most of it.

We met in the summer home of her young daughter Maria – formerly married to Mussolini's son Romano – at Marina San Nicola on the coast not far from Rome. It was a furnace of a July afternoon. The stone path to the porch grilled white in the afternoon sun. Maria Mussolini led the way into the living room. She was fuller in the face than her elder sister Sophia, shorter too, but the family resemblance was unmistakable. She acted as interpreter. Her mother Romilda Villani was dressed for the beach. The red hair shimmered in the Mediterranean sunlight. A heavy gold medallion swung across her bosom as she walked, her cork heels clacking on the marble floor. The carefully accentuated eyebrows and the pale lipstick still conveyed an uncanny resemblance to the great Garbo. She spoke first, in Italian. Clearly La Signora intended to take charge of the proceedings.

'Tell him I am going to speak my mind. Tell him that!' she commanded her younger daughter, drawing fiercely on a king-sized cigarette.

Maria promptly obeyed.

I asked Romilda about the man who fathered her two daughters.

'I never liked him!' she snapped. (Maria frowned at her mother in disbelief.) 'That's right – you tell him so!'

'How did you meet?'

'It was pure accident that I met him. One of those chances in life. Incredible things can happen. And you must tell him so.'

'OK, I tell him, Mamma.'

Romilda waited warily for her words to be translated.

'Now you tell him it was also just by chance I had two daughters from him. It was the case of a young girl from the country who finds herself in a big town. She meets a man. And she makes a mistake. I was a concert pianist when I came to Rome. Then I met Riccardo. In the street. He saw me from far away and ran up behind me and spoke

to me. He said he was in films and as I was such a beautiful girl
[Romilda growls on a laugh] he said he could help me. We met again
sometimes and after three weeks we went to bed together. After a
month and twenty days I am carrying Sophia. I had the baby quickly,
easily, like an animal.'

'Where did you go when you were seeing Riccardo?'

'In my room. Where do you think, in the street?'

'Was he a handsome man?'

'No. Very thin, very tall, with a big nose.'

'For all that, you stayed with him and had a second child by him?'

'What do you expect? I was hoping he would marry me. It is the
mentality of a small village. If you have a baby you marry the father
of your child. I'd abandoned myself to the situation. I wanted
Riccardo to marry me even though I didn't love him, for the sake of
my children.'

'Why didn't Riccardo marry you?'

Maria began to translate Romilda's sharp response, then trapped
the words behind her hand.

'I can't say.'

'Tell him!'

'It means *sonofabitch*.'

'*Grazie*,' Romilda beamed, satisfied.

I left, and drove to the Villa Ponti. Film-star homes usually reflect
their owners' egos, riches and wacky eccentricities. The Villa Ponti, in
the Alban Hills outside Rome, was a labour of love by Carlo Ponti for
his wife. He engaged a vast army of plumbers, electricians, artists,
painters, restorers and horticulturalists to refurbish the villa, whose
foundations were more than two thousand years old. Glossy images of
film stars by their pools in Beverly Hills are now a cliché. Compare
it with the rare and priceless setting that Carlo had created for Sophia:
the sixteenth-century marble fountains; the Louis XVI bedstead and
console table made in Tuscany; the invaluable Etruscan pottery; azalea
plants bought on a trip to Hamburg; the thirteenth-century baptismal
font; the white birch trees from Russia and the enormous seventeenth-
century-style swimming pool; the twelve-foot-high entrance
dominated by 400-year-old cypresses. All this lush and exquisite

antiquity, along with the Picassos, Renoirs and Henry Moore sculptures, amounted to the greatest love token of the century. But any idea that all this monumental luxury might go to La Signora's head can be instantly dispelled.

One day, during some major discussions involving several million dollars, producers, lawyers and others converged upon the villa for urgent talks with Sophia. They were told to wait. It was a long wait. They sat frowning at their watches around the enormous Roman pool. They naturally assumed the 'empress' was engaged on even more vital business. She was. Some distance away, outside the fumed-oak door of a toilet, she was engaged in an intimate dialogue with her baby son Cipi:

'Cipi, darling, it's Mamma.'

'Yes, Mamma?'

'Have you done good business?'

'Si, Mamma, very good.'

'Bravo, Cipi, ciao.'

'Ciao, Mamma.'

Sophia then strolled into the conference smiling broadly at the agitated moguls. 'OK, gentlemen, shall we start?'

CHAPTER THIRTEEN

The Ultimate Survivor

'Look at that beautiful Jewess over there eating pork!' – Richard Burton to Elizabeth Taylor, Shepperton, Middlesex, 1964.'

The 1960s was the decade to remember. Four lively extroverts named John, Paul, George and Ringo leaped out of a Liverpool Cavern and changed the world; a former Edinburgh milkman drawled over a curl of cigarette smoke, 'My name is Bond, James Bond' to launch a billion-dollar legend; and one sultry afternoon in Rome Richard Burton touched flesh with Elizabeth Taylor and Cupid found himself in mortal combat with the devil. The Beatles of course were fun to be with until that momentary insanity on a New York pavement shattered everything. Meanwhile, 007 soars into its 21st sequel, a cinematic miracle that brought unimagined prosperity to a string of James Bonds.

But the life and times of Elizabeth Taylor and Richard Burton have a resonance far beyond the incredible statistics and glittering occasions. Think of them now. Burton remembered more for his drunken capers than for his superb gifts as an actor and writer of some style; a huge talent plummeting via cirrhosis of the liver into an appallingly premature oblivion. By contrast, Elizabeth Taylor remains a life-battered triumph of a woman. A spectacular survivor who conquered obesity, alcohol and several frightening near-death encounters to become the First Lady of Hollywood. In their most tumultuous years they played out in their personal lives more erotic mayhem and lurid dramas than any self-respecting screenwriter would dare to put his name to. They loved, they fought, they all but devoured each other. Observing it all from scene one to the final curtain – his not hers – I found it hard to predict who would be the ultimate survivor. That accolade as we've seen belongs to Elizabeth Taylor. She reigns supreme now in that exclusive enclave of Bel Air – a screen goddess turned Lady Bountiful, using her influence and undiminished charisma in the fight against AIDS.

At a sassy 71, she is the miracle heroine of countless battles marital and medical. She was pronounced officially dead on four occasions. (Twice I was hauled in off a golf course to write her obituary only for the patient to emerge from a coma, flutter her eyelashes and ask for champagne.) She endured nineteen operations. She suffered the emotional havoc of widowhood and a bruising continuum of eight marriages not to mention the life-threatening addiction to alcohol and pain-killing drugs. Yet here she is, as provocative as ever, a phenomenon of bright and defiant womanhood. The owner of that renowned bosom, sculpted for bliss and now for comfort, is cherished by the nine grandchildren and one great-grandson she adores. I always enjoyed her company, even though I would frequently get the worst of the argument. As I related earlier, in the back seat of her Rolls one day in Rome, she said with infinite sweetness, 'You know, you're a shit, Donald, dear,' which, as expressed, was high in the canon of Liz Taylor compliments. She reacted furiously to my review of her *Cleopatra* ('fifty-seven varieties of bosom pall after a while...'). But I was paroled for good behaviour following my rave notices of *The Taming of the Shrew* and *The VIPs*.

There are many unassailable truths about the lady. Some of them if explicitly uttered in a 'confessional' would shatter the stained-glass surrounds. At her foul-tempered worst Liz Taylor is a virago to be reckoned with. Fifty years within earshot of Hollywood moguls, agents and others have given her a line in expletives second to none. But in her melting, pianissimo moments no man, child or stray dog can resist her. (Her friend the late Rock Hudson put it well: ' Elizabeth is very extreme in her likes and dislikes. If she likes, she loves. If she doesn't like, she loathes.') Uniquely, Elizabeth Taylor never traded her sensational beauty or feminine clout for headlines or critical acclaim. Those husbands of hers I knew over the years did not regret a single moment of the chaotic bliss that passed for holy matrimony. She could earn several fortunes for 'kiss-and-tell' revelations about her life, notably the men intimately featured in it. But she has rejected all offers as stubbornly as Frank Sinatra did. She was, and is, one of the few superstars in total possession of herself.

(When the late billionaire Howard Hughes offered her a million dollars' worth of diamonds as a declaration of intent, they were returned to sender with a curt 'thanks, but no thanks'.) But it is in the last few years that this Oscar-winning Dame of the British Empire has won the most cherished plaudits of her life. When Rock Hudson died of AIDS in 1985, she was one of the few major celebrities to go public fundraising for AIDS sufferers. It was not the most popular of causes in an industry pathologically obsessed with its public image. But Elizabeth Taylor leaned on friends, financiers and politicians, raising more than $50 million. (The fact that she also launched two perfumes, Passion and White Diamonds shows Madame has a fragrant regard for the priorities.)

If she is particularly generous with her compassion it is because there have been heavy demands upon it over the years. Those familiar with her history will recall how she cradled her co-star the late Montgomery Clift in her arms following a violent car crash on a canyon road. His teeth had been knocked out and were lodged in his throat. He was choking. Elizabeth managed to prize them free with her hand so that he could breathe. He gave them to her afterwards as a souvenir. Clift, like James Dean before him, found solace in Liz Taylor's special brand of compassion. Both were bi-sexual. Rock Hudson was gay. All three actors at various times experienced the pain of rejection. But never with Elizabeth Taylor. Unconcerned about her own image and reputation, she gave them tea and sympathy or whatever else they needed to see them through the night.

Now, as she looks down on the city that created her, she is entitled to a frisson of satisfaction. God knows, she scarcely got off to a happy start. By the time I moved into her orbit the ravishing young girl inevitably tagged as a 'child in a woman's body' was already making headlines. For those who've come late to the Elizabeth Taylor saga, the early years make a fascinating backdrop.

In 1950 she had married, at eighteen, Conrad Hilton Jr in a ceremony of unerring bad taste at the Church of the Good Shepherd. She wore a $3,500 wedding gown courtesy of MGM who, I was told, later demanded its return. She became pregnant and miscarried. A divorce followed on the grounds of extreme mental cruelty. Enter the languid British actor, Michael Wilding. They were deliriously happy for a while and had two children, Michael and Christopher. But the debonair Britisher was never at ease in Hollywood. He took to the place like cashmere to barbed wire. At parties, puzzled hostesses baffled by his strangled English accent would ask me, 'What's this guy saying?' Michael never shared his wife's passion for animals, then five cats, four dogs and a couple of house-broken ducks. He was frequently alone while Elizabeth worked. To sit around and have a duck waddle insolently along the wall-to-wall carpet while she earned the family money compounded his gloom.

When I was invited for dinner at their home one evening, drinks were served and constantly replenished. Through a wall of plate glass I could detect a banquet-in-waiting. Candles lit, wine cooling, music playing, cutlery a-gleaming. I looked at my watch. Wilding responded. 'Let's go, darling,' he drawled sliding his foot along the carpet to trip the switch that triggered open the doors. No luck. Madame joined in. Nothing happened. I stomped the floor the way coyotes tease out buried rodents. Soon three grown adults were skating over the carpet in pursuit of the elusive switch. Finally it required an urgent call on the intercom to bring the cavalry in and the glass doors opened.

Reality followed. By July 1956 the marriage had struck a reef. Their joint declaration had all the intimacy of a Foreign Office communiqué: 'We are in complete accord on an amicable separation...much careful thought has been given to the steps we are taking.'

They were divorced soon after. Michael Wilding came home to England and back to his Mayfair chums. Elizabeth Taylor stood by him in hard times, particularly later, when he became desperately ill. There was much mutual love and respect. But the generating current of the marriage had burned itself out. After the doldrums, the hurricane. The producer Mike Todd, a brash entrepreneur with a lot of cash and even more chutzpah, became Liz Taylor's third husband. Born to call the shots, he told her he loved her and grabbed her hand in marriage. As I recall it, he flashed a couple of eighteen-carart gold teeth which went well with Elizabeth's weakness for anything that gleamed. He installed a double bed in his private plane so that Cloud Nine could assume a more tangible meaning. They had a daughter christened Elizabeth Frances Todd, Liza for short. It was a great love story, though, considering the temperaments and the tempers of both parties, there were fireworks along with the frolics. Todd was proud of the fact that his father had been a rabbi. (At the Dorchester Hotel in London he introduced Elizabeth to assembled guests as 'my beautiful little Jewish broad'. Not exactly in the class of 'Shall I compare thee to a summer's day...' but then Shakespeare's father wasn't a rabbi.) Todd bought two cinemas in Chicago and named them His and Hers. Emeralds, rubies and sapphires shimmered as further testimony to his devotion. Asked what it was like having a beautiful young movie star like Elizabeth Taylor in love with him, Todd responded, 'Let me tell ya. Any minute this dame spends out of bed is wasted, totally wasted.'

If the Michael Douglas/Catherine Zeta-Jones wedding was the bash of the new millennium, it had nothing on the Todd nuptials in Acapulco, Mexico, in 1957.

Fifteen thousand white gladioli and 26 bushels of white orchids formed the fragrant backdrop. A Niagara of champagne helped wash down the caviar specially flown in from Havana. (The champagne was served in split coconuts brought down from the tops of giant palms climbed by a tribe of Indian boys.) How long that marriage would have lasted was, tragically, academic. We know of course what happened. On 24 March 1958, Todd's plane, *Lucky Liz*, crashed in the Zuni Mountains, New Mexico. The occupants were burned beyond recognition. Todd's twisted gold wedding ring was brought back to Elizabeth. She was 26, a widow with two sons and a daughter. She suffered excruciating grief. She all but committed suicide. She slept at night in the shirt Mike wore before he flew off. She kept his pyjamas under her pillow. The story goes that she refused to change the sheets he had slept on, wanting somehow to retain the last vestige of physical contact with him. She somehow managed to wear the blackened, twisted wedding ring salvaged from the crash, declaring she would never take it off her finger. The hit tune at the time was the theme from *Around the World in Eighty Days*, Todd's award-winning blockbuster. Elizabeth switched off radios and televisions for fear of hearing it played. It was two months before I could reach her by phone. She was seated by a pool in Tucson, Arizona. She picked up the receiver and said, 'This is Mrs Michael Todd.' She sounded stronger than I'd anticipated.

'Remember this,' she said, 'I have something to be strong for. I have the memory of Michael's love. That kind of love happens once in a lifetime and I will hang onto it all my life.'

Tears dry fast in the Californian sun. Consolation came speedily in the shape of Eddie Fisher, a glossy-haired singer with the soft boyish touch plus the additional cachet of being Princess Margaret's favourite crooner. He had been a close friend of Mike Todd's and hero-worshipped the showman to the point of imitating his mannerisms, the gambling, and the locker-room language. He was Mike Todd writ small. But he offered a soft shoulder in hard times. I once shared a trip with him and his wife, the singing star Debbie Reynolds, on the *Queen Elizabeth* and found Fisher a dour, deep customer behind the night-owl pallor.

The Taylor–Fisher love affair and marriage thrust Elizabeth into the full blast of that most dubious aspect of public indignation – moral outrage. The powerful Mothers of America lobby, infuriated at Fisher for apparently walking out on his wife, turned their fury on to Elizabeth. 'Husband stealer' and 'home wrecker' summarises the hysteria of the times.

(Ten years or so earlier those same battalions were mobilised against the wonderful Swedish star the late Ingrid Bergman. A cultivated beauty with a half-crooked smile, she had left her husband Peter Lindstrom for the Italian film director Roberto Rossellini and bore his children. It was, to the media at least, the juiciest scandal of the decade. In Hollywood, Ingrid was socially ostracised, professionally persecuted and eventually hounded out of America.

'Apostle of degradation' was added to the hyperbole of hate specially reserved for the 'other woman' in the leading scandals of the day. The attacks followed her to her home in Italy even after the first child, Robertino, was born. She was virtually under siege in her Rome apartment. The Vatican was drawn into the attack. Cinemas boycotted her films. Yet nothing I found in this woman remotely resembled the lurid picture presented to the world. Her marriage to Lindstrom had cooled long before she and Rossellini met to fall instantly and all-consumingly in love. She took the flak that followed with a shrug of the shoulders. But the anger she expressed when we met in her home was focused entirely on her children, Pia Lindstrom and Robertino. 'Haven't I been punished enough? Do they have to punish the children as well?' Ultimately, perhaps inevitably, the affair blew itself out. Rossellini, by all accounts, deserted Ingrid. She was married again to the taciturn Swedish producer, Lars Schmidt. They led a serene and happy life in his mansion in Paris. Bergman was, of course, a superb actress – *Casablanca*, *For Whom the Bell Tolls*, *Gaslight* (an Oscar), *Anastasia* (another Oscar) etc – but she was also a woman of style who wore her martyrdom lightly. In 1974 she was told she had cancer. 'Well, I'm not the only one,' she said to me. In 1981, the last year of her life, she gave a memorable performance playing the Israeli leader Golda Meir. By then the cancer had spread. Her right arm swelled so massively it had to be hidden under a shawl. She still managed a crooked smile. 'I call it my dog,' she wrote to a friend. 'I joke with it: "Come on let's go walking to see the sun, the trees and the people." I say to myself, "Just think, Ingrid – you could have gone blind and be incapable of seeing the sun."' She died in London 1981 on her 67th birthday. She was a strong and companionable beauty who totally eclipsed the hypocrisy of her times.)

So, as acres of fulsome headlines informed us, Elizabeth Taylor became Mrs Eddie Fisher, 12 May 1959; much to the disgust of the novelist Robert Ruark, who attacked the bride somewhat sanctimoniously as in 'this monument to busting up other people's homes', and 'this solid statue to the ignoring of the ordinary tenets of widowhood,' adding (because she and Eddie had been married in a Jewish temple in Las Vegas), 'It's a little gamey for a temple.' The storm raged at the time when Elizabeth's film, *Cat on a Hot Tin Roof*, became one of the biggest money-earners of the year (1958). But the notoriety over her marriage to Eddie Fisher turned her triumph into a blood sport in which she was the prey. The National Theater Owners of America gave her their Star of the Year Award, only to withdraw it later with the mealy mouthed defence, 'the movie industry is at the mercy of public opinion.'

But notoriety sells tickets. Elizabeth was now one of the top ten box-office stars of the year. Eddie Fisher was not. There were some fun and good tunes in the marriage. But not for long. Here again one career (his) fought to survive being engulfed by another (hers). Moreover, *Cleopatra* had struck a reef even before the cameras turned. Costs had rocketed into the fiscal stratosphere. The script was being rewritten every hour on the hour. Six thousand extras, horses, donkeys, elephants, slave girls, hysteria, resignations, hirings and firings – the budget soared as hearts sank. Hold-ups, arguments, front-office shooting matches, capricious elephants and an unpredictable Cleo caused an in-shock studio executive to mutter, 'The inmates have taken over the asylum.' In recognition of the stark truth that without Elizabeth there was no movie, the then mighty MGM provided a Rolls Silver Cloud to take her to and from the studios. Two penthouses were reserved for her and her entourage at London's Dorchester Hotel. The personal hairdresser, secretary, chauffeur and an array of other perks were standard issue for a queen. Eddie Fisher of course was on hand as husband, carer and supervisor of the Villa Papa outside Rome, wherein they lived in some style. This appropriately pink marble mansion had fourteen rooms with a swimming pool and tennis court and was set amid eight acres of pine trees. She and Eddie Fisher shared it with the three children, ten dogs, four cats, two secretaries, three maids and two butlers. 'It's the first real home Eddie and I have ever had,' Elizabeth Taylor is reported to have said.

But, by now, events were spiralling down towards disaster. From Eddie Fisher's standpoint, it was a disastrous free fall from pink cloud to rock bottom. A friend phoned me from America to say that Eddie had had a nervous breakdown and was being privately sedated in a

New York Hospital. Two psychiatrists were said to be in attendance. Whatever the cause, it was clear that the marriage, which had been shakily constructed on a widow's grief, had struck a reef. It was briefly salvaged when he Fisher joined Elizabeth in London. Then she was suddenly struck by what was thought to be Asian flu. In fact she started choking. An anaesthetist who happened to be in the hotel gave here emergency oxygen by pushing a tube down her throat. He said only an emergency tracheotomy could save her. She was rushed by ambulance to hospital, where a doctor gave her an hour to live. For three days world events were pushed off the front pages. 'Condition grave', 'Fighting for her life', 'An hour to live', 'The queen's physician called in' – in newspapers around the globe obituaries were rushed out in readiness.

As I remember from my own vigils at the time, Fisher was not the only one weeping. Even some of her nurses shed a tear for the pale legend sustained only by a tube through a two-and-a-half inch slit in her throat. But Elizabeth Rosemond Taylor was not ready to quit. Somewhere in that diminutive but devastating body throbs a survival kit second to none. It was around this time that she received a Best Actress Oscar for her role in *Butterfield 8*. She gave a fine performance, but there were many who said the vote had an element of sympathy and answered prayers. Eight months after the tube was removed from her throat Cleopatra was back in Rome with a Greek chef, a French butler, an English valet (for Eddie Fisher), a governess for the children, five servants and quarters for the animals so that they could continue to live in the style to which they had become accustomed. All was set for the great luscious, if not ludicrous, centrepiece of the film: the 6,000-strong procession bringing Cleopatra to her Antony.

Mr Richard Burton, the hero in question, made his own more mischievous entry onto the scene.

'Well I guess I've got to don my breastplate once more to play opposite Miss Tits,' he blithely declared as he left London for Rome. Ill-fated humour as events unfolded. For the scandalous fallout from their first meeting under the scorching Italian sun would shatter lives and induce virulent reactions on a global scale. As a subplot to this, the most brazenly defiant love affair of the decade, there was Elizabeth Taylor's critical and sometimes near-death collapses. Trying to keep up with it all was hard work for the peripheral characters who would be caught up in the fallout. I mean journalists, analysts, doctors, nurses, divorce lawyers, bodyguards, accountants – all the formidable influences on the body and the soul, including the Vatican in Rome. As soap opera, it was *ER* out of *Dallas*. As a sex saga, it was a steamy scenario by Jackie Collins with additional dialogue by Tennessee Williams.

Put at its most elemental, two sex-driven extroverts with passion to spare, fused into a studio love scene and Life began imitating Art with a vengeance. Their appetite for each other was, according to Burton at least, total and insatiable. Vatican Radio scathingly described the affair as 'the caprices of adult children'. The newspaper *Il Tempo* called Elizabeth 'an intemperate vamp who destroys families and devours husbands'. *L'Osservatore della Dominica* condemned her for 'erotic vagrancy'. Eddie Fisher booked a flight to New York and flew back in anger. He called a press conference during which he telephoned Elizabeth in Rome. He asked her publicly to kill the rumours about her and Richard Burton. It was a desperate gamble and it failed. She answered him with the simple truth. 'Well, actually, Eddie, I can't do that.' Thus with dark inevitability the marriages with Eddie Fisher and Sybil Burton ended. Both were swept off stage as Burton and Taylor walked deliriously and defiantly through the exotic minefield of their affair. In a parody of the best fairy stories, they loved, fought and were reconciled to live hellishly ever after. Lunching with them, or just sitting in on their explicit encounters required resilience and a fair hold on the profanities.

I remember one lunch at a riverside restaurant near Shepperton Studios, Middlesex, which was typical. Elizabeth arrived seductively beautiful, but in a temper. There had been some sort of foul-up over the lunch arrangements. The atmosphere calmed. The meal was served. Richard roared across the table, 'Look at that beautiful Jewess over there eating pork. Overfull of calories but magnificent just the same.' Burton was bent on mischief. But, as ever, the World's Most Famous Welshman hoped the sheer magnificence of his oratory would redeem him. And, as ever, he failed, on two counts: first, the liquor had blunted his style; secondly, Elizabeth Taylor, who knew the nature of the beast, wasn't rising to the bait, merely observing. 'You deliberately intend to make me appear nasty to inflate your own ego.' Further words were exchanged across the table. I said, 'If you two would prefer to be alone...' 'Not at all,' boomed Burton, 'Elizabeth is just doing a little trottin', dancin' and prancin'.' She was of course doing no such thing. She was striving, as she would through the tumult of their partnership, to save a great actor from disaster.

She was fiercely involved in trying to rescue the Burton she had fallen in love with – the multi-talented genius, who was an actor and scholar with an alert ear for the poetry and cadences of his native Wales. But it was hard and humiliating at times, notably when Burton was dangerously drunk. I was with him once in his dressing room at Cinecitta in Rome. Richard had already dispatched a bottle of vodka and was now drinking Chablis out of a beer glass. This triggered him into mischief. Elizabeth entered, looking her chic and voluptuous self. A shaft of afternoon sunlight caught the violet eyes beneath the brushed charcoal eyebrows. But it was the famous bosom upon which Burton fixed his clouded gaze. 'Isn't she smashing!' the Welshman roared. Elizabeth flinched as he reached out his hands and squeezed her breasts like an old-time cabby. 'Honk, honk,' bellowed one of the finest Hamlets of his times. Elizabeth reacted with the resigned smile of an old campaigner.

There had been similar displays before. There would be many more in the years that followed. When Richard Burton was in his uproarious mode, blue-grey eyes glinting over puce, pitted features, nothing was sacred and nobody was safe. I asked him once why, considering his huge acting achievements, he played this kind of game. (I was being a shade disingenuous, since this kind of Burton was the most quotable character in the business.) His answer was significant: 'The truth is, we live out, for the benefit of the mob, the sort of idiocies they've come to expect. They expect that any moment some enormous vulgarity is about to be thrust upon the world either in our marriage or in our behaviour.'

In other words, give the public what they want. Burton, not Elizabeth, was happy to oblige. Fine for other performers, including those in the oldest profession of all. But not for this theatrical giant with the most thrilling voice of the age. Laurence Olivier had warned him, 'Make up your mind, Richard, a household name or a great actor.' Burton, with his pale-blue basilisk eyes open, took the soft option. He went out and grabbed the money and the notoriety on offer to a lusty, and thirsty, superstar. In the event, Stratford-upon-Avon lost out to the Valley of the Dolls. 'Rich', as he was known to his friends, could have called upon several demons in his own defence. One was a pathological fear of poverty. He was a miner's son from Pontrhydyfen, South Wales, and his family lived on a pittance during the Depression. Another was a nagging fear of a premature death. I have a note of what he said to me on that subject more than thirty years ago: 'Being happy and contented in this world is a very dangerous thing. Death is likely to pass by at any second, regardless of status or age.'

There was an inevitability to the chronology events. In 1974, his ten years of marriage to Elizabeth Taylor ended. A year later, a repentant Burton with all the fervour of a Welsh pastor, swore he'd finished with the demon drink for ever. Using all his guile and eloquence, Burton persuaded Elizabeth to marry him again. She flew out to join him on the set of *The Klansman* in Oroville, North California, scene of one of the first gold stampedes of the early 1800s. But that stampede was a minor event compared with the mayhem that struck this peaceful place of small homesteads set amid almond blossom. The fact that Burton's co-star in the film was Lee Marvin, whose drinking was the subject of legend, was a lively element in the fracas. As the director Terence Young was to say at the end of it all, 'There were moments in this film when really I was tempted to throw myself out of the window. In one week, we had Elizabeth Taylor deciding to divorce Burton [again]; he was running around with a waitress; the husband of another woman was threatening him with a gun; and Lee Marvin was contributing to the general entertainment.'

Elizabeth had had enough. Burton saw his humiliated wife off at the airport knowing that she would soon divorce him again. Terence Young made frantic efforts to get the film completed. 'Richard was making a great effort,' he told me later. 'He had to force his whole body just to get the words out. His shook like a man with the ague.

He was white, he was blue, he was yellow. I got a doctor down, who said, "This man will be dead in three weeks."'

But the actor, who in his youth had trained to be a prizefighter, was not ready to make his exit. An emergency flight to a Los Angeles hospital saved his life. Massive blood transfusions and urgent 'drying out' won the battle. A slow recovery followed, and miraculously a final comeback in *Camelot* on Broadway. He met and married Susan Hunt, former wife of the racing driver James Hunt. A tall shy beauty, Suzy played Chopin on the piano and kept Richard on the wagon. It was not enough to sustain the marriage. His fourth wife, Sally Hay, a talented writer, brought him tranquillity and considerable contentment. But everything was over-shadowed by Burton's rapidly failing health.

He died in 1984. He is buried in a small cemetery at Céligny, Switzerland, where he and Sally lived. The inscription on the stone says simply, 'Richard Burton, 1925–1984'. He was 59 years old. All his wives were vastly contrasting women. But there was unanimity in their grief and in their gratitude for the scintillating times they had with this extraordinary human being. Elizabeth Taylor was as devastated as she was following the death of Mike Todd. She had loved, and cherished, the actor, but couldn't save the man. But she herself was scarcely unscathed by the several traumas of their marriage. And the marriages that followed – first to the Republican senator John Warner and later to a one-time truck driver and cement mixer, Larry Fortensky, a fellow patient at the Betty Ford Clinic. If, then, Elizabeth Taylor is a miracle of survival, it begs the question: how has she managed it? Back in June 1985 I wrote,

You could accuse her of indulging in sexual overkill, discarding husbands and lovers like thrown hands in a poker game. You could argue that for sheer self-indulgence, this jewel-encrusted goddess has upstaged all the pampered playmates of history. Add to that her unchallenged supremacy in exquisite bitchery, ear-shattering profanity and keeping escorts hanging around until they sag at the knees and Miss Elizabeth Taylor, for sure, is no shrinking violet. But I defy anyone to fault her on the one outstanding feature of her beleaguered life – her miraculous flair for self-preservation.

That view is shared by the distinguished biographer and critic David Thomson, who recently listed among Elizabeth's fighting qualities 'candour, common sense, tough realism and irony'. What the records also reveal is the ability to quip rather than quake in serious or solemn occasions. (Told by an eminent surgeon that she had a foreign body in her eye, she wondered if it was anyone she knew.) When a justice of the peace asked her on her sixth marriage to list her previous husbands, she is said to have retorted, 'What is this – a memory test?' So here she is at 71, allegedly retired from acting, though one ought not to bet on it. She has expressed no desire to marry again, though I wouldn't bet on that, either. She had hip replacements in 1994 and 1995. A benign brain tumour was removed in 1997. She had further successful treatment for a form of skin cancer.

'I'm a fighter,' she says, 'a prevailer.' But more than that she has been a renowned comforter of some of Hollywood's most celebrated misfits. Her public display of loyalty to Michael Jackson when he was ridiculed and under siege revealed Elizabeth Taylor at her best. She can look with satisfaction at her magnificent home, the priceless paintings by Goya, Monet, Renoir and Picasso and the two Academy Awards. She can also look back on her life and consider that that, too, was quite a performance.

CHAPTER FOURTEEN

'Four Long-haired Schnooks from Liverpool...'

One afternoon in September 1963 the Beatles dropped by my home for tea. A bland enough statement, which in retrospect is as understated as Stanley's casual 'Doctor Livingstone, I presume.' For in the frenetic six or so years that followed, John, Paul, George and Ringo needed no surnames to identify them as the greatest musical icons of the age. They were smart, they were funny, and they relished their presence on this planet, producing many memorable songs to celebrate it. For apart from the revelation of their music, these four breezy young minstrels with the (then) Stone Age hairdos, were the loud and irresistible voice of millions of their age. A voice that offered a refreshing challenge to a perceived drab, clapped-out and sex-repressed society.

If the influence of this refreshing and remarkable group is a formidable entry in the history of the sixties, the accompanying statistics awesomely underscore it. Within a year or so of their exploding onto the scene, the *Wall Street Journal* reported that $50 million was spent in the US on Beatle products alone. In February 1964 10,000 screaming fans greeted their arrival at JFK airport in New York. In the same month 73 million viewers watched them live on *The Ed Sullivan Show*. 'Beatlemania' was born. And even now, some forty years later, their music still resonates with today's young, and anything they might have touched, worn or otherwise anointed, is a serious collector's item. When they left my home after two exhilarating hours,

196

a half-eaten sandwich remained on a plate with John Lennon's bite marks clearly visible. If I had been smart I would have fast-frozen it, Andy Warhol would have painted it, Saatchi exhibited it, Max Clifford marketed it, and I could have retired on it.

The day the Beatles swept into my home is especially memorable in the way that being struck by lightning isn't easily forgotten. The enthusiasm and sheer energy behind the cheeky, self-confident smiles was intrinsic to their magic. We need only to glance at their picture to get the flavour of it. They were then approaching the best years of their lives – before the group broke up and John Lennon died an appalling death on a New York pavement. John Lennon, the joker in the pack, was 23; George Harrison, the 'quiet one', was 21; Paul McCartney, even then a powerhouse of ideas, was 21, and Ringo Starr, a cheerful primitive who beat the drums, was 23. The clippings of that long interview record a happy foursome hugely enjoying their success. As well they might have. When the first part of my series on them appeared the following day the circulation figures soared. (There had been a bizarre incident during the night. Thousands of billboards bearing the Beatles' faces had been placed outside newsagents around the country. And just as many thousands of fans had crawled out of their beds to steal them in the wee small hours.)

By now the Beatles were a phenomenon that politicians, pundits, even royalty ignored at their peril. The Duke of Edinburgh presented them with important musical awards. The late Queen Mother, whose favourite tunes had nestled in the 'Just a Song at Twilight' category decided she was 'quite a fan of the Beatles'. Britain's Alamein hero, the late Field Marshal Montgomery, a champion of moral rectitude, suddenly joined forces with the 'Yeah, yeah' brigade. Sir Alec Douglas-Home, briefly prime minister at the time, claimed some sort of oblique credit for the Beatles, drawing from the Labour leader Harold Wilson in the Commons a sardonic 'Is nothing sacred?' (though Wilson himself could never resist a passing bandwagon). Then Madame Tussaud's immortalised the Beatles in wax, standing them alongside other great figures of the age. This was the ultimate accolade.

The Beatles were of course catalysts as well as innovators. Historically, they *were* the 1960s. When John Lennon teasingly claimed, 'We're more popular than Jesus now' it was a mild blasphemy that had a crude validity to it. The established church, by definition, offered no social solutions because it was perceived as being part of the problem. The Bible's 'Thou shalt love thy neighbour...' couldn't hold a candle to the Beatles' 'All You Need Is Love'. Churchmen attempted to get into the act by wearing long hair and blue jeans, and enlivening their words with hip phrases. They were about as convincing as politicians who did the same. This was the age when the young craved something new to believe in, driven by an irrepressible urge to dump the stuffed-shirt hypocrisies of the day. It had its beginnings in 1961 with the penetrating satire of *Beyond the Fringe*. The late Peter Cook, the master of the genre, mercilessly parodied the then prime minister, Harold Macmillan, every night on the London stage. Macmillan's 'We've never had it so good' speech came to haunt him (though, as with Bogart's alleged 'Play it again, Sam', he never actually spoke those words).

Infinitely more damaging would be the notorious Profumo Affair (1963) which almost caused the complete meltdown of the Conservative Party. John Profumo, a handsome and likeable government minister, had been linked with a tarnished female in the affair, a showgirl named Christine Keeler. He initially denied it, was forced to recant and subsequently resigned. (There would be echoes decades later with Bill Clinton's defiant declaration, 'I did not have sexual relations with that woman!') The Profumo Affair had all the ingredients of a raunchy paperback as co-written say, by Harold Robbins and the Marquis de Sade. Here in lurid close-up was a picture of the rich and the powerful – and a Russian spy named Eugene Ivanov – at play at secret house parties, engaging in high jinks involving young female playmates with caning and horsewhipping being part of the services on offer. This 'entertainment', it was alleged, was provided by a fashionable osteopath and talented artist named Stephen Ward.

Throughout the affair the British public were given a keyhole view of the sleazy undercurrents of political life. The fallout paralysed the government, dominated the headlines and was the talk of every pub, club and home in the land. As compulsive entertainment, it eclipsed

anything then on offer in film or on the West End stage. Stephen
Ward was charged at London's Central Criminal Court on three
charges of living on the immoral earnings of prostitution; also of
inciting Christine Keeler to procure a girl under the age of 21 for
unlawful sexual intercourse.

The key witnesses were Christine Keeler and Mandy Rice-Davies,
a self-styled 'Lady Hamilton'. I was in court to capture the
atmosphere of the trial and the demeanour of the main participants.
It was fascinating to see the chic and bejewelled ladies of Mayfair and
Belgravia jostling for the best view of the good-looking defendant,
Stephen Ward. It is likely that he had painted portraits of some of
them. Others had certainly had a more tactile relationship as his
patients. Nothing intrigues the aristocracy more than a juicy scandal
involving one of their own. There was much nodding and whispering
in the gallery. Christine Keeler was not so much in court as on stage.
She was then one of the most talked-about women in the world. She
had slept with men who were household names. The attraction was
plain to see. The long dark-red hair fell around her face, the parted
lips a slash of vermilion against the sallow features. She was smartly
dressed in a mustard-coloured cloak over a matching dress. In a voice
as casual as a clerk's listing the items on an invoice, she talked of
having sexual intercourse with well-known figures in society. Yet, far
from being embarrassed, she seemed faintly irritated by it all as
though a series of irksome parking offences had been brought to her
notice. The hours rolled on, and so did the formidable catalogue of
her sexual enterprises. Slowly her composure faltered. The mask fell.
One began to get a glimpse of the wretched girl, humbly born in a
London suburb.

The next day she was followed in the witness box by Mandy Rice-
Davies, an eighteen-years-old nymphet all *sauce piquante* and soot-
black eyelashes. One could see why the men of Belgravia and
Whitehall were tempted. Here was a tallish, baby-doll of a female with
a blonde, razor-cut fringe, snub nose and well-constructed body. Her
evidence, like Keeler's, listed endless encounters with men who must
have flinched to have read their names in the paper the following
morning. Unlike Christine, Mandy seemed to be enjoying her day in

court. Her mouth widened into a flare of scarlet as she bestowed friendly smiles around the court, including leading counsel and the judge. His lordship, Mr Justice Marshall, was not amused. Glinting through his spectacles he warned her, 'This is not a laughing matter.' Soon she was thumbing the wet blackness of her eyes and was relieved to make a wilting, tear-streaked exit.

Then Stephen Ward, pleading not guilty, took the stage. He was fifty years old but looked much younger. The darkish wavy hair was brushed well back from a high forehead. The heavy-lidded eyes were sombre behind the thick lenses of his spectacles. If all the sordid revelations shocked the courtroom and the world outside, they did not appear to unnerve the defendant. With his sober suit, russet tie and matching pocket handkerchief, he looked what he was: suave, confident and self-assured. But not for long. On 31 July 1963 after an eight-day hearing he was convicted on two of the charges of living on immoral earnings. On the same morning he was rushed to hospital after having taken an overdose of sleeping pills. He died three days later. No sentence was therefore passed by the court. That role would be left to posterity.

History is unlikely to judge John Profumo too harshly. The extra-curricular behaviour of the upper classes had long been tolerated by the Establishment. His error, like Clinton's, was to deny it. A straightforward *mea culpa* might have saved him, and perhaps the government. He made a swift exit from public life and devoted his energies to charity work. Christine Keeler has turned her experiences to some profit. She has published the story of her life, in which there were two failed marriages, an estrangement from her mother and much bitterness over the attacks made on her. Mandy Rice-Davies has become a writer. She has been married three times. The past does not appear to haunt her, since she is doing very well in the present – in luxury, in Florida, according to last reports.

Meanwhile, Beatlemania raged on in Britain and just as irresistibly across the United States. This was extraordinary, since the world of rock and roll had long been considered as exclusively American. But the Beatles' music transcended it by far because of its incredible creativity and inventiveness. There was genuine artistry at work. The pronouncement by a distinguished music critic that they were 'the greatest songwriters since Schubert' had plausibility. Not only did they compose some wonderful songs, they made inspired additions to their orchestrations. They added unusual instrumentation in the form of Indian instruments and string quartets. Two of their greatest hits, 'Eleanor Rigby' and 'Yesterday', were beautifully balanced, the vocals backed by very classy string quartet arrangements. It will always be hard to determine who was the most creative of the group. Lennon was unique, and certainly Paul McCartney has demonstrated a touch of genius in the prodigious body of work he has produced since he went solo. His televised concert in April 2003 was a stunning and at times moving experience. But we ought not to underrate the contribution made by the late George Harrison. He was pivotal for much of the Beatles' success. But his input was, like the man, quiet, deep and restrained.

With the phenomenon came the wealth. The sales, the concerts, and the spin-offs guaranteed them and their dependants an infinity of riches. Not that anyone in the first frenetic months had any clue of the mega-excitement to follow. The day after my first article on them appeared, I took Cubby Broccoli to lunch. I told him about the girls climbing out of bed at night to steal the bills outside the newsagents' shops. I had no personal axe to grind, I said, but I suspected that a Beatles film with a script even torn out of the *Yellow Pages* would be a sensation. He agreed, though they were then busy preparing a film with Bob Hope. He raised the idea with Harry Saltzman back in their office in South Audley Street. Without success. Saltzman said, 'Let me ask you something, Cubby: would you rather make a film with four long-haired schnooks from Liverpool – what's their name...?'

'The Beatles,' said Cubby.

'...the Beatles, who nobody's ever heard of, when we've got Bob Hope – Bob Hope! all ready to go.'

'Put like that,' Broccoli recalls in his autobiography, 'I wasn't sure I could give Harry an argument. By the normal rules of the game he made sense. Could we gamble on four relatively unknown kids?'

But Bud Ornstein, the production chief for United Artists in London, who had taken a sober look at the ticket sales, phoned his bosses in New York. Their response was a cool, 'Look, go ahead if you want to, but no serious money, you understand.'

So UA made *A Hard Day's Night* on a shoestring. Bud Ornstein flew to New York with the can of film under his arm, and a nervous sweat. How would the men in suits react to this delirious, tearaway nonsense, the Scouse accents meaningless in Manhattan? It was shown to the chieftains in the company's screening room. When it ended there was a silence. The bosses' mouths appeared to be open but no words emerged. ('I wanted to shoot myself,' Ornstein told me long after.) He looked pleadingly around the screening room for a reassuring glance. None was forthcoming. All the subordinates present were taking their cue from the boss, Arthur Krim. He happened to be a kind as well as powerful mogul. He rose and put a comforting arm around Ornstein's shoulder. 'OK, Bud, you've got this out of your system. Now go back and make some movies.'

One year and some $75 million later – the film had cost less than a million – Ornstein was the Flavour of the Month. The film's producer, a genial former press agent named Walter Shenson, was driving a Rolls with a personal number plate. The Beatles had conquered America and Mr Harry Saltzman had revised his opinions about those 'four long-haired schnooks from Liverpool'.

To be fair, no ordinary film producer or conventional entrepreneur could have foreseen at the time that the world of entertainment was about to be knocked off its axis. But there was one man who did. He was the Beatles' manager, Brian Epstein. In a sense, he was no less a phenomenon than the extraordinary foursome he created. A handsome young introvert living in reclusive style in London's Belgravia, he was the complete antithesis of your average show-business guru. I say he 'created' them, though, with a rare kind of honesty, he vehemently refused to take the credit. I remember his telling me in his apartment (Beatles photos and a silver-holster and gun, a gift from Elvis Presley, on the silk-lined walls), 'What I want to nail once and for all is the myth that I made them what they are. This is absolute nonsense. They are what they are and nothing would have held them back. All this', he added, glancing at the surrounding luxury, 'I owe to them. I didn't make them, they made me.' Yet, despite the modesty, he had clearly seen something dynamic and unfathomable and given it wings.

Epstein's quiet demeanour was misleading. There was a managerial iron fist inside the velvet glove. When the big agents, those cigar-chomping Titans of the ten per cent talked money with him, they found him no pushover. This soft-voiced thirty-year-old with the light-blue eyes revealed a shrewd understanding of the fine print of residuals, percentages, grosses and all. But, though he could steer an astute course through a million-dollar contract, his path through life was a minefield of drugs and sexual confusion. Over the horizon was an appallingly premature death. His was no rags-to-riches story. He was born to the middle classes; became a student at the Royal Academy of Dramatic Art; ran a record shop; found the Beatles; became a millionaire and, being gay, enjoyed the company of other beautiful and successful young men. An eight-foot blow-up of his friend El Cordobes, idol of the Spanish bullring, grinned down from his bathroom in Belgravia – an image much relished by another friend, the great dancer, Rudolf Nureyev. John Lennon once declared publicly that he and Epstein had 'almost had an affair'.

To be a self-confessed gay – and a powerful celebrity – in the still-unenlightened mid-1960s compounded Epstein's psychological hang-ups. He became a willing participant in the pervasive drug culture of that 'turned-on' era. He entered the largely uncharted world of experiments in 'mind expansion'. Asked once whether he was aware of the danger in the misuse of LSD, his response was, 'I took the risk but it was a calculated risk. I think LSD helped me to know myself better.' But not to save him. He died a drug-induced death in August 1967. He was a friendly if somewhat diffident companion. But there was much gentleness and kindness to the man. He was, as I wrote after his death, 'of the Beatles, by the Beatles, and for the Beatles'. They loved him as he loved them. And the 'Fab Four' were unlikely to survive without him.

'Give us answers!' was the battle cry of the disillusioned young of the 1960s. But the Establishment, notably the politicians, offered bromides in return. So the kids 'turned on, tuned in and dropped out' in their thousands. 'Flower Power' and 'Transcendental Meditation'

as espoused by the Maharishi Mahesh Yogi offered an alternative route
to personal happiness and fulfilment. It is easy to understand why the
Beatles, or a couple of them, seized on this mystical lifeline to an inner
peace. Born into the sensible reality of the North, they were now
worshipped as demigods blessed with the Midas touch. Cheques of
unimaginable sums arrived by every post. They stashed away their
wealth, collected their glittering prizes, bowed to the great ovations,
and rewrote the riotous history of show business.

They were awarded the MBE – which I criticised at the time, but
realise now that I was out of line. This was a modest accolade,
considering the knighthoods subsequently showered like confetti on
lesser talent. Moreover, they possessed the staying power of the true
artist and with it dominated what was arguably the biggest social
upheaval of the century. Everything they touched made money. This
brought the seductive spin-off of hordes of over-eager 'groupies'
throwing explicit invitations outside stage doors, hotel rooms, by
phone or through the mail. This was pretty head-turning stuff even
for these street-smart Liverpudlians, who were, to use a Richard
Burton phrase, 'as sane as bootlaces'. So even as they bought their
mansions and contemplated their wealth, they had the bewilderment
and unease that huge wealth and sudden celebrity can inflict on the
intrinsically humble. They changed visibly and internally. The four
cheerful characters who bounced into my home four years earlier bore
no resemblance to the new 'disciples' of that amiable guru, His
Holiness the Maharishi Mahesh Yogi. There was John with his
Mormon-style hat and ten-cent spectacles; George with his beads,
purple-embroidered coat and yellow shoes; Ringo in a lilac silk coat;
and Paul a psychedelic study in lime green, blue flowers, velvet and
multicoloured wool.

This was no publicity stunt. The world's most famous foursome
were – at the time – totally sold on the Maharishi and the spreading
cult of Transcendental Meditation. It was some quantum leap from
the banks of the Mersey to the shores of the Ganges. There would be
two Spartan months in cold-water chalets with bad plumbing for the
joy at being at the feet of the Master. (The actress Mia Farrow would
later follow in their footsteps to the Himalayas.)

To understand the 'message' it was essential to meet the messenger. His Beaming Holiness struck me as being the genuine article behind the beard, the beads, the aura of serenity. He greeted me in his hotel suite at Falsterbo, near Malmö, Sweden, cross-legged on a couch, barefoot, hands clasped, smiling hugely. We talked awhile about Transcendental Meditation and then he asked – and answered – the question of the hour: 'Why are the Beatles turning to meditation? Because there are certain things that cannot be gained from the outer sphere of living. They know they lack something in their lives but they cannot pinpoint it. They have millions, cars, fine houses – then what... then what?' he repeated spreading his hands. 'They have told me they have been seeking for something more – maybe a greater peace and serenity. They have told me there is no one in the Western world to whom they can turn.'

The Maharishi's words help to explain a bizarre period in the history of the Beatles. Their success had been miraculous. They were now required to perform miracles. This nutty aspect of their fame was spelled out to me by John Lennon one moonlit night on location in the Bahamas: 'On our American tour, theatre managers kept bringing blind, crippled and deformed children into our dressing room. This boy's mother would say to us, "Go on, kiss him, maybe you'll bring him back his sight." Well we've got as much compassion as the next feller and we'd give anything to help the poor kids. But we're entertainers not faith healers, and if you flinch they snarl at you, want to half murder you. We're not cruel,' he said. 'We've seen enough tragedy on the Merseyside. But when a mother shrieks, "Just touch him! Maybe he will walk again!" we want to run, cry, and just empty our pockets.'

That anecdote revealed the best, and the worst, aspects of Beatle-mania. They were wonderful lads, the schnooks from Liverpool, but they could not perform miracles. They did, however, possess genuine compassion, and Lennon in particular, half saint, half screwball, tried to embrace the world. Artist, songwriter, author and deep-thinking extrovert, he was the Beatle with the bite. That head-shrouding coiffure, and the faintly idiot grin beneath, were deceiving. Deep in the recesses of his mind was a turmoil of ideas, anger and disillusion all hidden behind that sardonic smile.

A degree of mutual disillusion was developing in our own relationship. By now he was divorced from his wife Cynthia and had married a Japanese film producer named Yoko Ono. A wildly extrovert, powerhouse of a woman, she shared Lennon's radical slant on life with just a touch of the screwball to enliven it. They decided to spend their honeymoon in bed, in public, in Amsterdam. In room 902 at the Hilton Hotel to be precise. This conjugal absurdity was projected as a 'bed-in for peace'. It drew, as was intended, the world's press and other 'interested parties'. I was certainly interested. It was the sort of lunacy that professional observers like myself grab at with delight. Around that time their campaign for peace included the two of them getting into a large bag and later revealing their bare backsides on the sleeve of a Beatles record. (Yoko's whimsical preoccupation with naked buttocks – 365 to be exact – had already been recorded on film.) All of which seemed an appropriate prelude for the hairy double act in room 902 at the Hilton. Dressed in sepulchral white robes topped by long, black, guru-styled hair, they grinned sheepishly beneath hand-drawn logos proclaiming HAIR PEACE, BED PEACE and similar signs. Then came the joint declaration, 'We're staying in bed as a protest against all the violence and war in the world. It's a happening. A bed happening. We want people to stay in bed and grow their hair instead of getting involved in violence. Hair is nice, hair is peace.' (These laudable sentiments amused me – I had been peacefully bald for decades.)

Yoko Ono, as likeable as any kook I've known, read from the Bible while Lennon played with his toes. 'Second chapter of Genesis. And they were both naked, the man and his wife, and were not ashamed.' She developed the theme, 'Think – if all the world dropped its pants, who could make war then?'

John Lennon thought a start could be made in Vietnam, then, 'The Russians could drop their trousers, and the Arabs, and the Israelis...' and so on.

Naïve and harmless stuff from two blissful newlyweds rich enough to indulge their well-intentioned capers. But they were now on a completely different wavelength from the rest of the group, cutting themselves off from them and seemingly the rest of the world. The partnership ended sourly in the High Court in 1971. It was the end of the Beatles, though not the extinction of their music. Whatever Lennon might have achieved later in life became tragically academic. In December 1980 he was gunned down on a street in New York. 'Hey, Mr Lennon,' his assailant called, then shot him five times. The grotesque incident was over in seconds. Lennon was forty years old. The irony, of course, was that the violence that he had fought against with public clowning, serious intent and hard cash should have been the instrument of his destruction. Nothing in the exuberant scenario of his life from Amsterdam to the Himalayas could have foreshadowed this monstrous finale in Manhattan. A few crazed shots near Central Park and a quarter of a century blown away. His death devastated Paul, George and Ringo. Big business had split them. But they shared the heartbeat of that Cavern in Liverpool.

Of all his songs, John Lennon considered 'Imagine' his most important. He wanted it to be his epitaph. One of the verses goes,

> Imagine no possessions,
> I wonder if you can,
> No need for greed or hunger,
> A brotherhood of man.*

That brotherhood was as elusive as ever. Overshadowing the 1960s was the war in Vietnam. Forty years later transport planes of the American Air Force and of the RAF would be bringing back the bodies of servicemen killed in the war in Iraq. In April 2003, watching on TV the coffins being carried down from the transport planes was an echo of a day I spent in a town called Culpeper in Virginia in January 1968. I had been in New York, scheduled to fly to Los Angeles. One evening in a bar off 42nd Street, we watched the scenes on TV as giant C141 Lockheed Starfighter jets flew in with the bodies of American heroes. There were inserts of the young men's faces and of their families waiting on the tarmac. It was wrenching to watch. I went back to pack; but the thought of Hollywood, the pampering and the punchlines didn't sit too well with the scenes I'd just witnessed.

---

*Copyright Northern Songs Ltd.

I wasn't getting into the 'holier than thou' business. I was a reporter reacting to the only story in town.

Hollywood's sober stance on Vietnam has led to come classic motion pictures. But Vietnam was a major issue in a deeply divided America. It was an awesome fact that every soldier killed in Vietnam was flown back under military escort to be buried in his own home town. This massive operation, reflecting the compassion and perhaps the conscience of America, was efficient but sensitive. An airlift of dead heroes, flown at five hundred miles an hour, halfway across the world. I felt an urge to be a witness to it. I wanted to experience one such homecoming of a soldier in small-town America. I decided that celebrity could be put on hold for a while, and flew to Washington. Unlike its frowning equivalent in Whitehall, the Pentagon told the serious enquirer all he wished to know about the Vietnam casualties. The young officer I talked to in Room 23 at the Pentagon, Colonel Howard Smith of Public Affairs, had all the right qualities for the job. He was candid and typically American: friendly to the stranger. Nevertheless I half expected a hint of suspicion as to my motives. Here was a British journalist touching a particularly sensitive nerve; probing an almost exclusive American tragedy. But the colonel was there to help. He gave me the latest casualty figures, adding a personal touch: 'I cannot look at a single name without thinking of the heartache it brings with it.' I asked if it was possible to attend the homecoming of one such casualty. He consulted a list. His finger stopped at the name 'Spencer'. He quoted the citation: 'Private First Class Edward O Spencer died in the province of Hau Nghia from wounds received while on perimeter defense in a forward base camp.' He was being buried that same week in Culpeper, Virginia. One unknown private soldier was being laid to rest, yet the whole town closed down in sympathy. Given an extra touch of brass and military splendour, this could have been the funeral of a much-loved general. The town was almost totally silent. Everyone spoke in whispers. This is a brief extract of my piece written under the dateline 'Culpeper, Virginia':

> It is uncommonly quiet on Main-street. There is a noticeable absence of customers in the Kut and Kurl Beauty Salon. The

counter-hands at the Gay Heart Drug Store and the Ritz Hi-Hat Restaurant eye each other bleakly through steamed-up windows. In Payne Brothers' Tonsile Artist Parlour the mugs are dry, the chairs empty. The notice in a window advertising a 'Grand Groundhog Supper' barbecued by the men of the local Baptist Church, attracts no loiterers. For the regular or potential clientele have important and sombre duties a quarter of a mile away. They are burying Private First Class Edward Odell Spencer, US 52914242, born in Virginia, killed in Vietnam a month short of his twentieth birthday.

Just why this bespectacled, crew-cut youth should have been required to die 11,000 miles away in the province of Hau Nghia, Vietnam, can be left to the scrutiny of history. What can be said now is that though he went out in humble company, young Spencer came back in style.

One day in Virginia. One of fifty thousand such scenes. Hollywood later grimly underscored the mood with such classics as *Good Morning Vietnam*, *Apocalypse Now* and *The Deer Hunter*. John Lennon's universal 'brotherhood' was still, as the song said, to be imagined.

CHAPTER FIFTEEN

Any Friend of Cubby's...

Soon work will begin – incredibly – on the 21st James Bond film. I say incredibly because, by any normal criteria, this character – who, its creator Ian Fleming once told me, was invented in a moment of intense boredom – should have long been pensioned off. Instead, it goes on and on as a miracle in motion-picture history. More than half the world's population is said to have seen a Bond film. Its gross earnings at the box office covering the twenty films is close to $3.6 billion. Its sleek array of 007s achieved international stardom and riches beyond their wildest imaginings; and the man famously identified with Bond – the late Cubby Broccoli – is now himself a legend. If I write about him with particular regard it is because he was like no other film producer of his time.

Veterans of the Hollywood scene will have been familiar with the stereotype. Loud, aggressive and ruthless, they ruled by a volatile mix of intimidation, flattery and the occasional crocodile tear. Albert Cubby Broccoli was the complete reverse of the stereotype. A large, affable Italianate character (his forebears came from Calabria), he was actually *liked*, if not loved, by hundreds of the assorted talents who worked for him. He enjoyed life more than power. The devotion of family and friends meant infinitely more than his widely acknowledged triumphs and the prodigious wealth that inevitably followed. That statement is easily made and means little unless one has been a close observer, and caught the resonance of affection that embraces the whole family. One afternoon in the UA offices on Fifth

Avenue, Cubby took a call on the conference phone. Mike Beck, a company executive, and I waited while he talked: to his wife Dana Broccoli in Beverly Hills; to his daughter Tina a few miles further along Sunset Boulevard; to his son Tony who lived nearby; to his stepson Michael Wilson at his home in Hampstead; and to his daughter Barbara in Chelsea. All conversations ended with 'I love you too.' That mission accomplished, Cubby Broccoli turned his attention to lesser matters like making movies.

I spent forty lively years as his friend without in any way feeling my impartiality was being threatened. ('But you don't have to slam my pictures in order to prove it!' Cubby once said, not unreasonably.)

The rise and rise of the James Bond Empire began, as most aficionados know, as the joint creation of Cubby Broccoli and the late Canadian producer, Harry Saltzman. But sustaining the series once Saltzman had departed; resuscitating the magic after the Fleming source material had dried up; above all keeping Bond alive and menacing, despite the blockbusting rivalry of his imitators, demanded more than the usual qualifications. Beyond these was the character of the man. Crucially, that character was rooted in the Italian soil. Cubby's family were farmers. It was his uncle Pasquale de Cicco who brought the broccoli seed to America. This vegetable, according to the experts, has strong roots and flourishes under the most adverse conditions. The same might be said of the family whose name it shares. Cubby's most poignant memories are of his mother Cristina, on her knees pulling the weeds on the modest family farm on Long Island.

Even when Broccoli was a major figure in motion pictures, she remained a gentle little soul with dark-ringed eyes and smooth features, her feet firmly on the ground. One night in New York Cubby took her to a lavish James Bond premiere. He wanted her to enjoy the buzz of seeing the name 'Broccoli' up there in lights, the excited crowds and the celebrities milling around the foyer. When they both emerged after the showing the proud son expected a reasonable display of motherly pride. But Cristina was thoughtful. 'Tell me something, Cubby. What happens to all those clothes after you've finished the film? There must be a lot of poor people who'd be glad to wear them.'

Broccoli's pride in his origins is reflected in his autobiography, *When the Snow Melts.* That title came from the rough Calabrian warning his father Giovanni gave him on the eve of his departure for Hollywood. He wanted Cubby to beware of charlatans. 'Remember, Cubby,' he cautioned, 'when the snow melts you see the dog shit.' Could Aristotle have said it better? Broccoli was the genuine article, with the gift of making friends and influencing people. Prince Charles and Diana called him 'Cubby'. He was 'Cubby' to President George Bush Sr. (On record as having been forced to eat broccoli, which he hated as a child, Bush sent a framed photo of himself to Cubby inscribed 'Now this is the Broccoli I *really* like.') Ronald Reagan was a close friend before, during and long after his presidency. He confirmed it with a broad smile when I interviewed him in Sacramento (July 1967) in his office as governor of California. (I wrote afterwards: 'It is a whimsical if not uneasy thought than an ex-movie star of many films that escape instant recollection could one day become President of the United States.')

I was less whimsical years later. Reagan turned out to be a highly popular president during one of the most prosperous and self-confident periods in the Union's history.

And who would have imagined so preposterous a sequel – Arnie Schwarzenegger for governor and maybe, who knows, the next president? Howard Hughes, that eccentric and reclusive billionaire, chose the then unknown Broccoli as a trusted friend and confidant. In his younger years as a producer, Hughes, filming the notorious *Outlaw*, needed someone to keep his eyes on – and hands off – its full-figured star Jane Russell. Cubby, then a young assistant director, was earmarked for what was by no means an onerous assignment. Now when I think of my amiable friend – he once cooked spaghetti for an entire crew on location – it is the fun and the anecdotes that surface in the memory.

One morning in New York I checked into the Plaza Hotel and found that Cubby Broccoli, now renowned as the James Bond producer, was having brunch with friends in a penthouse suite. When Broccoli was in town the great and the good and other buddies flocked to pay their respects. These included his cousin, the late Pat de Cicco, who was once married to the heiress Gloria Vanderbilt. (He prospered less from that marriage than he did from one of his more successful enterprises, cornering the market in bat manure.) Also present was Greg Bautzer, a handsome volatile giant who, as we saw in Chapter 10, was Howard Hughes's personal attorney. There were others, strangers to me, including a couple of writers, and a lugubrious millionaire seated in the corner named Beldon Katleman. They had all been to the nearby Catholic church that morning in a ritual dubbed the 'Alka Seltzer Mass' because of the morning-after frailty of some of the worshippers. Though not all were Christians, friendship required them to meet faith to faith at each other's baptisms and barmitzvahs, Jewish weddings and confirmations, wearing *yarmulkes* or lighting candles, where appropriate. That morning they sat hidden behind menus large enough to cover the average character sleeping rough. I was introduced as Cubby's friend. Instantly one of the group, who I learned later was a consultant to Madison Square Garden, said, 'What are you doing tonight?' I said I planned to watch the Muhammad Ali–Frazier title bout, then billed as the Fight of the Century. Scalpers were hustling tickets at $500 or more. 'Where're you staying?' he asked. 'Two floors down,' I said. He made a note. 'There'll be two tickets at the front desk in your name,' he said. 'I couldn't possibly accept,' said I. 'Relax will you?' he frowned. 'I'm relaxed. And anyway I don't need two tickets. I'm here on my own.' He looked pained. 'You want somewhere to put your coat for heaven sakes...'

Meanwhile, I noticed that Mr Katleman had lowered his menu and appeared to be crying. It seems he had once owned the famous El Rancho hotel in Las Vegas. It was a highly profitable operation. One weekend the police phoned him at his home in Beverly Hills to inform him that his hotel had been mysteriously burned down and that maybe it was not a good idea for him to return to Las Vegas. But Beldon was not crying about that. He was crying because he had fallen in love with a British actress he'd met in Hollywood, but she had rejected him and had returned home to England (name omitted, as the lady is happily married and has deleted that file in her life). Beldon had done everything to entice her back, including sending an emissary with a million dollars in cash as a sweetener. The answer was still 'no' and the unhappy suitor was taking it very badly. Cubby, whose compassion extended to all creatures great and small, including rejected suitors, asked me to comfort his friend. My mind groped for a suitable platitude. Having been informed of Mr Katleman's considerable financial interests, I decided something analogous to the Stock Exchange might be appropriate. I leaned over and said straight-faced, 'In life you gain by learning from your losses.' Pure drivel, even as a jet-lagged platitude. Katleman's eyes widened at this flash of insight high above the bustle of Fifth Avenue. He blew his nose into a monogrammed handkerchief and said chokingly, 'That is so true! How long you gonna to be here?'

'I'm leaving for Los Angeles tomorrow.'

'You're going to stay with me.'

'Thanks, but I've made reservations.'

'No friend of Cubby's', he declared, 'stays in a hotel when he's in my town.'

'Thanks again, but no.'

The following morning I buckled myself into Seat A on the Boeing 747 to Los Angeles. Mr Beldon Katleman buckled himself into Seat B. 'Don't get mad,' he grinned. 'I changed my flight and had my secretary cancel your hotel reservation.'

We arrived in Beverly Hills at twilight. The Katleman house, discreetly secluded off Sunset Boulevard, had once belonged to Gary Cooper. It had tall, cathedral-like windows, a large pool, sauna, and at full moon you might glimpse the odd security guard lurking behind the bougainvillea. On entering I was grabbed by the valet, who insisted I remove my clothes so that he could press them. Meanwhile, the housekeeper, in crisp white, wished to know whether I slept on a hard or soft pillow; how I wanted my eggs in the morning; and would it be coffee or tea, and, if the latter, Earl Grey, camomile, mint or regular? A kimono embossed with a golden dragon was draped over my king-sized bed. But the night was young and Mr Katleman's personal hairdresser had arrived in a Cadillac, his manly fragrance preceding him. He pranced in wearing a shirt unbuttoned to the navel, gold medallions bouncing off his hairless tan. He did his stuff on Mr

Katleman's coiffure. In silence. This was obligatory, since Beldon liked to watch simultaneously on an array of TV monitors a ball game, the latest soap and the ceaseless update on stock prices in New York, Tokyo, Paris, Frankfurt and London.

Fifteen minutes later there is a tap on my door.

'Who's this?'

'The hairdresser.'

'What do you want?'

'Mr Katleman insists I do your hair.'

'I don't have any hair.'

'*Please...*' he begged.

'See for yourself,' I said and let him in.

'Oh...!' he fretted. But the disappointment was momentary.

'Sit,' he said.

I sat.

Then with comb, blow-dryer and squirts of lacquer he worked on the straggled remnants above my ears until they stood out like wheel spokes. The effect was alarming as though the lever had been pulled at San Quentin.

Satisfied, the genius packed his gear and left.

Twenty-four hours later I did likewise.

Fade out. Fade in. The lobby of a hotel in Las Vegas. Broccoli's latest Bond film had broken all records and he wanted to share his good fortune with family and friends. He strolled into the lobby and sat down before a one-armed bandit. He lost repeatedly. Suffering from glaucoma, he suddenly remembered he had to put drops in his eyes. He did so and put more quarters in the machine. He lost again. Meanwhile, the drops were having their effect. Tears rolled down his cheeks. A mature little lady beside him held out a handful of quarters. 'Here, take these,' she murmured to my far from penniless friend. 'Maybe they'll change your luck.'

Where do we begin to define Albert R Broccoli? He was born in a New York tenement (1909) apparently not without some difficulty. The newly born infant failing to breathe on cue, his grandmother, Marietta, a midwife, applied an old Calabrian life-saver. She thrust the beak of a live chicken in its mouth, which worked wonders for Cubby, if not for the chicken. As a youth he worked on the family farm on Long Island. He sold beauty products, costume jewellery. And then, as happened to his first 007, Sean Connery, he went into the undertaking business, rising, so to speak, from shrouds to riches. Invited to Hollywood by his cousin, Pat de Cicco, he fetched up one night at the famous Colony Club. He had a handful of silver dollars left over from a brief excursion to Reno, Nevada. Broccoli idly spun a silver dollar on the counter. 'Heads,' called the lean, tall stranger on an adjoining stool. Cubby lost. He spun again. And lost again. 'Try another spin,' the stranger said. 'Thanks, but no,' Cubby grinned. 'Not my night.'

How wrong he was. The stranger held out his hand. 'My name is Howard Hughes,' he said. This was a unique gesture from an obsessively private billionaire. The outcome for Broccoli was almost as miraculous as the genie was to Aladdin. The spin of a silver dollar spun him into the higher echelons of film production. He revealed the extent of it at our first meeting in London more than fifty years ago. He had bought, with his friend Irving Allen, the option on a book called *The Red Beret* (*Paratrooper* in the US) starring Alan Ladd. He had the story; he had the star. All he needed was the $100,000 guarantee to get the show on the road. Hughes, involved at the time in megadeals in aviation, oil and other enterprises, was hard to pin down. Cubby's deal had to be clinched within 24 hours. He drove to Hughes's home and cornered him in his toilet.

He tapped on the door.

'Who's this?' queried the busy billionaire within.

'It's Cubby.'

'What the hell...'

'I need you to sign this guarantee.'

'Can't it wait?'

'No.'

'Slide it under.'

Cubby slid the document under the door.

It emerged seconds later bearing the crucial signature.

Mr Albert R Broccoli had become an independent producer, courtesy of the tycoon in the toilet. The company was called Warwick after the New York hotel where Cubby stayed the night before he left for England. His early films were amusing capers from sexy safaris in 'darkest Africa' to blood-spattered derring-do in the Antarctic. All of which prepared him for the film he was most proud of, *The Trials of Oscar Wilde*, starring the late Peter Finch. A personable Australian actor, Finch had been much admired by Laurence Oliver; even more so by his then wife, Vivien Leigh. Their affair was just one feature in the ultimate disaster of that marriage.

Finch's rakish charm and mask of a smile fitted well into the Wilde character. His input went far beyond an actor's call of duty. He read all of Wilde's writings. At one point when he was reading some of the sadder poems he sobbed openly. He transformed himself from a slim, rugged ex-Australian soldier into the paunchy effeminacy of Oscar Wilde. This required additional ballast of bread, potatoes and half a bottle of whisky a day, the last no hardship for this notable tippler. He produced a unique and moving portrayal of the doomed genius. But there were problems with the script. Wilde's sensational courtroom admissions were considered too raw for cinema audiences in the homophobic attitudes of the day. That would be laughable today. But it was more than forty years ago. Much pressure was exerted on Broccoli by such moral crusaders as the Mothers of America and the Legion of Decency. They took particular exception to that (then) sensational moment in the trial of Oscar Wilde when the prosecuting counsel Edward Carson challenges him:

'Mr Wilde, did you know this valet?'

'Yes, I knew him.'

'Did you give him a cigarette case?'

'Yes, I gave him a cigarette case.'

'Did you kiss him, Mr Wilde?'

'Good heavens, no! He was far too ugly!'

The censors leaned on Broccoli to remove that scene from the picture. But Cubby refused to budge. It became a contest between 'the love that dare not speak its name' and a film that dared to speak its mind. Cubby won. The picture received rave notices and won awards around the world. Few people other than Cubby and Dana Broccoli, the raven-haired beauty he had recently married, knew how crucial that success was. Some months earlier Eros, the distribution company

Broccoli and Irving Allen had created, failed. In short, they lost their shirts. This meant that instead of the film being financed by a studio, Broccoli and Allen would have to put up their own money. Everything rested on the public's response, more crucially on the Los Angeles premiere. But the puritan campaign had struck home. Protestant, Catholic and Jewish organisations all came out publicly against the film (the fact that Oscar Wilde was required reading in almost every American school had apparently escaped them).

Then came the *coup de grâce*. The night the booking geniuses selected for the premiere at the Paramount Theatre in Hollywood was the eve of the Day of Atonement, the most sacred day of the year in the Jewish calendar. Most cinemas were empty, the temples packed – the penitents more concerned about their own sins than those of Britain's tarnished genius. The director, Ken Hughes, Cubby and Dana Broccoli sat together in the darkness of the vast theatre. They counted fifteen others in the audience. A film that would come to be regarded as a classic was dying, and with it, so Cubby thought that night, his career as an independent producer. 'We both wept,' he confessed to me afterwards. 'But my ever practical and devoted Dana pulled me away from the débâcle into a pub next door.' Their disappointment was temporarily mitigated if not drowned by a couple of Hawaiian stiffeners. They flew back to London to learn that the film had won three major British awards and seven in Moscow. But financially the film was a disaster. Broccoli felt under siege. He was close to ruin. To use a western analogy, he made a circle with the wagons and prayed the cavalry would come. Cue the arrival of Mr Harry Saltzman bearing an option on the books of Ian Fleming. But it was time-limited, and time was fast running out.

Long before Saltzman acquired the option, Cubby Broccoli had read the Fleming novels and was convinced they would make great cinema. (As the London *Times* would declare in its 1996 obituary on Broccoli, 'An American, it was his genius to perceive that the adventures of a British Secret Service Agent could make the stuff of international box office.' The several leading figures who subsequently tried to bring James Bond to the screen would all fall at the first fence. Their failure was largely due to a reluctance to invest millions in what was an essentially British character. In those days, with the exception of Laurence Olivier, a British star was considered a dangerous gamble at the international box office. Ian Fleming's attitude to show business, like Hollywood's (then) attitude to James Bond, was wary. Fleming likened the business end of motion pictures to being caught in a 'grisly maw'. Meanwhile the front-office suits in Hollywood dismissed James Bond as an anally constricted upper-class sadist who wouldn't sell a ticket in Milwaukee. The massive grosses would later remove the hesitancy from their faces. Moreover, when Fleming's bank balance began to fatten prodigiously, he found that 'grisly maw' to be a most seductive handshake.

In the early days, there were tensions, not least a clash of personalities. Producer Harry Saltzman had his soft centre, but this was not immediately apparent to those who didn't know him. And certainly not to Ian Fleming. The situation required much of Cubby's savvy and native goodwill to achieve the necessary rapport between Harry, Fleming and a highly cautious United Artists.

Saltzman was a gifted but somewhat abrasive Canadian, famous for discovering Michael Caine, and for what used to be called 'kitchen-sink' movies like *Look Back in Anger* and *Saturday Night and Sunday Morning*. It was an impressive track record. But as the sixties got under way audiences for such films were dwindling. Saltzman was short in what the trade calls 'eating money'.

His prime asset at the time was the film option on Fleming's Bond stories. It was the British writer Wolf Mankowitz who suggested he approach Cubby Broccoli. The partnership almost died at the first handshake. Saltzman produced a scrap of paper. 'You have forty-nine per cent,' he suggested cheerfully. 'I'll have fifty-one.' It was a good try. Bad thinking. He just managed to waylay the departing Broccoli at the door. Success came eventually as a result of a face-to-face meeting between Cubby Broccoli and the powerful head of United Artists, Arthur Krim. Krim shrewdly judged how volatile the triple-headed situation was. But he gambled on Cubby's ability to pull all the strands together. In the event his hunch brought huge revenues at a crucial moment in the company's history.

Fleming shared Krim's confidence. He took instantly to Broccoli, a friendship enhanced by a shared appreciation of beautiful women, fine food and the green baize of Las Vegas. Walking with Dana Broccoli one moonlit night along the banks of the Bosphorus, he revealed himself to be a very human soul behind the aristocratic air. The mind that had created the menacing Blofeld and the sinister SPECTRE also dreamed up the delightful *Chitty Chitty Bang Bang*, which the Broccolis fashioned into a highly popular film. The stage version is a major West End success and the magic car will soon be flying over Broadway.

Fleming was very much in character when we first met, at his chambers in Mitre Court off London's Fleet Street. The setting reflected the man. A gold-painted nude, one eye glancing coyly over an eighteen-carat shoulder, looked down from the Regency-striped wall. Other topless beauties were deployed among the rare books and *objets d'art*, or alongside a quill pen on a rare antique desk. The long cigarette holder, the spotted bow tie, well-worn dispatch case and the shiny revolver on the inkstand completed the image. Whether Bond was modelled on Fleming, or the other way round, was academic. It was clearly the two-tone decor of the esoteric, and the erotic was basic to 007. Fleming (Eton, Sandhurst, Boodles) relished the good life that his grandfather's banking house fortune ensured. Tall, sardonic, with hooded eyes, he was the archetypal product of the English public school, in which the flaying of bare buttocks was held to be good for the character and the survival of the Empire.

Fleming did not initially favour Connery as 007. He told me he always preferred David Niven. He wasn't convinced that Sean Connery, the former truck driver and assiduous coffin polisher, would have the touch of class that Bond required. He changed his mind after inviting Sean Connery to join him and friends for dinner at the Savoy. A young woman in the group said she almost had kittens placed within touching distance of the 'walking aphrodisiac'. Yet United Artists at first also thought Connery was wrong for the part, famously wiring Cubby, 'Keep trying.' But Broccoli was adamant. So too was his wife Dana, who on seeing some early Disney footage of Connery exclaimed, 'There's our Bond!'

Connery, six feet two inches of street-hardened independence, was a shade less euphoric. Negotiating with the two producers in South

Audley Street (he had SCOTLAND FOREVER tattooed on his arm), Sean fought his corner with the same tenacity that be brought to James Bond. His chequered history as Bond; the string of blockbusters like *Doctor No*, *Goldfinger* and *From Russia with Love*; his dispute with the two producers, and his eventual departure are now fading elements in the Bond legend. He departed amid some acrimony, claiming publicly that he had been short-changed by the producers. This was strenuously denied. But the atmosphere had been soured and in any event he was looking for pastures new.

It was never going to be easy to replace him. He had carved a defining benchmark whose subliminal message read, 'Follow that!'

Well, George Lazenby, Roger Moore, Timothy Dalton and Pierce Brosnan did so. I suspect most people, including Connery, would concede that they have done pretty well for the product and of course for themselves. George Lazenby, with little more than a famous chocolate bar commercial behind him, did surprisingly well in *On Her Majesty's Secret Service*. Roger Moore made a spate of successful Bonds, achieving as much with one raised eyebrow as Errol Flynn ever did with his sword. Timothy Dalton, the tall, lithe actor with jungle-cat eyes, made the most of his reputation as 'the thinking woman's James Bond'. He was followed by Pierce Brosnan, who, far from being inhibited by the ghost of Connery, has seen his films smash all previous box-office records. Both he and Sean reached out to women with contrasting magnetism: Sean with brawny, caber-tossing masculinity; Piers with a beguiling touch of the Blarney Stone.

How well would these actors have fared if they had never had played 007? No one can say. Certainly each one has proved he has the looks and the talent to carry a film or TV series (Roger Moore with *The Saint* and Pierce Brosnan with *Remington Steele*). But an actor needs a shop window and on that analogy Bond was as big as Bloomingdales. Even when time left its footprint on Roger's Riviera tan he managed – with a little help from Max Factor – to take Bond almost into a Zimmer frame. Moreover, as a roving ambassador for the United Nations, Sir Roger is turning the Bond image to valuable effect as a celebrity fundraiser. Timothy Dalton, living in princely style in Beverly Hills, goes from film to film. His deft touch and the darkly handsome looks of a younger Olivier will take him, like Connery, into lucrative middle age.

But it is Connery who has made the most triumphant transition of all. Defiantly bald, grey around the sideburns, this rugged 72-year-old hoots roguishly when told he's still voted the sexiest man in the movies. He is now Sir Sean Connery. What resonance that title must have for this beefy son of a Scottish charlady, born in a slum, a bottom draw serving as his crib. He has devoted much of his time and money in support of the country he loves. He has won an Oscar. He is one of the few actors whose names alone can carry a major film. All due to a gritty talent, and a most compelling screen persona. But there must be many watching those craggy features on the screen who also see a curl of cigarette smoke and hear a voice murmur huskily, 'My name is Bond. James Bond.'

Many directors, using Bond as their template, have made their individual mark on the genre. Steven Spielberg has generously acknowledged 007's influence on the big spy/action epics. He recently said he would like to direct a Bond film. A considerable accolade from one of the world's finest directors. Last May the *Independent* newspaper in its supplement *Empire* listed *Goldfinger* among the ten most influential action films of all time alongside *Lawrence of Arabia*, *Apocalypse Now*, *The Seven Samurai* and *Raiders of the Lost Ark*.

Cubby Broccoli died at his home in the early evening of 27 June 1996. He was 87. As she had been throughout his long illness, Dana Broccoli was at his bedside. The tributes that followed in London and Los Angeles were as substantial as the man. Much of a man's worth in life can be measured by the reaction to his passing. The actors, directors, writers and hundreds of studio personnel who assembled in his memory reflected affection as well as recognition. But there is more tangible evidence of Cubby's impact on his times. The much-coveted Irving Thalberg Award and the massive 007 stage at Pinewood studios are significant trophies in a lifetime of filmmaking. But beyond the world of motion pictures there is the St Francis of Assisi church at La Quinta near Palm Springs, which the Broccolis helped to build for their friend the late Father Ray Bluett. There is the Man of the Year Award acknowledging Cubby's support for the Variety Boys and

Girls Clubs of Queens (NYC), an echo of his boyhood in a New York tenement. Then there is the Dana and Albert ('Cubby') Broccoli Centre for Aortic Diseases at the world-renowned Johns Hopkins Hospital in Baltimore. Faith, Hope and Charity were never more substantialy expressed.

Now Michael Wilson, Dana Broccoli's son by a previous marriage, and her daughter Barbara as co-producers are carrying the legend and the legacy into its 21st incarnation. The significance of it would have astounded Ian Fleming. He lived long enough to witness his pleasant lightweight novels transformed into a motion-picture miracle. He died in August 1964. I have this vision of him, a tall impatient figure standing outside heaven's Pearly Gates.

'Name?'

'My name is Fleming. Ian Fleming.'

'Yes...?'

'You know, author, James Bond, Eton, Sandhurst, Boodles...?'

'So?'

'Look, I knew Cubby Broccoli...'

'Of course! Why didn't you say? Any friend of Cubby's...'

CHAPTER SIXTEEN

Facing the Music, with Sinatra and Others

Film stars and other attention seekers want to be loved, admired and respected. Failing that, they at least want to be noticed. It is an understandable craving. On stage or screen they are under the close scrutiny of millions who are just as fascinated whether they're a hit or die the death. Unfortunately, critics, columnists and other professional commentators can't always be as obliging as celebrities would wish. They are not in the business of nourishing egos or of window-dressing second-rate talent. Their job is to say what they like or don't like, describe what they see or hear, and hope that, when the dust settles, normal relations will be resumed with the performer concerned. But you cannot win them all. There are some characters who, to paraphrase Voltaire, 'detest what you say and will fight to the death to prevent your saying it'. They might have learned something from the late multi-faceted genius Andy Warhol.

No one understood the celebrity business better than he ('In the future everyone will be famous for fifteen minutes'). Artist, philosopher, filmmaker and photographer, Warhol was the patron saint of the sex, drugs and rock-and-roll sixties. A reticent whiz kid with an unruly platinum wig and matching eyebrows, he mixed with the greatest celebrities of the day. He therefore understood the nature of the beast. He learned the trick of having fame thrust upon him rather than courting it. He responded to the notoriety aroused by his highly controversial films with the cherubic smile of a born innocent. Even when he was nearly fatally shot in June 1968 by a kook named Valerie Solanas, leader of SCUM (Society for Cutting Up Men), Warhol was sanguine and philosophical about the incident. Henry Kissinger, Jackie Onassis, Jimmy Carter, Yves St Laurent, Federico Fellini and a cluster of stars like John Lennon, Liza Minnelli, Shirley Maclaine and others all came to his famous Factory on E47th Street, New York, to hang on his every word. This required considerable patience. Mr Warhol's words were as hard to extract as the last squeeze of toothpaste from a well-flattened tube. I discovered this in February 1973, when I phoned him in New York. Around that time there had been a major legal battle in the Appeal Court in London over the banning of a film the photographer David Bailey had made about him. I wanted to ask Warhol for his comments. This is an extract of what passed for our conversation:

Mind if I ask you a few questions?

'Oh, sure.'

Have you been kept informed about all this fuss over the David Bailey film?

'Yes.'

Can you understand it?

'No.'

What do you say about it?

'What's to say?'

Your paintings of Campbell soup tins and Coca-Cola bottles are supposed to be worth $100,000 today.

'More.'

Sorry.

'That's all right. Do you want the phone number of the girl who paints pictures with her breasts?'

Not especially.

'She's in the George Washington Hotel.'

Thank you. Are you painting other portraits at the moment?

'No.'

Was the Brillo box your last painting?

'No, it was Dennis Hopper's ex-wife.'

I thought it was the Brillo box.

'No. Dennis Hopper's ex-wife.'
I hear you may be coming to London for the opening of your film Trash.
'I don't know.'
You're expected.
'I know. I might go to Rome to make some three-dimensional horror movies, *Frankenstein* and *Dracula*.'
That's interesting.
'Or I may stay here.'
How's your mother?
'She's old.'
I'll take the phone number of the girl who paints with her breasts.
(Well if you must know, her name was Miss Brigid Polk. She was a full-bosomed artist who daubed her chest with paint and brushed against a canvas or two ('After Titian', quipped one critic.) Her response to my phone call was, 'I'm sick of the whole thing. I don't want to talk about Andy. I don't want to talk about my paintings. I just don't want to say *anything more!*' After which tirade I assumed she put her implements back in their cups, her inspiration shattered for the day.)

Those monosyllabic responses of Warhol's (he died in 1987) were less a case of being inarticulate, more a shrewd stratagem for handling what is now called 'the media'. It is a pity that the late and indisputably legendary Frank Sinatra never acquired that gift. It might have spared him (and us) many of the angry confrontations that marked his controversial appearances around the world. It all happened half a century ago. But the jury is always out on those the world deems immortal. And, since Sinatra's songs are still as magical today as when first they tugged the hearts of millions, the evidence is worth recalling.

There was the fist fight with the influential journalist, Lee Mortimer, in 1947 and a photographer, Eddie Schisser, in 1950. There were ominous threats against reporters in Mexico, and the records show at least one bartender being hospitalised as a result of not pouring the extra dry martini on cue. Sinatra was hustled away from countless brawls in which blood was occasionally spilled and teeth unsurgically removed.

It should be said instantly (in case Ol' Blue Eyes is somehow reading this) that an argument could be made for the defence. Some of the reporters covering Frank Sinatra's life and blistering times were crass, offensively intrusive and not too meticulous with their facts. They operated on the assumption – which no entertainer of class could accept – that a press card was an invitation to malign at will; that there's no such thing as bad publicity. This may be true for pop freaks, desperate bimbos or other 'overnight sensations'. But Frank Sinatra's profound contribution to the music of our time placed him way beyond the ordinary confines of celebrity. There was, of course, the kinder side to Sinatra. He was spectacularly generous to family and friends. His fundraising ran into several million dollars. When his friend, that fine actor Lee J Cobb, was rushed to hospital in 1955 suffering from a near-fatal heart attack, Sinatra's response was swift and munificent. He paid all bills not covered by insurance. He later moved him to a rest home for six weeks, paying all expenses and visiting him almost every day. But good deeds rarely make headlines. The image remained, of a volatile, all-powerful, short-fused performer whose path one crossed at one's peril. Bing Crosby, who saw the blue of his night fade into the gold of Sinatra's day, described him as 'a loyal friend and an implacable enemy – but then he's a Sicilian.'

He was born 12 December 1915 on the mean streets of Hoboken, New Jersey, and defiance seethed in the Sinatra bloodstream. Delivered by Caesarian, the lacerated ear and deep facial wounds he suffered as a result must have inflicted lasting psychological damage. Moreover, if you have been raised by a boxer-turned-bootlegger father and a battleaxe of a mother in an environment of poverty and swinging truncheons, Fauntleroy is not your middle name. But the street fighter in him enabled him to battle his way to fame. In 1944, it was the shape of the Beatles to come. Ten thousand kids queued line abreast along New York's 43rd Street at a concert they called the Columbus Day Riot. He was then, and would remain, supremely in a class of his own. How else could he have stayed at the top so long, singing his way through the lives of six American presidents, all of whom courted him at campaign time without blushing? He had been an Oscar-winning actor (diMaggio in *From Here to Eternity*), studio magnate and a relentless pursuer of women, from famous movie queens to 'What's that name again, honey?'

He could radiate, unexpectedly, great buddy-boy charm with a fierce shoulder hug to confirm it. If you were a guest at his closely guarded estate in Palm Springs with its helicopter pad and private chapel, you would be treated like visiting royalty but get no sleep. An audience with Sinatra, Jack Daniel's and all, required a zinc-lined stomach and round-the-clock insomnia. But his temper, following some real or imagined affront, was often close to being uncontrollable. He turned much of that fury against journalists, whom, in general, he loathed with a passion.

That hatred first blew up around his squally love affair and marriage to the Hollywood star Ava Gardner. A slim Southern beauty with chestnut hair and oval features, she had been battle-hardened by her marriages to the actor Mickey Rooney and the bandleader Artie Shaw, both of which lasted less than a year. The daughter of a tough hard-drinking North Carolina farmer, she smoked, drank and swore – which was fine with Sinatra unless he was the target of the profanity. They fought and loved with equal frenzy. They both liked blood sports: Frank, boxing, Ava, bullfighting. But, when their marriage itself became a blood sport and made the headlines, it was open war between Sinatra and the press. It cut no ice with Frank if his hellraising exploits were mitigated by rave reviews shimmering with adjectives like 'magic', 'sublime', 'bewitching' or 'unforgettable'. Praise meant nothing to him. It was only *his* opinion of his work that mattered. But his ego did not yield too well in a breeze of adverse criticism. The press were garbage. Period. Since I was more interested in his music than I was in the rocky landscape of his marriages, there was some fair weather between us. Until 3 August 1966 to be precise. On that morning a piece of mine in the *Mirror* criticised Sinatra's arrival in London. It was illustrated with a photo showing Sinatra and a friend leaving the hotel by a back entrance. It struck me as a somewhat paranoid display by an over-protected celebrity. Under the headline RELAX FRANK. NOBODY'S GOING TO BITE YOU, I wrote:

Furtive exits via the dustbin entrance. Much secret coming and going behind smoked-glass windows and a screen of muted hangers-on. Heads down. Sealed lips. Silenced hall porters, guarded doors. The whole grim apparatus of a total security clampdown: the bulging shoulder-holsters and yapping dogs.

And who is it all for? A visiting Soviet delegation? A NATO conference on Nuclear Strategy...?

Not at all. Frankie is in town. And Mia. Or if we have to be formal, Mr. and Mrs. Frank Sinatra are in England on their honeymoon.

We are accustomed to seeing police suspects being smuggled out of back entrances with raincoats over their heads. It puzzles us when our favourite stars feel it necessary to get up to the same stealthy malarkey.

Sinatra's response was a short and explicit telegram:

DEAR DONALD LAST NIGHT I REMINDED MY SECRE-TARY TO HAVE ME CALL ROBIN DOUGLAS-HOME DAVID LEWIN AND DONALD ZEC TO HAVE THEM COME VISIT ME ON THE SET BECAUSE I CONSIDER THEM THREE OF THE FAIREST JOURNALISTS I HAVE MET WHICH IS SAYING A GREAT DEAL STOP AS OF THIS MORNING YOU BLEW IT. SINATRA 5 GROSVENOR SQUARE.

Well, life went on. I was paroled for good behaviour. But then much of the fury if not the sound had subsided. His wife, Barbara, had a lot to do with it. A lady of wit and style, she was no competing ego and, though sparks flew occasionally, she never threatened the citadels of his power. He respected her the way Bogart revered Lauren Bacall: not a broad, but a woman of some importance. There is no doubt that this stunning and intelligent woman steered him on a more serene, more elevated course. They gave substantial support for the Desert Museum and the Desert Hospital near Palm Springs and the Sexually Abused Children Program in Coachella Valley. Barbara Sinatra serves on several charity boards, giving time, money and no little prestige.

The last time I spoke to Sinatra was one Christmas night in Beverly Hills. It was a year or so before he died. Our parting handshake bespoke goodwill if not brotherly love. It is sad, perhaps, that his superlative musical achievements should have been overshadowed by lurid tales of association with gangsters. The truth was that Las Vegas, the glittering Mecca to every live performer, was in the early years almost totally financed by the crime bosses led by the handsome hoodlum Bugsy Siegel. 'Playing Vegas' was (still is) the most lucrative gig in show business. The money paid to the top entertainers, not to mention the five-star lifestyle included in the package, far exceeded the pay cheques on offer outside Nevada.

But frequently, entertainers were made offers they couldn't refuse. That verstile entertainer the late Sammy Davis Jr was one of them. He once cancelled a lucrative Las Vegas engagement in order to appear at the opening of a nightspot owned by a crime chieftain named Sam Giancana in Chicago. He was interviewed by the FBI, who were investigating Giancana at the time. They asked him how he was able to cut short a highly paid engagement in Las Vegas to appear at the Chicago opening. Davis, who years earlier had lost an eye in a car accident, is reported to have replied: 'Baby, that's a very good question. Let me say this. I got one eye, and that one eye sees a lot of things that my brain tells me I shouldn't talk about. Because my brain says that, if I do, my one eye might not be seeing anything for a while.'

The implications were obvious. What the investigators could not know was that this was not the only time Sammy Davis Jr was nervous about his one good eye – or his two good legs for that matter. The other episode involved him and the actress Kim Novak, who had replaced an incandescent redhead named Rita Hayworth at Columbia Pictures. Their friendship unleashed much unsavoury comment in the scandal-sheet gossip at the time: 'Guess which sepia entertainer's attentions are being whispered as the Kiss of Death to guess which blonde movie star's career...'

The insult was nothing new to the Harlem-born Sammy Davis Jr. But it was offensive to independently minded Kim Novak. The daughter of a Chicago railroad worker, she was in 1956 second only to Marilyn Monroe as the biggest female star of the year. Harry Cohn, the scary megalomaniac who presided over Columbia Studios in the style of the Italian dictator Mussolini, whom he much admired, had big plans for Novak. She had all the basics of a screen goddess. The film director Richard Quine said she had the 'proverbial quality of the lady in the parlour and the whore in the bedroom'.

The 'Kim and Him' scandal, as it was dubbed in those prejudiced times, was snuffed out. Maybe the two principals involved recognised when they were beaten. But there was a more ominous explanation. According to Sammy Davis Jr in his autobiography *Why Me*, 'I looked through the papers and read: Sammy Davis Jr has been warned by top Chicago gangsters that if he ever sees that blonde movie star again both of his legs will be broken...'

An alternative, and more reliable, version relayed to me had this character warning the singer: 'Sammy, you've already lost one eye. D'you wanna go for two?'

Whoever instigated the threat was never revealed. It hardly mattered. Both stars went on to broader horizons. Sammy, whose tenacity matched his talents, would go on to earn the respect and friendship of Martin Luther King and Bobby Kennedy, both victims of the same ominous forces that had threatened the singer. Though Kim Novak went on to make some very good films opposite the very best screen actors, she never quite reached goddess status. She was certainly beautiful, but maybe too nice to make the waves and the headlines that superstardom seems to demand. She once sent a gracious note to me following something I'd written about her. Handwritten on a lavender card, the ornate style of the writing was interesting. I remember asking a handwriting expert to analyse it. Her verdict: 'An intriguing mix of innocence, independence and defiance.' No Hollywood tyrant could have stood for that.

One morning, 28 June 1959 to be precise, a taxi arrived at my London home bearing a large cardboard crate. It contained three dozen toilet rolls. The short and unperforated message inside read, 'Dear Donald – these foolish things remind me of you. Love, Mario.'

The sender was Mario Lanza, who was then – all too briefly – one of the most adored singing idols of the screen. He had a magnificent operatic voice and, until his calorie intake went out of control, had the handsome dark Italianate features to go with it. He accrued staggering wealth from his records, films and concerts. So I suppose he could well afford a crate of even the most luxurious toilet rolls (pink, as I recall). Their arrival coincided with a piece that was published that morning in which I criticised his notoriously temperamental behaviour with his co-stars and studio bosses. When this roaring rampaging tenor was offended, windows were shuttered, doors bolted; friends and other victims fled to the hills. Pavarotti's occasional and probably exaggerated outbursts were tranquillity itself compared with the verbal, and sometimes physical, carnage that raged around the life and times of Mario Lanza.

Mario's displeasure over my column lasted no longer than the toilet rolls. All things pass. Soon he was on the telephone inviting me to visit him and his family in Rome. It was a beautiful autumn weekend, the sunshine splashing the marble and terracotta façade of the forty-roomed villa where the maestro was installed. This monumental extravagance with its huge crystal chandeliers had been the Italian dictator Mussolini's gift to the gallant Marshal Badoglio for his bravery in bombing the spear-throwing forces in Abyssinia. I had barely said '*Buon giorno*' before Lanza was announcing the menu for lunch. 'We're gonna have the Mario Special,' he said, his dark eyes gleaming. I soon discovered – as did MGM not long after – that Lanza's obsession with eating, guzzling whole chickens at a sitting, was a catastrophe in the making. Compounding that obsession was a fiendish temper and an insatiable appetite for drink, drugs and women. None of this was touched on of course as we sat – Mario, his wife Betty and I – around the marble table where once Mussolini had entertained his mistress. 'Temperamental?' roared my host. 'Never! Impulsive, yes, devilish if you like. Sometimes I heave a bottle at a wall. But not much more than that.'

I said, 'Let's talk about *The Great Caruso*' (his classic film about Italy's legendary tenor).

'No! Let's talk about the "Mario Special",' he insisted as the waiter arrived with half an animal on a giant tray.

'What is it?' I asked him.

'What is it!' he echoed *molto fortissimo*. 'It is *Vitello à la Bolognese*! Listen, you take a select piece of veal, dip it in egg and breadcrumbs. [at which point Lanza endowed it with human form.] *She* is now a breaded veal cutlet. Across it drape two slices of beautiful ham and this you cover with slender slices of bacon. Now you must overlay it with mozzarella cheese.'

'And that's that?' I said, shaping up to applaud.

'Oh no!' he lilted *molto espressivo*. 'Now you make a sauce of five different kinds of meat. Then maybe a *zabaglioni*, liqueurs...' (after which guests may wish to take coffee in an oxygen tent). The afternoon had its lyrical moments. Lanza played a couple of his finest recordings, his voice soaring over the ancient rooftops of Rome.

We talked about his life in the Soho district of Philadelphia, where he was born Alfred Arthur Cocozza in January 1921. He conceded that he was a young tearaway who hated discipline, and was expelled from high school. But he loved singing and had a beautiful voice. Like drama students who sweep stages hoping to become actors, he got a job as a piano mover while continuing to study singing. He was heard by the great conductor Sergei Koussevitsky of the Boston Symphony Orchestra and, in the best showbiz tradition, zoomed to stardom.

Unfortunately, Papa and Mama Cocozza loved food and shovelled it into their son with a passion. He grew up to be big, powerful and thunderous of voice. 'Puccini and pizza!' he roared. 'That's a bigger partnership than Samson and Delilah.' Well we know what happened to Samson. But at least that warrior had God on his side. Lanza had the devil in his corner. His life was a brawling scenario of lightning success, dismal flops, fantastic wealth and a discordant marriage aggravated by jealousy over a secret mistress. His entry into movies began, he confessed to me, with a resounding flop. Produced by MGM's favourite filmmaker at the time, Joe Pasternak, it was called *That Midnight Kiss* (1949) and teamed him with a wavery-voiced soprano named Kathryn Grayson. The story, it may not surprise you, was about a hefty piano mover with a great voice which is heard by a famous conductor who happens to be listening at the time. It bombed. *The Toast of New Orleans* (1950) followed and also flopped, but one of the songs, 'Be My Love', sold millions.

It was *The Great Caruso* (1951) that which made a fortune for the studio and Lanza into a star. But trouble. Pasternak declared, in what turned out to be a considerable understatement, 'Lanza was difficult from the start. There was a wild, unpredictable streak to his nature.' *Time* magazine, not notable for revealing such intimate detail, disclosed a list of Lanza's unpleasant if not unhygienic habits. These included an antipathy towards soap and water, plus a reluctance to go to the men's room if he needed to take a leak. What else were potted plants for?

Lanza's lust for money was graphically illustrated by a friend of his, and mine, the late Hungarian photographer, Alexander Paal, as he related to me:

'Money burned right through his soul. At around 2 a.m. one morning he rang the doorbell at my home in Hollywood. I let him in – I always let him in – and he thumped up the stairs with a huge oak chest on his shoulder. "Get a load of this, Alex," he shouted. And flipping the lid open, tipped the chest over, and poured a great shower of dollar bills, silver dollars, even gold coins all over the floor. He grabbed a handful and threw it up to the ceiling. "Lovely beautiful stuff. I gotta feel it, touch it, hold it. I never held a ten-dollar bill in my fist till I was fifteen."'

But the hunger for money would not be as lethal as his lust for food and alcohol. Paal remembered one night when the nineteen-stone Lanza charged through the locked doors of a Hollywood delicatessen just to get his giant hands on a hunk of beef. He could drink a dozen cans of beer at one sitting. There was another incident which Paal swore was true. He said that, in a St Moritz hotel one morning, Lanza demanded cold roast beef for breakfast. A waiter put a plate of it before him but Lanza complained at full throttle, 'It's not rare enough.' Twice the waiter brought replacements. Finally the enraged tenor grabbed a carving knife and cut his arm until it bled. 'This what I call rare! Now bring me something with blood on it!'

Mario Lanza died of a heart attack in a Rome clinic, October 1959, barely five months after the day I spent with him. The pills, the empty beer bottles, the half-eaten caviar and the shambles of papers, letters and unpaid bills at the villa were a squalid epitaph to his short, explosive career. He was just 38 years old. In the end his own life story transcended all the lightweight scenarios he brought to the screen.

He was a legend. And so too was Judy Garland. Her lacerating career differed from Lanza's only in the clinical details. Otherwise it was a similar story of drink, drugs, temperament and studio mayhem all undermining, and eventually destroying, a fragile but spectacular talent. Perhaps an even more poignant analogy would be to Edith Piaf, whose doomed, drug-ridden life is haunted by the wrenching 'Je ne regrette rien' ('No Regrets').

With Garland, too, one song, 'Over the Rainbow', like Crosby's 'White Christmas', will be played and replayed as long as the world can listen. Even if you are too young to have seen *For Me and My Gal*, *Meet Me in St. Louis*, *Easter Parade* or *A Star Is Born*, That Song from the memorable *The Wizard of Oz* will clue you to the Garland magic. Two images of her hover in the memory. The first was 6 December 1939, seeing her as the shining-eyed Dorothy in *The Wizard...*; the second was almost thirty years later, backstage of a London nightspot, the Talk of the Town. She was 46 and had just acquired her fifth husband.

'Have you come here to say nasty things,' she asked as she wiped off her makeup, 'or pay me a compliment?'

'A compliment,' I said.

'Will you make it a long one? It will be nice to take with me on my honeymoon.'

For the record, it *was* a long one, a thousands words or so. I quote from it not because I consider the words particularly memorable. But the occasion certainly was. It was a classic reprise of one of the oldest dramas in show business – a legend fighting for its life.

She trips over the microphone lead, catches a stiletto heel in the long feather boa, struggles with a shoulder strap, occasionally murders the music. The urchin face is strong on pathos, eyes anxious-bright, the smile a torment, the deep lines souvenirs of battles, lost, won or still smouldering. Judy Garland, a defiant forty-six, refurbishing a legend...in a great assembly of uncertain well-wishers...for the volatile ingredients of this show are a mixture of magic and morbid fascination; of maudlin sentiment with overtones of danger.

Will she remember the whole of the lyric, part of the lyric, or none of the lyric? Will she be all sweetness and light or spit fire to the four corners of the room? Every tightrope walker knows the conflicting thoughts behind those upturned eyes...

No entertainer senses this more than Judy Garland. And no one but Judy Garland could exploit so magnificently the schmaltzy nostalgia and brittle humour which gives the show its nerve-racked fascination.

The audience that night, as I remember it, were old enough to have lived through thirty years of Judy Garland. Thirty years of breakdowns, lawsuits, trouble over performances and seemingly endless heartache. When she was filming *The Pirate*, directed by her then husband Vincent Minnelli, she commuted between the studio and a psychiatrist's couch. There was a half-hearted attempt at suicide with a broken water glass. Her pill intake included Seconal, Nembutal, amphetamines, and tranquillisers. According to Otto Friedrich in *City of Nets*, 'Her skin broke out in rashes. Her hair began to fall out. Yet another doctor put her in hospital and had her undergo six electric shock treatments.'

Not the life she had anticipated at the end of the rainbow. (Four writs had been served on her since she arrived in London a couple of weeks before the show.) On that fateful night she needed more than moral support. She desperately needed the sound of hands clapping; the roar of the crowd. The crowd obliged. Even before the first roll of the drums, all hearts – seven hundred and eighty to be precise – went out to this diminutive idol waiting in the wings, in a great burst of good intent. They were prepared to forgive her everything, pardon her musical transgressions, even give a pint of blood if needed, which now and again seemed possible.

The reward was a performance of precipitous magic – a kind of musical Houdini act in which we knew, fluffed phrasing and all, that the lady would escape in triumph. But the coup would be short-lived. She died on 22 June 1969. Vincent Minnelli had been the second of her five husbands. This brilliant and gentle filmmaker had done his best to protect the woman and the blazing talent within. The devotion remained. He was filming in London when his daughter Liza Minnelli phoned to tell him of her mother's death. How did he feel at the time? Minnelli smiled wanly. His thoughts were his own. It was the professional who responded.

'When I'm on a picture, I'm on a picture,' he said.

On with the show.

CHAPTER SEVENTEEN

The French Connection

One evening in a private Paris cinema I sat with the Hollywood actor Gary Cooper viewing a film called *And God Created Woman*. It was a psuedo-erotic romp, aiming for as much nudity as would get past the censors. It starred a frisky little mam'selle named Brigitte Bardot. At the end of the film Cooper, with a disapproving wriggle of the nose, said, 'I guess I should have watched this with a sack over my head.' When this quote appeared it did no harm to the film whatsoever. It became notorious overnight and, as happens when leading moralists are publicly disgusted, it was a sellout worldwide.

Bardot, sometimes known as 'Bébé' or the 'sex kitten' because of her feline sexuality, had all the juicy credentials required of the bankable superstar: a brace of husbands, a string of lovers, a capacity to outrage and one attempted suicide. With her provocative walk – the French called it *la démarche* – her long wheat-coloured hair falling around those large brown eyes and pouting features, she was to become one of the most photographed creatures on the planet. She revelled in her body. The American glossy magazines voted her 'The Best Undressed Woman in the World'. But even partially clad she could look stunning. She transformed frayed blue jeans into a chic fashion item. She put St Tropez on the map simply by living there. And it was Bardot, first discovered in Cannes in 1953, who made the town and its Film Festival the Mecca for every ambitious 'kitten' in France, if not the world.

The Cannes Festival has acquired a shade more gravitas since then. But, outside of its serious evaluation of world cinema, it remains a splurging, self-indulgent, tax-deductible spree for producers, writers and actors – and every kind of hustler with more chutzpah than hard cash. For fourteen days and frenzied nights La Croisette, with its open-air cafés lapped by the Mediterranean, becomes a slave-market-turned-jamboree. It is The Place to 'do the business', or indulge in those *liaisons dangereuses*. Here, veteran producers (and perspiring parvenus) talk in the jargon of the trade about foreign rights, DVD spin-offs, residuals and front money, knowing that their chances of actually getting a project onto the screen are slim to none. Away from all this fiscal vulgarity, the Cannes jury view the contesting films with serious deliberation. Words like *genre, avant-garde, nouvelle-vague, auteur, oeuvre* and other lofty terms waft around the table. Sometimes the comments are so esoteric, some producers cannot tell whether their films are being praised or excrementally inundated from on high. But it is what goes on outside the jury room that engages the paparazzi and the hordes of filmmakers, stars, the media and freeloaders who descend upon the town. For years the great Cannes show-stopper was the ritual bra-removing act by a star-struck unknown hungering for recognition. It rarely earned her anything more than goose pimples and the fare back home. She was not even famous for fifteen minutes. But be sure the ritual will continue as relentlessly as streakers at big sporting events.

The festival's focal point is, or used to be, the Carlton Hotel. But it is the chic Hotel du Cap along the coast where the characters with the real money are closeted. With gold chains dangling over their bronzed pectorals, they talk on their mobiles to New York, Los Angeles or London flanked by subordinates who nod eagerly on cue. Being invited to Cannes' glitzy premieres establishes your professional credentials; but an invitation to the many exclusive celebrity parties afterwards is the most coveted card on the Riviera. The producer Sam Spiegel, in the days when he temporarily upped his image by calling himself S P Eagle, threw fabulous bashes on even more fabulous yachts. To be invited aboard for lunch placed you among the immortals. Without that gilt-edged invitation you couldn't even get to the gangplank, since the Spiegel yacht was moored offshore, the guests being ferried out on motorboats. (An old friend, Art Buchwald, columnist on the *Herald Tribune*, came up with an ingenious ruse for would-be gate-crashers: go out on a pedalo within shouting distance of the yacht carrying a bottle of champagne and a megaphone and bellow, 'Why don't you all come down and join me for a drink?' No self-made mogul, he reasoned, could ever resist a hustle of that class.)

It was in this hedonistic paradise that Brigitte Bardot blossomed into the flower of French sexuality. By the late fifties she was one of the biggest box-office draws in the world. It was possible, from the many conversations I had with her at her home and on film locations, to make a plausible prediction as to what her future might be. But what I or even the most expert crystal-gazer could never have envisaged is the Brigitte Bardot we see today. Forty years on, Madame d'Ormale, as she now is, is a 68-years-old animal rights campaigner who adores anything that neighs, brays, barks, bleats or miaows. The mass culling of baby seals in Newfoundland sickened her. She created a Foundation for the Protection of Distressed Animals. She campaigned against vivisection and the killing of rare animals for their skins. She recently rescued a pack of wolves in Mongolia which were destined to be destroyed. She saved 100,000 stray dogs in Romania from being put down. For these and other kindly acts the former Sex Kitten is called 'The Madonna of the Strays'.

She is now accorded less benign descriptives because of her controversial politics. Married to an executive of France's National Front, Bernard d'Ormale, she is a fervent supporter of the Front's leader, Jean-Marie Le Pen. In May 2003 the *Guardian* reported that two anti-racist and human rights groups were taking her to court over her comments in a book called *A Cry in the Silence*, in which gays and illegal immigrants appear to be the target for her extreme right-wing views. I find it hard to equate all this with a woman who can weep at the sight of an injured mongrel or at the cries of a fox caught in a trap. But even more puzzling – to me if not to her – is that Madame d'Ormale should be the same person who inspired Picasso, the eminent author Simone de Beauvoir and the poet Jean Cocteau. When I knew her she was delightful company, and probably still is – on the subject of cats, dogs, mice and men. But I doubt if I would find an hour or so in the company of the high priestess of the Far Right an agreeable experience. Paradoxically, in her early years rebelling against the conventions of sex, fashion and marriage, you would have marked her as the French equivalent of Jane Fonda ('Hanoi Jane' to her detractors), which is an irony since Brigitte's first husband, the brooding film director Roger Vadim, went on to marry Fonda. (Both Brigitte and Jane had at least one ritual in common: they both walked barefoot along the vertebrae of a prone Vadim to help cure his chronic back pain. I witnessed the Fonda Technique in their Paris apartment one night. It worked wonders for his back, but not the marriage.)

My early encounters with the young Bardot were all fractured English and *sauce piquante*. In February 1955 she breezed into Pinewood Studios, England, to film *Doctor at Sea* with Dirk Bogarde. Coquettish and revealing, she put blushes on the faces of the film crew and happy smiles on the faces of the producers. I recall little of our lunchtime conversation except her telling me that her dog was a Cocker Spaniel. In December 1957 at the studio in Paris she showed signs of the nervousness and fear that comes with being the most famous woman in France. The set was closed. There were security guards all around. One cameraman disguised himself as a waiter, another as a Turkish diplomat. Both were tumbled out onto the boulevard.

The one happy face belonged to the producer Raoul Lévy. It was he who produced *And God Created Woman* and made a fortune out of it. He was given to acting like a Mandarin and wore a gold-embroidered Chinese robe to emphasise it. I dubbed him 'Chiang Kai Lévy', which pleased him right down to his ornate sandals. After lunch we visited an art gallery. He asked me which of the two Picassos on offer he should buy. 'Hard to choose,' I said. '*Absolument*,' said he and bought them both. Sadly Monsieur Lévy did not continue to enjoy success for long. Many of his later film projects failed. The yacht he invited me on for a jaunt on the Mediterranean was soon sold. He could never repeat his first, and only, real triumph with *And God Created Woman*. He tried frantically to pull off the ultimate coup, a film teaming Bardot with Frank Sinatra. It came to nothing. He had nothing left to hustle. He took a revolver and shot himself.

Bardot went into acute depression. There were real fears that she might take her own life. She had tried once as a distraught lovesick teenager by putting her head in a gas oven. She tried again years later at a friend's villa near Menton. Neighbours found her one night at the bottom of the villa's garden covered with blood. In despair, she had slashed her wrists. She was rushed to the St Francois clinic in Nice. The doctors discovered she had also swallowed a quantity of sleeping pills. She had scrawled a suicide note. Roughly translated it read: 'I am fed up. I am desperate and unhappy. I am changing my ideas. I am suffering and I may as well suffer for something. So long. B.'

While the doctors fought to save her, at the Hotel Negresco her mother pleaded with the hordes of reporters to take the pressure off her daughter. In the public outcry that followed the 'usual suspects' were blamed – notably the too-intrusive newspapers and the ruthless rat race of show business. Even the chemist who had sold Bardot the sleeping pills was attacked. He told the police he had failed to recognise her. 'How could I know it was her? In my shop I serve hundreds of Bardots every day.' Bardot's own explanation ('I was at the end of my tether') failed to convince the cynics. One even suggested that it was a publicity stunt to boost her film *La Vérité*, which featured a suicide scene. It was a sick thought, which most observers rejected.

Soon she was back in her villa, *La Madrague*, near St Tropez with bandaged wrists and the warm embrace of public sympathy. Fully recovered, she asked me over to Paris to explain the episode of her attempted suicide. I found her on the floor of her studio dressing room playing with a set of toy trains. When she wasn't playing with the trains, she told me, she did jigsaw puzzles or strummed a guitar, all activities useful therapy, she explained, following her breakdown and apparent attempted suicide on the Riviera. 'That incident', she said firmly, 'can never happen again. I admit there was one time after the terrible breakdown of my marriage [to Jacques Charrier] when I wondered why I should go on living. But, now that catastrophe is behind me, I can see that it is good to be alive now.' Not that she had any notion of changing the pattern of her life. 'I had to have the experience, the cost was high, but it was worth it. I know now exactly the kind of woman I am.' This begged the obvious question. Her responses were entirely in character.

'I must be in total control...I am what Nature made me...that is how I am made and I cannot help it. For me marriage must be a paradise, not a prison. I cannot live only for one man, I have to live for myself too...Marriage must allow me to enjoy exactly the kind of life before the ring was put on my finger...I am not ashamed of revealing what I am and the way God created me...What is it for me to be a star? My two houses in Paris, villa on the Riviera, my diamonds and my furs. They are nothing. I may wear mink, but I think blue jeans.'

There were further variations on the theme in Paris again, and later on location in Cualta, Mexico. These revealed the (then) two dominant themes of her life: sexual freedom and cruelty to animals. The first was typical Bardot: 'I love freely, I give freely and I leave freely when love is gone. I only do openly what women crave secretly.'

The second might be a salutary reminder to the formidable political activist we see today: 'I hate injustice. I hate any creature being made to suffer – man, woman, child or animal.'

It is only in this context that I quote the late Willi Frischauer, one of Bardot's several biographers, who wrote, 'The only coherent conversation Brigitte Bardot had with a British film writer was with Donald Zec, to whom she responded better than most.' What, then, would be her response to this: does the justice that she claims to champion extend to the whole human race, as well as to 'All Creatures Great and Small'?

Whatever Brigitte Bardot did for Cannes was mere window-dressing compared with Grace Kelly's gift of life and lustre to the cliff-hanging principality of Monaco. Before she touched it with her magic, this glitzy anachronism on the Côte d'Azur was sorely in need of an heir and a miracle makeover. Grace, the resolute daughter of a no-nonsense Philadelphia builder, expertly obliged in both departments. She produced three spirited and independent children and turned a sybaritic cash register of a kingdom into a prestigious watering hole for novelists, dramatists and poets. She transformed Monaco as triumphantly as she re-created herself from Hollywood star to a zesty and hard-working princess of a revitalised dynasty. She died, as we remember only too poignantly, in an appalling car crash in the South of France in 1982. She was only 52. She had accomplished miracles and had dreams of more to come.

As with Humphrey Bogart and Marilyn Monroe, my interviews with Grace transcended the conventional question-and-answer routine. She used those encounters as part of a ceaseless exploration of herself. She was marvellous – though not easy – to know. She was of course jaw-droppingly beautiful. Those actors with whom she was successively in love, and they with her, were thrown every which way by her ice-and-fire sexuality. The fact that the sexuality was concealed behind a cool, poised, immaculate exterior was all the more tantalising if not maddening to the actors who were considerably smitten. They were confused by the hint that the inaccessible was not necessarily the unavailable. Since I was merely a professional observer, I was accorded the cool, assured, freshly ironed treatment. This could have fooled me, and it did. It was not until long after our first meeting at her apartment in New York that well-authenticated stories revealed a more seductive Grace Kelly behind the lily-white image. She could be different things to different men. But essentially it was this subtle mix of poise and passion that sent their senses spinning. I saw her as a kind of 'Madonna of the Seven Veils' (though you might prefer Gary Cooper's reported comment: 'Looked like she was a cold dish with a man until you got her pants down, then she'd explode.')

To her friend and Riviera neighbour, the distinguished novelist Anthony Burgess, 'There was nothing glacial about that blonde elegance. She had wit, intelligence... and was one of the great European hostesses... able to overwhelm state dignitaries as well as cool the ebullience of Republican characters like Frank Sinatra.' (I suspect cooling Sinatra's ebullience was quite a feat of thermostatic control.)

Grace Kelly's ascent from being a classy New York model to becoming Her (incredibly) Serene Highness the Princess Grace of Monaco, continues to fascinate the millions – as will the life and unhappy times of the late Princess Diana. Both married princes. Both died in car crashes in France. But with Diana there was more tragedy than triumph. She was more the victim than the victor. Grace Kelly on the other hand laid the ground rules for her life, which Hollywood, and Prince Louis Henry Maxence Bertrand Rainier III would be obliged to follow. Hollywood knew how to handle its screen goddesses – but not this mettlesome daughter of an Irish bricklayer who could sing all the words of the lustier Irish ballads.

The director Alfred Hitchcock was the first to unleash the Kelly magic. 'The others', he chuckled, 'just didn't know how to melt the ice and find the sexual elegance beneath.' More expansively, over dinner at Chasen's restaurant in Hollywood, he said, 'With Monroe you have sexuality written all over her. With Grace you have to fight for it, but it's there all right. It's rather like losing your virginity at Fortnum and Mason's' ('customer services' acquiring a whole new meaning). Still, it was worth a flight to New York to check on the Hitchcock handiwork.

The apartment high over Manhattan was the perfect reflection of its owner – cool, stylish, elegant and securely guarded. Even the outside brickwork had a touch of class, having been supplied by an expert, John Kelly, the Irish farmer's boy from County Mayo. But if this self-made millionaire enjoyed trowelling his way through the New York skyline, it was nothing compared with the almost awesome pride he had in his daughter Grace. There was much to be proud about. She was raw but compelling in the classic *High Noon* opposite Gary Cooper. She was even more stunning in *Mogambo* with Clark Gable. But it was *Country Girl* in which she played the long-suffering wife of an alcoholic (Bing Crosby), where Grace produced the rare portrayal that won her an Oscar. (The fact that she fell in love successively with all three leading men – William Holden would have to wait a while – merely confirmed how the make-believe in Hollywood can so easily become the Real McCoy.)

It was almost fifty years ago when I rang the bell at her door in Manhattan. But the vision remains. After three clicking deadlocks and a rattling chain Grace appeared, poised and smiling. Here without question was the Queen of Hollywood, already pencilled in as the future Princess Grace of Monaco. I could see what Hitchcock meant by 'sexual elegance'. No makeup, no nail varnish, just a hint of colour on the lips, a youthful, athletic figure beneath pink shirt and green skirt. She could make the fleeting vision of an ear lobe beyond a tress of golden hair as sexy as a full-frontal assault from her rivals. She had that commanding demeanour that drew this accolade from Frank Sinatra: 'Grace was a princess from birth.' She had all the qualities that made Hollywood moguls uneasy – intelligence, good taste, backbone and pride. The front office preferred its hired goddesses to take the money along with the facelifts, silicone implants, and teeth straightening by which the lacklustre becomes the sublime. Well, they had tried to do that with this natural beauty, colliding head on with a battling Kelly. As she put it that March day on E66th Street, 'I told them if it was quantity not quality they wanted, they had plenty of big-bosomed creatures to choose from.'

Her use of the word 'creature' in relation to oversized bosoms might have given the odd analyst something to think about. She may well have had a complex on the subject. At one Cannes Film Festival, watching a starlet fling off her bra on cue, Grace turned to me and teased, 'It must be quite a change for you talking to an actress with her clothes on.' (A score of possible answers flashed through my mind at the time, which, perhaps over-cautiously, I rejected.) As it happened she had invited me over partly to express her anger over a particularly crass manoeuvre by her studio. They were about to release her film *Green Fire* and aimed to present her as some kind of 'sexy siren' (their words). They used her face on the posters but superimposed it on someone else's more voluptuous body. Grace was furious. 'I told them I would never be able to compete in that department; that I had no intention of trying, and if they persisted I would tear up my contract. I have no desire to become another piece of excess baggage of the movies.'

I didn't speak to Grace again until the night before she boarded the SS *Constitution* on the eight-day voyage to marry her prince in Monaco. 'I hope I'm going to have three children, which I consider the ideal family.' What Grace wanted, she achieved. Her other plans were shattered in the wreckage of that fatal car crash.

The frenzied crowd scenes on the New York waterfront on 4 April 1955 when Grace Kelly boarded the liner were a press agent's dream. Reporters' questions were on the following level:

Q. Will Miss Kelly have a crown?

A. No.

Q. Prince Rainer has said he was so excited he has to pinch himself – does Miss Kelly feel the same?

A. Yes, she pinches herself once in a while.

Q. (to Grace) Will you be studying books on protocol?

A. No. I'll be studying the prince.

The eight-day voyage from New York to Cannes was a penance for the hordes of reporters aboard hoping for juicy eve-of-wedding stories to file back to their newspapers. In fact Grace became increasingly apprehensive behind the self-assured smile. Hindsight suggests that she was hoping to erase all lingering feelings about her previous love affairs, the latest being William Holden, so that she could present herself to Rainier with a clean slate. Even at a distance of four thousand miles, the stern Grimaldi influence was having a subtle effect. When occasionally we walked her black poodle Oliver along the promenade deck, I could see minders lurking behind lifeboats and in doorways. Every day afloat she became less a Hollywood movie star, more the princess. (Her poodle, as I recall, was also having illusions of grandeur. He ate first class, had already received diamond-studded gifts from rich and royal dog owners around the world, and was not giving interviews.)

What I did discover in the verbal fencing that passed for our conversations was that Grace was seriously into astrology. She was a Scorpio, read her horoscope every day and frequently consulted astrologers. (Depending which guru you rely upon, Scorpios have an embarrassment of characteristics, which include 'secretive, stubborn, well-organised, tenacious with a strong sexual drive and personal magnetism'. Just after the midnight before the liner's arrival in Cannes, Grace leaned over the rail gazing at the twinkling lights on the French shoreline. 'I'm going to need a lot of strength in the next seven days,' she murmured. 'But I'm optimistic. I've been studying my horoscope very carefully.'

'What does it say?'

'Here, have a read,' she said, handing me a copy of *The American Astrology Digest*. 'You'll find me under the sign of Scorpio. My birthday is November 12.' The forecast for the princess-in-waiting read: 'You are destined to be a target for love and marriage of a deep, true and idealist nature. Because of this great love potential it might be well for you to look inwards upon yourself for a bit of serious analysis...'

I read on and we both laughed at the rest of it. 'Don't let money slip through your fingers but don't be miserly to the point of starvation...'

Hunger pangs were the least likely symptoms one could have forecast for the megastar-turned-princess. She had been wealthy before she became a star. Her father John Kelly's bricks were part of the skyline of New York. Both he and his son John Jr had been Olympic scullers. Prince Rainier, with his score of titles and even more decorations, impressed him not at all. After the engagement he told Rainier that royalty didn't mean a thing to him and that he hoped he wouldn't play around the way some princes do otherwise he'd lose 'a mighty fine girl'. As it turned out, he had nothing to fear about this prince.

At 6.30 in the morning of 12 April 1956 Rainier boarded his yacht *Deo Juvante II* ('with God's help') to sail out to meet the SS *Constitution*. Twenty thousand Monegasques, tourists, sightseers and journalists packed the harbour. As whistles and horns blew and cannons fired salutes, a seaplane owned by the oil magnate Aristotle Onassis dropped thousands of red and white carnations on to the yacht. Meanwhile, at the 220-roomed Palace of Monaco, the final preparations were made for the luncheon at which the bricklaying Kellys and the dynastic Grimaldis would hopefully bond as strongly as sand and cement. Two butlers were stationed behind every chair in the dining room. 'The servants had so much gold braid,' Jack Kelly said, 'you couldn't tell them from the generals.'

None of her numerous obituarists would deny that her 26 years as Princess Grace of Monaco were anything less than a triumph. She well understood what was expected of her. She would be required to do no more than inject good healthy Kelly blood into the bluer stuff of the Grimaldis. Without an heir this mini-kingdom would revert to France and be forced to pay French taxes – the ultimate calamity to the sun-bronzed natives. The crucial importance of providing Monaco with an heir was underscored by Grace Kelly's consent to undergoing a fertility test. It was not something Rainier himself would have asked for. But the Monegasque courtiers made it clear that without the guarantee of Grace's fertility there could be no wedding. The test was kept secret from Grace's parents, her Irish father's likely reaction being too awesome to contemplate. The test was admirably positive if not positively admirable. The House of Grimaldi heaved a huge sigh of relief. Sex and Sovereignty were fruitfully conjoined.

Monaco's prime asset – apart from its tax-free status and tourism – has always been its casino. When last I saw it, it was a pockmarked and peeling edifice at which rich old crones holding cards in skeletal, age-mottled hands lived out their days and nights over green-baize tables. Grace did more than make the place leakproof and damp-free. She turned a gloomy palace into the semblance of a home. More urgently, she managed to clear out some of the dissolute characters who were giving Monte Carlo a bad name and a string of bad debts. But above all she persuaded the world to take seriously this oddball principality occupying five square miles on the Mediterranean.

Dutifully, nine months and a couple of days after the wedding, Grace honoured her commitment and bore a daughter, Caroline. The prince, presumably to ensure the squawking infant didn't get ideas below her station, squeezed two drops of champagne on her lips from a fountain-pen filler. Rain seeped into the cannons scheduled to fire a 21-gun salute. They choked on an embarrassed silence at 19. But nobody was counting the salvos, only the silver. Hundreds of silver spoons rattled into the palace with such additional necessities as a Louis XV commode and a mink-handled toothbrush. If years later Caroline and Stephanie became royal dropouts, fleeing from stifling protocol and mothballed ermine, Grace was the first to understand it. As she herself was to say in telling understatement, 'During the first years of my marriage I lost my identity...I tended to let my husband and his life and work absorb my personality. I had to find ways of finding myself in this life.' Not much time for that. A son, Prince Albert, was born in 1958 (a 101-gun salute against his sister's misfired 21). The discrepancy was more than male chauvinism. This was the Big One, the Heir to the House of Grimaldi, the green light to Monaco's future – *Mesdames et Messieurs, Fâites Vos Jeux...!*

In May 1958 Prince Rainier invited me to the Palace of Monaco to explain to me a decision he'd taken that caused a furore at the time. This concerned a couple of rich eccentrics, Sir Bernard and Lady Nora Docker. Invited to the christening of Prince Albert, the Dockers, famous for their public extravagances and their Daimler limousine with the solid-gold radiator, asked that their son Lance be invited too. The palace refused on the grounds that the guest list was complete and that letting in one son would unleash an avalanche of requests for other uninvited offspring. Nora Docker, not used to being refused, took a paper replica of the Monaco flag and tore it apart publicly. Their enormous yacht, like that Russian ship heading for Cuba, was warned off the Monaco coastline. The Dockers, for whom the casino was like a second home, would not be permitted to come ashore. It may have been Rainier who signed the order. But Princess Grace's newly acquired patriotic fervour was certainly behind it. Astonishingly, an anonymous American made an offer of £6,000 to the Monaco Red Cross if Rainier would lift the ban. Scarcely a smart move, since the princess was the charity's prime patron. Rainier killed the idea at birth, then invited me to the palace to give his reasons: 'The Princess and I are not interested in bribes or bargaining. Supposing a Frenchman had torn up a Union Jack in England. Grace not only reacted as my wife but as a human being. The principality is no idle playground. We have our pride and our independence.'

More importantly, they had Grace. True, she had been absorbed by Monaco but not devoured by it. She had given it a cultural edge that to some extent silenced the whirr of the roulette wheels. Rainier's devotion to her was touching to witness. He laughed at Hitchcock's description of her: 'an iceberg with a raging furnace inside'.

'She can boil,' he smiled, 'but is not constantly on the simmer.'

The rest we know, told across a vast acreage of print in newspapers, magazines and books by the score.

There were the marital problems of her daughter Caroline: those sensational poses of her semi-nude on a yacht. The startling cleavage displayed with un-royal abandon around the world's night spots. The gamut of famous boyfriends with a brief intermission for an impetuous disaster of a marriage to a rich and rampant playboy. Meanwhile, her younger sister Stephanie was destined to have her fling too – flung out of a stern, uncompromising finishing school for daring to have the odd illicit cigarette while Ma'am's straight back was turned. Caroline soon sailed into calmer waters. At 24 she could point to two university degrees, proving that to go topless is not necessarily to be mindless. Grace had been tempted to return to Hollywood to 'recharge her acting batteries'. But the family, and loyalty to Rainier, remained her sole priority. She developed a special empathy for Monaco's elderly, solitary figures in wheelchairs looking out onto the Mediterranean. She could not only speak to them in French but in the local dialect. She had a theatre named for her. There were plans to build an Open University. And it would have happened, for Grace Kelly, like her father, loved to build and build what was meant to last.

The dreams ended on 14 September 1982. A sudden brain spasm, the swerve of a steering wheel, and a princess and an era lay shattered in the wreckage. In her last television interview, Grace said this: 'I'd like to be remembered as a decent human being and a caring one.'

On that score, this fine and lovely woman may rest assured.

CHAPTER EIGHTEEN

The Misfits

Ten days before boarding the SS *Constitution* taking the Kellys to the Grimaldis, I received the following telegram at the Beverly Hills Hotel, California:

MARCH 30 1956...THANKS LIBERACE PIECE STOP ONE THING NOT CLEAR STOP. IS HIS LAVATORY PIANO-SHAPED QUERY REGARDS RANDALL.

Now I'm not saying that there were not other matters of equal importance at the time: trouble looming in Suez, anti-Soviet demonstrations in Warsaw and so on. But to appreciate the significance of the feature editor's query we need to remind ourselves about Mr Wladiziu Valentino ('call me Lee') Liberace. Before he shimmered into the gaze of an adoring public with his pompadour hair style and sugary Milwaukee sentiments, there had been nothing remotely like him at the piano before – or since. Clad in a succession of sartorial nightmares in gold lamé, rhinestones, furs and other fripperies, he sat at the piano and sang of love with saccharin sweetness and schmaltzy chords. Diamond cufflinks, rings and other jewellery, all shaped in the piano motif, gleamed in the flickering light of a huge candelabra that became his stock-in-trade. And, though he refashioned Chopin, Listz and Beethoven to suit his own syrupy style, millions loved it. He became the most adored, ridiculed, publicised and lampooned idol in Hollywood's gaudy history. He made *The Guinness Book of Records* as the world's highest-paid entertainer of the 1960s and 1970s. He played with devastating success to a vast amplitude of blue-rinsed matrons and those fiercely protective mothers of America upon whose collective bosom he rested his beautifully coiffured head. He traded in fantasy love – mother love for preference.

The music he played; the outrageous kitsch ensembles he wore; the cloying, 'couldn't you love me' smile and the coatings of verbal marsh-mallow he ladled all over it were aimed at one target: the heaving bosom of mature and generous-hearted matronhood. It enthralled many, but nauseated more than a few. To those dissidents, our thick-skinned hero uttered the immortal phrase, 'Well, I'll just have to cry all the way to the bank.' And while we cynics in the media derided, for example, his lightning version of Chopin's 'Minute Waltz' (37 seconds give or take) we could not ignore the statistics. Thirty years of golden discs, two Emmys, several television blockbusters, concert hall sell-outs and fan mail by the truckload, had put him at the pinnacle of show business. A precarious place for entertainers, as the Rise and Fall of Liberace sadly, and controversially, revealed. It became a Drama in Three Acts.

I was personally involved in the first two. Scene One takes us to the Liberace home high in the mountains above Hollywood. Nothing on the outside prepared the visitor for the visual and audible eccentricities within. I rang the bell. It played a tune. The door was opened by the dimpled maestro himself with a broad smile and a honey-sweet 'come on in' that would have disarmed a serial killer. (If I go into some detail about the Liberace lifestyle as I witnessed it that day, it is because that lifestyle was central to the sensational lawsuit that would later involve him and a colleague, the late Sir William Neil Connor, who wrote a forthright column under the pseudonym 'Cassandra'.)

A quick glance around the Wunderkind's living room might just have clued you into the owner's profession. The cushions were shaped like pianos, the ashtrays resembled pianos, coffee tables were shaped like pianos; his huge bed-back was an entire keyboard; in the bathroom there was 'Liberace' embossed on the mats, piano motifs on the towels. (No, the toilet was not piano-shaped but maybe Steinway should give it a thought.)

'How can you sleep nights,' I asked him, stubbing my cigarette out on F-sharp, 'with eight octaves hanging over you.' 'The bed-back was given to me,' he said candidly, 'like almost everything else in the house.' (I could well believe it. The pope gave him a silver crucifix and a lock of hair from the great Liszt himself.) Wondering how far I could go, I asked Liberace if he was sensitive. 'Only to beauty,' he said with feeling. 'The sight of a lovely ballet dancer brings me out in a cold sweat.' The condition was catching. 'Could it be', I suggested 'that the public are beginning to get a little restive about the candelabra and the music-for-the-boudoir routine?' He rose and did a springy little walk around the piano. 'I dedicate myself to the common people. I make them forget the drab reality of their lives.'

'But you probably irritate thousands.'

'Yes, but I please millions,' he flashed back with dimpled glee.

No one denied that Liberace was a brilliant self-parodying performer and a competent piano player who at twenty had performed with the Chicago Symphony Orchestra. When he was eight he was taken to a concert given by the legendary pianist Paderewski. The maestro later visited the Liberace home, heard the boy play and is reported to have said, 'Some day he may take my place.'

But Paderewski might have revised his opinion if he'd sat in on the rest of my interview chez Liberace up in the mountains over Hollywood. I asked him why he had never married. (The question was innocent enough at the time, his gender preferences not then public knowledge.) 'I suppose I will one day, when the right girl comes along. I'm singing a song about that in the show I'm going to put on in Las Vegas. It's called, "The Girl in My Life".' He sat down at the piano and sang it for me. It was all about fancy dames, including Gloria of the Waldorf Astoria, who was thrilling – and willing. Then he did a soft-shoe shuffle, followed by an imitation of a showgirl lifting a skirt to show a wicked garter. That is to say he lifted one trouser leg to reveal a wicked sock. Maybe it was jet lag or the thin mountain air, but my stomach responded badly to the demonstration. It hardly mattered. As with the conjurer who can confidently twist a balloon into a thousand shapes without bursting it, there was no puncturing this self-adoring but shrewd entertainer – until a fateful week in September 1956.

Liberace arrived on the boat train from Southampton to London's Waterloo Station. Six carriages of the train had been reserved for him and an entourage that would not have disgraced a visiting monarch. More than two thousand women crowded onto the platform, some spilling over on to the track. They squealed and screamed in a frenzy of mostly middle-aged hero worship. Some women fainted on the spot. Others who did not swoon just stood there and wept at the delirium of it all. One eager fan actually pressed her trembling lips to the carriage window with Liberace obligingly doing likewise on the opposite side. If it was pure joy to the singer and his hysterical fans, it was stomach-turning stuff to my late colleague Cassandra. He turned a baleful eye on the hapless Liberace and threw the book at him. In an unusually savage piece of journalism, Cassandra wrote,

He is the summit of sex, the pinnacle of masculine, feminine and neuter. Everything that He, She and It can ever want. I spoke to sad but kindly men... who have met every celebrity arriving from the United States for the past thirty years... they all say that the deadly, winking, sniggering, chromium-plated, scent-impregnated, luminous, quivering, giggling, fruit-flavoured, mincing, ice-covered heap of Mother Love has had the biggest reception and impact since Charlie Chaplin arrived at the same station, Waterloo, on September 12 1921.

This was unquestionably the most calculated demolition job ever written about a performer, but a fairly inoffensive one at that. He was a freakish but good-natured extrovert who sincerely preached mother love and confected a little happiness for millions of lonely wives or widows who hung on his every sigh and murmur. Bill Connor was kindly by nature and a supremely gifted writer whose columns were quoted throughout the world. But his splenetic attack on Liberace was scarcely appropriate: it was a huge artillery barrage aimed at demolishing – a meringue. Even Liberace, raised on the showbiz credo 'There's no such thing as bad publicity' could not shrug this one off. He sued, and he won. The legal giants involved, the astonishing scenes in the court, Liberace's own impressive performance in the witness box – made it the case of the decade. But the most remarkable moment in the trial came just moments before the verdict was delivered. Called in as a witness for the defence, I had a close-up of the incident. As the jury returned to their places, a woman among them who had been eyeing Liberace intimately throughout threw him a brazen wink, signalling an unmistakable 'You've won.'

Liberace was awarded £8,000 damages, of which £2,000 was for the allegations of homosexuality. Unfazed as ever, Liberace went on performing in the same gaudy, glitzy manner. He set new box-office records at the Radio City Music Hall in New York, selling a total of 82,000 tickets. He was driven onto the stage in a silver-mirrored Rolls-Royce; he alighted wearing a $300,000 rhinestone-studded blue-fox cape with a sixteen-foot train. Fans rushed the stage to kiss his rings. 'I feel like the pope,' he gushed.

But the euphoria was fleeting. Behind the mask and the shimmering rhinestones, a darker picture was emerging. The veiled hint of homosexuality on which the libel trial focused now seemed to have substance. But what blew the roof off Liberace's gaudy paradise was a sensational lawsuit brought in 1982 by his former chauffeur Scott Thoron. This tall, young, blond Adonis had worked for Liberace for six years. But he was not suing his former employer for wrongful dismissal. His massive, $65 million damages claim was for palimony – whereby a cohabiting partner can claim the same rights as a wife or husband. (It was reported that Liberace paid a plastic surgeon to have his lover's face remodelled in his own image.)

The case opened in rollicking style. The judge, Irving Shimer, ruled that the writ had not been properly served. The process server said that he had served it personally on Liberace, who, he said, was dressed in a brown suit. 'Liberace wouldn't be caught dead in a brown suit,' snapped the judge, to the merriment of the court and Mr Liberace. The court was told that, when Thoron ended his employment, he received, by agreement, $75,000, an interest in a house in Las Vegas and some of its furniture, a Rolls-Royce, another luxury car and two dogs. Not a bad pay-off for a chauffeur. But a bitter Liberace accused the plaintiff of character assassination. The judge appeared to agree with him. The case was eventually reduced to one of breach of contract and settled out of court for $200,000. Despite the lurid revelations of the case, Liberace lost none of his popularity among his loyal fans. He merely had to play the opening chords of 'I'll Be Seeing You', swivel his smile around the auditorium, and the audible sigh from the darkness told him that, in their eyes at least, he could do no wrong.

In his last few years Liberace was stricken by a variety of illnesses, which were undoubtedly AIDS-related. He is quoted as having said, 'I don't want to be remembered as an old queen who died of AIDS.' Perhaps that would have been too harsh a judgement. Nevertheless, he had become a lonely, unhappy ghost of the flamboyant character he once was. Yet a flicker of the showman remained. 'Make sure my toupée is in place', he said as he was dying. He died in February 1987 and was interred at Hollywood's prestigious Forest Lawn cemetery, where his mother and brother George were buried. He was 67.

Despite the unpleasant revelation of the ex-chauffeur's court case, history will leave Liberace's reputation largely unblemished. Rock Hudson will not be so fortunate. For him, a wretchedly unhappy movie star who died of AIDS, only the debris remains of one of the great careers of Hollywood. I'm glad I knew Rock Hudson through his best years – that golden period when he took his boyish and beefy image through a string of successful films like *Magnificent Obsession*, *Giant*, the appealing double act with Doris Day in *Pillow Talk* and the immensely popular TV series *McMillan and Wife*. But I am even more pleased, and relieved, that he did not live to witness the ultimate shredding of his reputation in one of the most squalid cases ever dredged through a Los Angeles courtroom. Not even Elizabeth Taylor, who publicly, defiantly, supported the stricken actor, could save this posthumous assassination of his character.

The case lasted seven weeks, and threw America, let alone Hollywood, into a frenzy of disbelief and disgust. It was brought more than three years after Hudson's death by Marc Christian, a six-foot-two former lover and live-in partner. His case was against the multimillion-dollar Hudson estate. He claimed that Hudson had deliberately and outrageously failed to inform Christian that he had

AIDS; that he had encouraged his secretary Mark Miller to join the conspiracy to prevent Christian from finding out; and that he irresponsibly continued to have high-risk sex with his companion even after AIDS was diagnosed. The jury of twelve – seven men and five women – found in his favour. He walked triumphantly from the courtroom loathed, admired, but an unrepentant millionaire. I say unrepentant because even by the standard of the most lurid kiss-and-tell-revelations, the clinically detailed intimacies of these two men were scarcely for sensitive ears. The case induced shock, not because Hudson was revealed as being gay. That fact had been cocktail-hour talk in Hollywood for years. The most chilling aspect of what was virtually the Trial of Rock Hudson was the Dorian Gray portrait it painted of him: the private agony of one of the most likeable and popular stars in motion pictures.

To appreciate Hudson's thirty years of torment we must see it in the context of the early 1950s. This was an industry in which all the perceived virtues were enshrined in happy, healthy heterosexual marriage, as evoked by the wholesome Doris Day and the music of Irving Berlin. Those genial tyrants Louis B Mayer and Sam Goldwyn gave the millions what they wanted, reworking that age-old plotline: boy meets girl, boy loses girl; boy finally gets his girl. (It would be some time before boy meets boy, boy loses boy, etc. would be an acceptable scenario to the audiences of middle America.) The young female stars of the 1950s were mostly variations on a theme of Debbie Reynolds or Ann Blyth – squeaky-clean American beauties who could dance, sing, giggle or weep on cue. The men were picked straight out of lumber camps, the army or the navy, chosen mostly for what the trade called their 'beefcake'. Acting talent was a shade less important than their glistening pectorals. And if there was a matinée-idol smile to go with it, then a star was born.

This was what happened to Rock Hudson, born Roy Scherer, Winnetka, Illinois, November 1925. A six-foot-four truck driver turned postman, he became, in the words of one commentator at the time, 'The latest rooster to be bred especially for the Hollywood barnyard'. (What nobody knew at the time was this rooster's sole preference for other roosters.) Thus the whole star-making machine of the studio was geared to making Hudson into a handsome, debonair leading man in the style of Cary Grant. He was photographed with various young beauties on his arm at premieres, on the beaches, dancing in night clubs, apparently enjoying all the delights of heterosexual manhood. It was all a pretence of course, but the actor in Rock Hudson enabled him to fool most of the people most of the time.

But the rumour mill began to grind. 'With all these beautiful women around him, how come this guy never married?' was the question persistently raised at dinner parties or on the beach at Malibu. Henry Willson, the Hollywood agent who discovered him (postman Hudson was delivering letters to his home), decided his protégé needed to be married, and fast. (The fact that it was the agent's secretary, Phyllis Gates, Hudson married suggests happenstance was helped by a little gentle arm twisting.) The marriage lasted a couple of years, and was a sham. In between his unconvincing moments as a husband, Hudson was irresistibly drawn to gay bars, bath houses and massage parlours, many of them little more that pick-up joints and brothels. That was his scene, and it's not for me to judge him. Moreover, in all the years that I knew him, he was that rarity – a gentleman actor and a very good-natured one at that. Time-warped to the twenty-first century, where the word 'gay' is not the stigma that it was, Hudson might have been able to walk out of the shadows. But, in his day, no handsome leading man could confess to being a homosexual and expect to get another day's work in Hollywood. As Kitty Kelley wrote in her biography of Elizabeth Taylor (Rock Hudson was her co-star in *Giant*),

> Homosexual male stars posed a problem for the studio [MGM] publicity department because of Louis B Mayer's frenzy on the subject. MGM men were encouraged to marry so that he would be assured of their masculinity. Mayer was rabidly suspicious of any male star who did not chase women.

This was, of course, breathtaking hypocrisy considering LB's clandestine advances to some of his contract artistes. But Rock Hudson got the unequivocal message and was forced to live an excruciatingly complex double life, suffering agonies of guilt and confusion. He was imprisoned in a lie. He never spoke publicly about it, fearing a backlash from his studio chiefs. But one day he decided he wanted to talk and invited me to his home on a ridge high above Los Angeles. That interview – it was nearly thirty years ago – is worth recalling because of what it says about the subliminal homophobia of his day. I knew Rock's invitation was probably made with some reluctance. He was painfully shy even when he was on every magazine cover and netted three thousand fan letters a week. But the professional in him required him to submit to what he hated most – talking about himself and his life. What emerged was intriguing both for Hudson's candour and also for the ambivalence of his replies. Part of him went on autopilot as he reiterated the myth of his healthy, happy heterosexuality. But the more honest man within hinted at his inner rage at not being able to be the person Nature had made him.

We began the interview over lunch at the Bistro restaurant in Beverly Hills, then continued it at his home atop the mountains. Coldwater Canyon, which snakes up from Sunset Boulevard to Mulholland Drive at the crest, presents a fascinating picture of the different levels of accessibility. On the safer, lower slopes, the richly timbered architecture reflects security, stability and a kind of selective availability. These are the homes of the Establishment, where like tends to mix with like. All homes carry warnings of 'armed response' and Dobermans prowl restlessly behind the wire mesh. But those who crave solitude favour the almost unreachable peaks at the summit. Marlon Brando, Hollywood's superannuated rebel, resides there frowning down upon a Hollywood he has frequently derided. This was where Rock Hudson chose to live, far enough away from the whispering and the accusing glances. Alone, attended by his houseman James behind closed doors, he could live his secret life with some tranquillity.

I asked him what he missed most in life. 'Children, children,' he said quietly. 'I think I might have made a good father. I love kids more now than I ever did. When I lived in Newport Beach there were four kids who lived next door. Their father was dead. Once when I came home for a few days the house was empty. I learned their mother had choked to death. The children were sent to an orphanage in Milwaukee. I tried to adopt them. But because I was single the answer was no.' There was a long silence. He stood, and stared thoughtfully out into the distance. 'I've had my share of unhappiness like everybody else. But I don't think about it. I don't wallow in it.'

I asked him about the rumours and the inevitable questions that followed the fiasco of his marriage to Phyllis Gates. 'A lot of people speculated. Let them speculate. It's none of their business. What do I care? Terrible things have been written about everybody in this town. But with maturity comes the knowledge of when to get upset and when to say the hell with it.'

Rock Hudson's sex education acquired some fairly colourful input from his grandfather: 'When I was about sixteen working on his farm in Southern Illinois he used to have me drive him into town once a month. I'd drive him to this whorehouse and he'd ask me to wait an hour – or two hours on a good day. He was eighty. He looked terrific. "Don't tell your grandmother," he'd say as I drove him home.

'My parents divorced when I was five. My mother remarried a man named Fitzgerald and that's what I was called before the bullshit department renamed me Rock Hudson.'

'How badly did your parents' divorce affect you?'

'Well I loved my daddy and one day he wasn't there.'

That thought visibly pained him. He went on: 'I never enjoyed being a young man. I never went to the beach. Never went to parties. Those were the Dark Ages for me. I didn't know anybody. I had no friends. All this was happening when I should have been going out, having a ball, sowing my wild oats.' He laughed loudly at what those words implied.

'Let's dispose of a few myths that probably offend you...'

'No let's give 'em some more!' He declared with a savage grin. 'Oh, Christ. Sure it offends me. If people want to think that way they're gonna think that way. I'm not going to waste my time trying to prove myself, for Christ's sake. What am I supposed to do? Take some broad on the stage and invite everybody to watch? I suppose it goes back to Louis B Mayer in the thirties, anybody that the studio was backing or pushing. Their public image demanded that a young man always had to be seen with a beautiful girl. A young girl had to be with a good-looking guy. So the accent was on never going alone; never go anywhere with somebody of the same sex. You and I could never go to a restaurant – there always had to be a beautiful girl in tow. Ladies lunch together, don't they? Does that make them lesbians? But to tell you the truth I no longer care. It used to hurt; it doesn't any more.'

'It was once said of you you're the man everybody loves but nobody knows. Is that true?'

'Yes.'

'Do you want to keep it that way?'

'Yes.'

'What would you most like to achieve in the future?'

The answer was a long time coming.

'Anonymity,' he said finally.

Too late. AIDS and the court case had turned celebrity into notoriety. In the year before he died, Hudson weighed barely seven stone. To see this gaunt, skeletal figure huddled in pyjamas and silk robe was a terrifying ordeal for the few friends who knew him in his matinée-idol years. The most frequent visitor was Elizabeth Taylor. It said much for her strength of will and devotion that she held back her tears until she was alone.

Rock Hudson died on 2 October 1985. He was 59. His body was cremated, the ashes scattered secretly at sea. Anonymity at last.

Rudolph Nureyev differed from Liberace and Rock Hudson in one essential: all three made headlines, but it was the fabulous Russian ballet dancer who made history. From the moment he made his spectacular leap to freedom in the West at a Paris airport in June 1961, he galvanised British ballet. He transformed its polite and sometimes prissy image into a visual and erotic turbulence, most memorably in that magical partnership with the late Margot Fonteyn. At their sensational debut at Covent Garden in 1962, they took 22 curtain calls. As one critic put it, 'The impact was as though a wild animal had suddenly entered a drawing room.' Whether or not Rudi was the greatest male ballet dancer since the legendary Nijinksy was irrelevant. This would be argued about for years over vodka in St Petersburg or coffee in Covent Garden. What no one would dare contest was that

Nureyev in his prime was the most awe-inspiring dancer of the century. All the uncompromising arrogance of his Russian blood was distilled in his performance. There was an audible gasp whenever he took that famous leap in which he appeared to loiter awhile before descending. He dominated, he took command; his proudly raised head, Slavonic glances and explicit body language totally hypnotised his audiences. 'Watching him dance', panted one bedazzled female at Covent Garden, 'is to feel one is present at an orgy.' (When I quoted this to him one day in Paris, he laughed aloud, asking mischievously, 'Did she say which ballet it was?') When he died, the one-minute silence observed by a hushed and tearful audience at Covent Garden was more significant than all the many ovations he was given in his lifetime.

I spent some hours with him on a studio set in Paris, where a film was being made of his life. One thing was obvious: Rudolph Nureyev was no closet gay. He would never have submitted to the Rock Hudson-style charade of pretended heterosexuality in order to project a bogus public image. For him, sexual orientation was one of the less important facts of life. His body was an instrument for all kinds of exciting expression in which the classical was infinitely more important than the biological. But mostly he preferred young males as his companions. A Tartar born and bred, he hated all convention – whether sexual, artistic, moral or political. It was this temperamental genius, remember, who once deliberately stamped on the foot of a male dancer who had offended him. He is also reported to have defecated in front of judges at an Italian arts festival because they had dared to award him a *second* prize. The message of that little demonstration was unmistakable: Rudolph Hametovich Nureyev, dancer, director and choreographer, born Razdolnaya, Lake Baikal, 17 March 1938, was second to no one. (On the weekend before I met him in Paris he had danced in TV's *Sunday Night at the London Palladium* to a standing ovation such as the world of ballet had never witnessed. 'It was good' was the most this ruthless perfectionist would say about it.)

Close up, Nureyev was a compelling figure. He could manipulate his deep-set eyes, flared nostrils, and wide sensuous mouth into a variety of expressions, from the gently disarming to the blazingly bad-tempered – notably when some manoeuvre was a tad short of perfection. He had something of Marlon Brando's brooding, Olympian disdain for the cheap or second-rate. But in his more genial mode, as he was that day in Paris in 1970, he was as gentle a Tartar as you'd ever meet on the Steppes.

'We Tartars', he explained, 'have much in common with untameable animals. Quick to catch fire, yet sometimes as cunning as a fox.' I reminded him that even his closest friends have said that he could also be 'a veritable sonofabitch'.

'*Bien sûr,*' he laughed, 'but isn't everyone a veritable sonofabitch at times?'

He was born, he told me, on a train. 'My mother was with child with me as she journeyed across Siberia.' There was a hint of sadness as he spoke about the family – he had three sisters – he was forced to abandon when he defected to the West.

The KGB never gave up trying to persuade him to return. 'I received many phone calls. There were threats, constant pressure and persuasion. I had so many nightmares. I dreamed often that I was being followed. Sometimes I was being shot.' Joan Thring, Nureyev's personal assistant and devoted friend, remembers when they were in Beirut. 'We could see Russian ships in the harbour. There were whispers of a possible kidnap attempt. Rudi had a bodyguard and I carried a revolver in my handbag.'

Nureyev had bitter memories of his home life. 'Home' was a single room of nine square metres shared by three families. Rudolf recalled 'constant, gnawing hunger'; a few pounds of potatoes had to last a week. His soldier father needed to sell his civilian clothes to buy food. Nureyev distinctly remembered fainting from hunger at kindergarten, and being teased by other children because he didn't have proper shoes or clothes.

A glimpse at his upper lip revealed a sizeable scar. 'I once fed a dog from my mouth,' he smiled. 'It taught me my very first lesson in life – never be kind to anyone.' A joke of course, since the one thing I learned from other dancers – male and female – was Rudi's extra-ordinary generosity as a coach, adviser and in the many opportunities he created for them. 'I live to dance, and dance to live,' he said. 'All I ask of my other dancers is that they do the same.'

That dedication brought him celebrity and riches beyond anything he might have dreamed of in that crowded one-room home beneath the Ural Mountains. After 27 years the hard-faced authorities finally allowed him a fleeting visit home; tragically, his mother was too ill to recognise him. Nureyev returned to Paris, heartbroken.

The essence of Nureyev's unrivalled hold on an audience was the fact that he appealed to both men and women with equal intensity. Gay pubs in London, Paris and New York displayed semi-nude posters of their hero. But there was equal adoration in the squeals of anticipation from the waiting women outside stage doors. 'He couldn't of course tell them he was gay,' an associate said, 'or how terribly lonely he was.' It was in that loneliness that Nureyev found his only solace – in the company of young men. Many recall this solitary figure in a long overcoat, swaddled in a scarf, prowling the dark deserted streets of Paris or Covent Garden. There was no doubt about his homosexuality or his promiscuity. He contracted HIV, which would develop into AIDS. But he insisted it be kept a secret. Rock Hudson had now become, in the words of one biographer, 'the poster-boy of AIDS. But Nureyev did not want to be identified by his illness.'

Put simply, he just wanted to go on dancing to the death. He continued to perform, even though those once sturdy footballer's calves could barely support him. Sometimes his performances were so technically poor there were some in the audience who demanded their money back. But for the majority it wouldn't have mattered how badly he danced. The moment he took the stage all bets were off. This was Rudolph Nureyev. It was enough that he was standing there. Even motionless he was magic. But at last this resolute Tartar found even walking beyond his powers. In 1991 his cherished partner and mentor, Margot Fonteyn, died of cancer. Between them, her classic elegance fused with his animal verve, they had conquered the world of ballet. Now she was gone and he was dying.

His last appearance in public was for his staging of *La Bayadère* at the Paris Opera. He had first appeared in 1960 with the famous Kirov Ballet. There was an almost audible sob as this frail legend with staring eyes walked down to the front of the stage supported by two principal dancers. The audience stood cheering, or visibly weeping.

Nureyev smiled with delight, bringing a hint of colour to his pallid features. The ovation seemed to give him strength. It was a magnificent though intensely moving farewell. Thinking back on our conversations in London and Paris, I can see that death and loneliness were constantly in his thoughts. More than once he said, 'We're born alone, we die alone.' And in his autobiography he wrote, 'Death is at the end of the road, one knows it, yet one continues along it.'

That journey began on a train crossing Siberia and ended in Paris on 6 January 1993. It was far too short. But no one can say it was not memorable.

CHAPTER NINETEEN

The African Queen – and the Ex-Marine

One of the pleasures of being an old campaigner is that you can look back at some memorable episode and say, 'I was there!' I was there at the opening of *Funny Girl* in New York when the newcomer Barbra Streisand, with an awesome display of raw talent, stole the show and the heart of Broadway. I was also at Number 21404 Pacific Coast Highway, California, when Lee Marvin, the former fighting Marine, relived his war in as savage a monologue as you wish you'd never heard. Both experiences were vastly different in essence, but equally shattering in their impact. For Lee Marvin, the battles were long past. Barbra Streisand's were yet to be faced. In the euphoria of that night on Broadway, this so-called 'ugly duckling' had stopped the show. An enthralled audience leaped to its feet. She turned those asymmetrical eyes up to the heavens and mouthed an unmistakable 'thank you.' She was 21.

Reviewers, this one included, ran out of the conventional superlatives. *Funny Girl* was not the greatest musical ever. But this multi-talented performer had brazenly used it as a shop window for all she had to offer – which was plenty. The ultimate accolade came from Frank Sinatra, who brushed past me backstage and hugged her, saying 'Magnificent. I love you.' Like Sinatra's, her voice had its own unique hallmark, defying imitations. But, if we seek comparisons, well, she sang with the heart-touching passion of a young Judy Garland, and when the numbers called for it, with the blazing rhythms of Lena

Horne or Peggy Lee, with Edith Piaf looking down approvingly from above. In texture, the voice had everything from the schmaltzy to the unashamedly raunchy; with a power range from murmuring tenderness to the full-throated Tannoy.

When I first met Streisand she was married to the actor Elliot Gould. They lived in an apartment high over the streets of Manhattan. I remember her standing there in a muu-muu, visibly ecstatic over her success and not noticeably displeased at being Barbra Streisand. Confronted by this glowingly mature female, I instantly forgave the kitsch decor – the black, patent-leather kitchen walls, the 300-year-old Jacobean bed with a built-in fridge; and the chewing-gum slot machine; just the sort of innocent indulgences you'd expect from the kid from Brooklyn who to her freckled-faced astonishment had suddenly conquered the world.

Any intimate participant in the early years of Barbra Streisand would have had a variety of reactions in which exasperation, agitation and consternation were all secondary to an overwhelming admiration. She had plenty to overcome as she clawed her way to an Oscar, an Emmy a Grammy and a Tony as a singer, actress, producer and director. The impresario Billy Rose dismissed her as a 'pushy little broad' and then handsomely recanted. It is true she earned a reputation for being difficult – an understatement for an uncompromising persona, which transmitted a message straight off the Brooklyn streets: 'I won't take crap from anyone.' Or as one battle-weary mogul at MGM declared, 'She's a man-eater. A regular ball-breaker. A female Orson Welles. She wants to control the picture, the timing, the editing, she wants it all. And I have to tell you, I'd give it to her. If you want Streisand you bite on the bullet. You did it with Marilyn. You do it with Brando. And you did it with Streisand. Period.'

So they 'bit on the bullet' with such films as *Funny Girl, Hello Dolly, On a Clear Day You Can See Forever* etc. with no toothache but plenty of dough.

Much of Streisand's so-called prima-donna histrionics were no more than self-protection and concern for her work; a form of self-defence in a jungle where only the toughest predators survive. When she was playing her assertively Jewish persona, there was an element of parody in it. She knew the stereotype and if you wanted Fanny Brice she could 'give it to you wholesale'. But she was quick to shed the Brooklyn image. As hip on Bach and Beethoven as she is on the blues, this intelligent woman would one day talk politics to American presidents and other leading world statesmen, with a deep consciousness of the troubled world around her. I saw elements of this on location in Kenya, where Streisand filmed scenes for *Up the Sandbox*. I'd covered many steamy safari epics and was intrigued at the thought of seeing Hollywood's gorgeous predator at work. Let's take a short digression into the jungle.

Ever since the first Tarzan swung from a tree emitting the Cry of the Great Ape, Hollywood has been obsessed with 'Darkest Africa'. That formula of lions, loincloths and lust has made the Bwanas of Burbank and Culver City very prosperous indeed. Not exactly in the Oscar class, they happily settled for such lesser souvenirs as elephant-foot doorstops and horn-handled back-scratchers. Dressed safari-style by Abercrombie and Fitch of New York, accessories courtesy Saks, Fifth Avenue, they strode into the jungle hell-bent on finding Dr Livingstone or the source of the Nile. Gulping on their malaria pills, stomach pills, vitamin pills and salt pills, they were ready for the great experience. The call of the wild. Almost invariably the storyline of their films has the white hunter coolly dropping a charging rhino with one shot as the cowardly husband flees, and the disillusioned wife (38, 22, 36) softly asks the hero, 'Is there room for two under your mosquito net?' Or,

> 'Stand perfectly still,' he commanded as the tarantula inched slowly up her thigh. Then with a flash of his hand and a stamp of his boot it lay dead at her feet. She felt a strange dizziness. Less than a week ago she was just a bored biology teacher from Boston; now every fibre of her being yearned for the rough passion of his embrace. It was madness, and yet...

Admittedly, the genre has come a long way since those primitive 'Me Tarzan, you Jane' days. *African Queen*, *Mogambo*, *Snows of Kilimanjaro*, *Out of Africa* were but a few of the epics that made fortunes for the fearless producers who risked everything to bring the film back alive. Installed in tented, four-star encampments, strictly off-limits to anything that roared, hissed, charged or stung, this was Nature in the raw. Here was Africa at its most primitive: brightly hued Cadillacs gliding silently through the trees; the droning hum of electric generators; the mating call of a full-breasted starlet in the undergrowth – all beautifully evoked by Mr Sol Lesser, Mr Sy Weintraub, Mr Sam Spiegel and other intrepid Bwanas of that ilk.

But I suspected that all would be different when Barbra Streisand betook herself to Africa back in June 1972. And I was right. Dressed African style in a swaddling of colourful robes, beads and cartwheel earrings, she relished every moment of this African adventure. She wanted to know everything about the music, the customs and the lifestyle of the women of Samburu, Kenya, where the film unit was located. But there was one appallingly crass moment when the girl from Pulaski Street, Brooklyn, revealed some of the anger that could send subordinates fleeing to the hills. She was told that one hundred Hebrew National sausages had been shipped from a New York deli and were now awaiting collection at Nairobi airport. The genius responsible for the stunt had planned to hand out these kosher frankfurters to a hundred selected 'warriors' taken from the local tribesmen. He also calculated that Miss Streisand, born and raised in a nice Jewish home, would be amused by the gesture. The fury in her slightly diagonal eyes told him she was not. She pointed out icily that (1) the Samburu 'warriors' did not eat meat, (2) that this was 'the most tasteless, offensive, humiliating stunt, she'd ever heard of, and (3) 'Those hot dogs stay where they are at the airport.' Since it was her company that was producing the film, it was She Who Must Be Obeyed. But, fortunately for the hapless press agent, Barbra was quick to forgive. She was too enthralled by everything around her. An insatiable explorer, Barbra wanted to devour everything she could about Africa: the smells, the colours, the strange melancholy of the music, the high-pitched harmony of the women's voices over the beating of the drums.

Sired by the late Emmanuel Streisand who had a PhD in education at Columbia University, Barbra had – still has – a voracious appetite for knowledge. She demands answers. She wasn't just fascinated by the costumes and exotic makeup of the ultra-beautiful Senegalese dancers hired for the film. At one point she asked one of them to put some of the dancer's blue eye makeup on her own eyelids. 'She broke a twig from a tree,' Barbra explained, 'took a long thread from her husband's skirt, made like a Q-tip, broke off a piece of soft-blue rock, spat on it and put that on my eye with the Q-tip. Now I put all my eye shadow on that way.' (Eminently marketable, I would have thought, given a skirted husband, a chunk of rock and spit.)

Soon Barbra and the dancers were doing what many women do in these situations. They gave each other freedom of the wardrobe. Streisand, as excited as a child, allowed herself to be costumed, necklaced and turbaned in the style of an African princess. Given her own Nilotic features, the Nefertiti comparison became irresistible. Standing there, shielded from the blazing equatorial sun by her personal umbrella man, Streisand blended superbly into the African setting. Of course, good manners obliged her to offer the Senegalese troupe reciprocal hospitality. They homed in on her *haute couture* with the discrimination you would expect from sophisticated artistes used to staying at the George V in Paris or the Dorchester in London.

It had been only eight years since I first saw her on the Broadway on stage in her sensational *Funny Girl*. Now, here in Africa, there was a more thoughtful Streisand. It was early evening when we sat down to talk. It was the sort of perfect African sunset film cameramen pray for, the stillness broken only by the splash of a crocodile sliding down into the river. 'This place teaches you the absolute lunacy of possessions. Look at these people. They prove that extreme poverty does not mean unhappiness, and I've had plenty of that. We have our inhibitions and sexual hang-ups but that's no big deal to them. To them it is natural and innocent. They own nothing except themselves. I can't wait to unload all the fancy things I've bought over the years. If I feel the need I can always go visit a museum.'

Everything about Barbra Streisand then, and now, underscores the immensity of her achievements. Whether, as some claim, she was the most popular female vocalist in the world is irrelevant. What matters is that she has always been a class act with all that goes to make a

legend. Not all her films were great but she was terrific in most of
them. Moreover, despite those asymmetrical features, which I admit I
had my fun with, she was always a joy to look at. Whoever it was who
likened her profile to that of an anteater should have seen, as I did,
this African Queen standing proud in the gold-tinted sunset. My
admiration must have shown. Her warm but mocking smile
acknowledged it. She went into her teasing mode.

'I think I'm terribly graceful and sensuous, don't you?'

'I do.'

'Then say so.'

'I will.'

Barbra returned to Hollywood via Tel Aviv. She met the Israeli
leader Golda Meir. The two hit it off immediately like a couple of
cousins from Brooklyn. This was Barbra demonstrating political rather
than spiritual interests. She helped George McGovern in his
presidential campaign, appearing in a fundraising concert in the Los
Angeles Forum. She would do the same for Bill Clinton as well as
campaign for other causes that concerned her. Subconsciously
perhaps, everything she has achieved seemed designed to honour the
father she barely knew. The Oscar and other major awards, not least
that highly personal film *Yentl*, missed that one ecstatic element – 'not
bad, eh, Pop for your homely looking kid from Pulaski Street?'

But there were compensations, not least of which is her son, named
Jason Emmanuel, thus perpetuating her father's subliminal influence
in her life. She is sixty now, and happily married to the actor James
Brolin. Their secluded life in Malibu is shrieks away from the sensual
adventures of Streisand's earlier relationships. After her divorce from
Elliot Gould, Barbra's friendships covered a lively spectrum, which
included the Canadian premier Pierre Trudeau for dinner and Ryan
O'Neal for breakfast. Jon Peters, the semi-delinquent who became in
turn a fashionable hairdresser, then successful producer, moved in for
a while. The relationship had all the scorching overtones you would
expect from a union between a half-Italian half-Cherokee ex-reform
school tearaway and the spirited fighter from Brooklyn. (A close friend
of Barbra told me how she was forced to intervene during one of their
spats by stubbing a lighted cigarette on his backside.) The actor Don

Johnson was a welcome change from the Peters's roller coaster. Her husband James Brolin, and the wisdom accumulated as a singer, actress, political campaigner, wife and mother, have brought this superstar a fair degree of tranquillity. But hold the lights and keep those cameras turning. The scripts are still coming in, and there's music in the air.

Drive down from the Streisand homestead at Malibu and you hit the Pacific Coast Highway, which follows the coast four hundred miles north to San Francisco. The villas hidden behind the palms and dense foliage look fairly nondescript from the road. That is because all the 'action' is on the beach beyond. Here is where Hollywood goes barefoot and walkabout at weekends. The 'beach house at Malibu' is a status symbol of some magnitude. An invitation to Sunday brunch at one of the more exclusive hideaways on the Pacific raises you above the serfs. Conversation over the Bloody Marys, hot dogs or pastrami on rye is mainly concerned with 'trade talk': who is making which film, with what star and for how much money – $30 million merely the opening bid for some of Hollywood's most bankable stars. But there was no such shoptalk when I was last at Number 21404 Pacific Coast Highway.

The man who lived inside was the actor Lee Marvin. He was as flawed a superstar as ever wrecked a fancy dinner party or drank his way to lesser glory. But he was a legend nonetheless. Whatever role he played, whether the lead or supporting, the actor was so blazingly effective his sometimes more distinguished co-stars just prayed the audience would remember they too were there. Complex, intimidating with an almost contemptuous self-assurance, Marvin possessed the essential personality bait that hooked an audience – of thousands or of one. The face, with its hard bony features, looked like a reject from Mount Rushmore. But once seen, never forgotten. His violent screen persona became all the more threatening because of the laconic, loose-mouthed grin that was its trademark. You would of course have had to have seen *The Wild One, The Caine Mutiny, Bad Day at Black Rock, The Dirty Dozen* and *Point Blank* to appreciate the subtle mind behind those Cro-Magnon features. But then there was *Paint Your Wagon, Cat Ballou* and *Monte Walsh* to confirm that tenderness, humour and sensitivity were also part of his acting resources. His power was generated from a lean, taut, physical dominance. From the hard high battlement of his forehead and the basilisk grin, down to his combat boots, he was always in control. For more than twenty years he had been the definitive bully of the screen. Terrorising widows, taunting cripples, shooting, knifing, maiming and raping, he was the consummate psychopath. Off screen, it must be said, Marvin was no shrinking violet. His drinking escapades were notorious but colourful. Even when fully stewed he could bring a delicate touch to the proceedings. Only a man of sensitivity could, when confronted by a beauty at a party whose right breast had waywardly dropped out of its bra cup, gently reseat it on its plinth, then bow out like Raleigh from the first Elizabeth.

You may detect some grudging admiration in all this. You would be wrong. There is nothing grudging about it. Marvin stood high on my list of top-notch performers. The more so because I believe his talents were seriously underrated. There was far more to Marvin than his drunken-buffoon image conveyed. He was certainly in the Bogart class as an actor. And like 'Bogie' he was the complete professional, always ready to work in the morning despite the social carnage of the night before. But he was also a man of considerable courage, winning a Purple Heart as a Marine in World War Two. Not surprising, perhaps, given that his father, Captain Lamont Marvin, served with the American Expeditionary Force in France in World War One. But the lineage had even more distinguished roots. Matthew Marvin became the first chief justice for the State of Connecticut. A General Seth Marvin fought with the North in the American Civil War. Ross G Marvin served with the great Arctic explorer Admiral Robert Edwin Peary on two polar expeditions, dying on the second in 1909. All impressive stuff set against the perceived image of the man I was visiting on the Pacific Coast Highway. Further surprises were imminent.

'The door's open. Come on in to the back deck. But don't make too much noise. I'm bird-watching.'

And there he stood, bent over the rail, eyes peering out over the Pacific. 'That bird, unless I am mistaken, is the lesser marbled godwit. Not to be confused', he warned, 'with the Hudsonian godwit.' He digressed momentarily to point out a *Baywatch*-type beauty on the beach with, 'That's the best piece of ass I've seen today,' then continued, 'And that is my favourite bird, the sandpiper. Hey, and there's another godwit.' This seemed a lot of godwit at the time, particularly since it emerged from the least likely ornithologist on the face of the earth. But probing further into Marvin's CV also revealed an expert knowledge of oceanography, marlin fishing and the history of warfare. A six-foot-three intimidating giant with an acerbic wit, Marvin was never going to be a screen idol in the Gable or Redford class. As he himself admitted, 'I'm not exactly the type of guy women throw themselves off the cliffs to get at.' Yet that most sophisticated French actress Jeanne Moreau – his co-star in *Monte Walsh* – would later rhapsodise, 'Lee Marvin is more male than anyone I have ever acted with. He is the greatest man's man I have ever met and that includes all the European stars I have worked with.' The fact that these ecstatic declarations followed hard on their famous love scenes in *Monte Walsh* may have just been a coincidence. The critic of the London *Spectator* noted that Marvin and Moreau 'have a presence, a palpable magnetism...'

A more persuasive testimony came from Michelle Triola, Marvin's Sicilian-French partner, who won a palimony suit against him – a landmark decision that sent America, Hollywood in particular, into shock. 'Jeanne was absolutely mad about Lee,' she insisted. As for the actor himself, it was clear to me that he found the first lady of the French screen as intoxicating as anything he'd ever drunk in his life. The most intriguing aspect of it all was that, having cast them for the film, the producers decided it would be prudent to keep their unpredictable hellraiser away from Moreau as long as possible before the picture started. The danger, as the director William Fraker saw it, was that 'Lee might not feel comfortable with her; that he might just go off and get drunk and say something devastating as he does when he drinks – he's a killer – and she would say, "Well fuck you, Monsieur Marvin" and walk off.' In the event, the two stars stood face to face, and measured each other to their evident mutual satisfaction.

Betty Ebeling, Marvin's first wife, recognised the intelligent and thoughtful individual behind that somewhat uncouth image. A tall slim woman with auburn hair, she had the sort of elegance that made men guard their language. A music graduate of UCLA, she had composed the music for several theatrical productions. They had met by accident. Left stranded alone at a party – her escort had ditched her for an eager starlet – she asked Marvin to give here a lift home. She discovered that he was far more gentle and soft-centred than, say, *Bad Day at Black Rock* suggested. For his part, Marvin detected the warm, vibrant woman behind the gown-and-mortar-board reserve. However, their marriage in Las Vegas, as related to me by the bride, suggested a brief reversion to Marvin's screen persona. You've seen similar episodes in a score of Hollywood films.

Halfway along the nine-hour drive to Vegas they pulled into a filling station. Marvin went to the men's room, came out with a fresh shirt and tie on. 'Here comes the bridegroom,' he warbled. It was around ten o'clock when the bridal pair drove on to the garishly lit main street of the gambling town. They stopped outside the Wee Kirk o' the Heather, that nuptial phenomenon of Nevada – on offer, the fastest wedlock in the west. In the best tradition of those old Universal comedies, they hammered on the door of the kirk. It was opened by the sleepy-eyed incumbent in a nightshirt. You would just know that his name was the Reverend Loveable.

'We want to get married,' Marvin said.

'So I figured,' yawned the Rev. Loveable. 'You got witnesses?' Lee looked blankly at Betty as though it was her fault. She did the packing.

'OK, no witnesses,' the reverend said wearily. 'I'll have to get the wife.'

Mrs Loveable was asleep. 'Wake up, honey,' her husband announced close to her ear. 'We got a wedding.'

'A wedding,' Mrs Loveable intoned as she rolled out of bed. She threw a muu-muu over her head but flatly refused to be seen. 'I'll witness from behind a screen.'

The ceremony began, Lee and Betty standing in front of the Rev. Loveable, a pair of aged, pallid insteps inside slippers being all that was visible of the witness. The reverend went through his routine, not too articulately as Betty Marvin remembered it.

'When it was over Lee kissed me and said, "Well I don't think I could have done better..." and that was that.' Well not quite. On the drive back to Los Angeles their headlights picked up a soldier walking erratically along the highway. Lee jammed on the brakes. 'Wanna ride with us?' enquired ex-PFC Marvin of the US Marines. The soldier grinned like the happy drunk he was. 'Get close,' Lee said to Betty. She rested her head on Lee's shoulder and fell asleep. The soldier rested his head on Betty's shoulder and also fell asleep. The bridegroom, sleep-starved and emphatically juiced, craned forward trying to focus on the road, or just focus. There were two priorities: to get the drunken warrior back to his regiment and his new bride into bed. In that order. Marvin jettisoned his tottering comrade at a bus station. The two men embraced, slapping each other's back as a sliver of sun glinted over the distant hills. 'You'd have thought they were the ones who'd got married,' Betty laughed. 'When we got home Lee was too pooped to carry me over the threshold,' she remembered, 'and I was too pooped to care.'

The records show that they lived happily, but not for ever, after. Betty began to find the worst side of Marvin, the drunken buffoonery in particular, too exhausting to live with. But the divorce after fourteen years of marriage was dignified, with both parties striving to be as generous as they could be to each other. By contrast, the palimony case brought by the mistress exploded into Hollywood history and revolutionised the entrenched laws of marriage and divorce in the USA. More particularly, it established a 'rights for mistresses' charter, which would make the cost of clandestine love even more bruising than your good old-fashioned alimony. This was the historic achievement of Michelle Triola, the dark, attractive daughter of a French mother and Sicilian father. This sexy, large-eyed 'chanteuse' at the smarter supper clubs had hit big in Las Vegas, singing the blues at the plush casino hotels like the Sands and the Riviera. It was this that brought her a small part in *Ship of Fools*, where she met Lee Marvin. They met often, traded heartaches, and the affair began. It ended when, to everyone's surprise, but mostly Michelle's, Lee suddenly decided to marry a former childhood sweetheart, Pamela Feeley. 'It absolutely destroyed me,' Michelle said. Well, not absolutely. She composed herself sufficiently to call that astute Beverly

Hills attorney Marvin Mitchelson. He issued a suit on her behalf which Hollywood's extra-curricular lovers must have seemed sacrilegious, namely, 'that though she lived with, but did not marry Marvin, she was still entitled to all the rights of a legally divorced wife' (which at the time meant half his assets).

The case with all its intimate and juicy revelations spared no one, least of all the two main contestants Marvin and Michelle. In essence the scenario of Mitchelson's suit went something like this:

> Beautiful young singer with promising career falls hopelessly in love with big, tough, famous actor. She gives up glittering future to be his long-suffering mistress, nursing his hangovers, hiding his liquor, enduring his wild eccentricities, aborting her pregnancies, all out of selfless devotion to the man whose name she had proudly adopted. And now discarded like an old glove, she was merely asking for fair and decent recompense...

Judge Arthur K Marshall didn't quite see it that way. His ruling, on 18 April 1979 was a triumph of judicial whimsy, leaving everybody wondering who had won. He decided that Michelle Triola Marvin had not established that a contract existed between her and the actor during the time they lived together. So she would not get the million and a half dollars plus she had demanded. Instead he awarded her $104,000 for 'rehabilitation purposes so that she may... re-educate herself and return from her status as a companion of a motion picture star to a separate... but perhaps more prosaic existence'. (The word 'prosaic' never surfaced in my recollections of this outspoken, glinting-eyed mistress.) The Marvin-versus-Marvin case, the longest-running spectacular in public linen-laundering, certainly raised the status of the live-in mistresses across the United States. Palimony is now accepted as a just compensation for mistresses who are wives in everything but name. I met Betty Marvin years later. She still talks about her life with Marvin with affection. Michelle Triola also has no hard feelings. 'Lee is a good guy,' she said through the mandatory tears outside the courtroom.

Lee Marvin died of a heart attack on 29 August 1987. He was 63. Too young to die, especially for an Oscar-winning actor who still had untapped resources to bring to the screen. But Marvin, who was badly injured in the war against the Japanese in the Pacific, was sanguine about his mortality and considered 'anything over forty is gravy'. It is almost exactly thirty years since I heard him say it on his veranda looking out on to the ocean. But it was the monologue that followed that I could never get out of my mind. It lasted for almost two hours. This was no longer an interview. Marvin was reliving his war and describing it with lacerating accuracy. I had asked him about his Purple Heart and how much he remembered of the action. 'You don't want to know,' he said with a harsh laugh.

'Try me,' I said. The tall, white-haired figure in blue jeans and heavy brown combat boots pulled a chair round to face me. He lit a cigarette and poured a drink. And began speaking. Outside, the limos from Beverly Hills or Bel Air were slotting into the ocean driveways like racehorses into their stalls. Bloody Marys were being mixed, jazz music wafted over the murmur of the waves. But inside 21404 Pacific Coast Highway it was the sound of one man talking, naming places now carved into the granite of American military history. Eniwetok, Kwajalein, Garrapan, Challantanoa and a 'bitch of a mountain' on Saipan called Tapotchau. Twenty thousand Marines, including Lee Marvin, slipped into rubber boats 1,500 yards off the beaches all wondering in the bright moonlight whether they would see another dawn. Then, as the second hands on blue-lit watches hit their mark, the paralysing bombardment made a multicoloured abstract of the sky. Marvin began.

We went in on Yellow Beach Two', he said. 'It was now dawn on the first day. On a beach south of a place called Challantanoa. We clawed forward and hit the basic scrub of the beach. Beyond it were those big open fields, thousands of sticks with sake bottles on top. My assumptions then were that they were used as insulators for wires that had been knocked down. But I was wrong. The Japs were using them as artillery markers. They had us nicely pinpointed on a checkerboard. They didn't miss. They just knew all these points we were on and started cranking in there. The artillery got very bad and all the bombing was coming down real heavy.

We finally got to a very large trench, I'd say about eight hundred yards inland. So we bailed into the trench and were just sitting there thanking God for this kind of cover when I noticed that the parapets of the trenches forward of us had firing slits and it dawned on me they belonged to them, not us. I happened to say this when they started opening up at us all along the trench.

So then the night came and we were very thinned out. There were only about thirty yards between them and us. They could have walked across and traded Sukiyaki. We lost quite a few that night. The next day we pushed towards Aslito airfield [re-named Isely field after its capture]. We got pinned down and lost some more guys going through those cane fields. We were pulled out and on the fourth morning we were heading up into what was called Death Valley and it looked it. We had to push up this mountain Tapotchau [an extinct volcano, rough limestone most of the way up to its summit at 1,554 feet]. Well, the mountain looked OK, I mean if you lived that long you could probably get to the top. Looked simple, really. But nobody could get up far enough to lick the bastard. They sent one company in and they lost a pile of men real rapidly. The residue was pulled back and they sent our company in. I was the point man of the assault company so I went with this guy Mike Harrison. We all climbed and suddenly Mike got nailed right under the heart or through the lung, most likely the lung because it was pink blood, you know. He went down and I didn't know for sure what to do, but anyway I stuck my finger in the hole to try to stop whatever it was that was coming out. But he was probably dead. We both had Browning automatics. I started firing at whatever was coming at us which was difficult when you've got one finger stuck in a guy's chest.

The Nips were hitting us with machine-gun fire at point-blank range. So then the captain shouted to fall in but I couldn't get in myself. We'd just got into a kind of knot, caught dead in an ambush, and, Jesus Christ, it was just decimation. We had started out with 247 men and fifteen minutes later there were six of us, 'I' Company, Third Battalion, 24th Marines. So anyway it was my turn to get nailed. There are two parts of your body in view to the

enemy when you flatten out – your head or your ass. If you present
one you get killed. If you raise the other, you get shot in the ass.
I got shot in the ass. I said 'Oh Jesus,' and I just came out of
rhythm. Then this guy knocked me in the ass, or spine, or
whatever. All I knew was I bounced off the ground and said, 'Jesus
Christ, I'm hit!' And somebody shouted, 'Shut up, we're all hit!'
'But *I'm* hit, don't you understand?'

Marvin creased up as he recalled the fine distinction he was making.

Then the ammunition dumps start blowing and we're getting
out. I wasn't sure I could move. You know how these things work.
You're stunned from the neck down. You start on your big toe first
and work up to your ankle, then your crotch, and maybe it's going
to be OK. They dumped some salt on my ass and the MO's big
bandages. He said, "Raise up so I can tie it." But there were
twenty-seven gun emplacements opening up on our position. With
all that shit flying around I am not lifting myself a sixteenth of an
inch higher than I need to.

We got to a clearing, must have been about twenty feet across
– say from maybe here to the kitchen – and it was a fire path ... and
I knew there was no way I could crawl across because I couldn't
move my legs ... I got behind this great big tree and figured, boy,
that's something at least. And there was a guy sitting behind it by
the name of Rose. He used to dye his underwear pink, you know.
He was just sitting there like there was no war at all. He said,
'Would you like some water?' I said, 'Jesus, yes.' So he leaned out
to get his canteen up. He gave me a gulp and as he leaned out to
put it back in again he got hit. He just went 'Oh' and fell right on
top of me. He was dead but he kept looking at me.

The stretcher bearers eventually take me away, and I get put
down on a real bed. Then a guy comes along and asks me, 'Would
you like some ice cream?' I'm lying there with a nine-inch hole in
my ass, souped up on morphine and he's offering me a dish of ice
cream, and – would you believe it? – 'Moonlight Serenade' is being
played somewhere on the piano. So then it all came in on me and

I started to cry. Yep, I was weeping because I felt like a coward, a deserter I guess. I felt just like I'd thrown down my rifle and run. That wasn't the way it was but, what with the morphine and the 'Moonlight Serenade', anyway I wept. Then I fell asleep. And that was about it.

But not quite. There were the thirteen months in different hospitals involving treatment for the severed sciatic nerve. It was in a hospital at Guadacanal that he was handed his Purple Heart. The memories hit him occasionally, 'like an exploding neutron in my mind'. Anything could trigger them off. A glance at a souvenir... the gold tooth he had off a Japanese soldier he'd killed, a vision of the face of the Marine sergeant he idolised. In those moments solace came sometimes from just looking out at the ocean, but most often from a bottle. Who would have denied him that?

Lee Marvin had a kind of craggy decency that was admired and respected as much by the profession as by his two wives and the eight children – four fathered, four acquired.

I drove away from the beach feeling emotionally concussed. I wondered whether even Norman Mailer at the height of his prose could have caught as shatteringly as Marvin did the deadly flavour of battle. I doubt if there's a plaque on the house at 21404 Pacific Coast Highway honouring the soldier, actor and sometime bird-watcher who lived there.

But there should be.

CHAPTER TWENTY

The Ultimate Legend

Well, we have seen the best, many of whom were great. But who were the greatest, and who decides? Self-evidently, the public who buy the tickets. As we saw earlier, 'Bums on seats' was how the late Laurence Olivier described to me his yardstick of success. By that test all the disparate performers arrayed in the earlier chapters were indisputably great. But none would have dared to have said so. Only those with a direct line to the Almighty or with an Olympian belief in their invincibility would have had the chutzpah to call themselves 'the greatest'. (That word, 'chutzpah', now part of the language, has best been defined by the late and highly gifted drama critic Kenneth Tynan as 'the untranslatable Jewish word that means cool nerve and outrageous effrontery combined ...' Well, he gave a pretty good demonstration of it himself with his show *Oh Calcutta!*. 'Outrageous effrontery' about summed it up. It was billed as 'An Evening of Elegant Eroticism' and Tynan, self-styled as the 'thinking man's voyeur', was furious with the negative reaction of many critics, me included. I headlined my review GARBAGE ON 12TH STREET much to Mr Tynan's displeasure. This taught me never to criticise a critic.)

But there was one supremely gifted performer who did have the nerve to describe himself as the greatest. That paragon was Muhammad Ali. He is not only a sports legend but was also one of the most respected boxers in history. Today, leading statesmen, including Bush, Blair and Nelson Mandela, are proud to shake his hand. Now painfully stricken with Parkinson's disease, he still contrives a smile and a faltering humour as he campaigns on behalf of others of life's victims. I always wanted to meet him. Boxing was out of my territory. But great is great. And the ability to pack a cinema, a theatre or a stadium requires the same dynamic – a magnetism that is exciting, unique and totally personal. So I set out to tackle this amiable and handsome giant, now a proud and dedicated follower of Islam. He was then (August 1967) heavyweight champion of the world. As Cassius Clay, as he danced on the resin under floodlights, his was close to being the greatest show on earth. But as Muhammad Ali, self-styled minister of the lost-found nation of Islam, he was far more circumspect.

To get to this 'mountain' it was necessary to go via Muhammad. Two Muhammads in fact. The first, Michael Muhammad in London, quizzed me closely on the phone. 'I would like to know why you wish to see Muhammad Ali. Also I wish to hear your voice.' I passed this hurdle, only to be further interrogated by a Mr Herbert Muhammad in Chicago. I received the 'pass friend' from him as well, which finally brought Muhammad Ali to my hotel entrance in Beverly Hills, but significantly not across the threshold. He sat yawning in the noon sunlight, a matchstick in his lower teeth. The biceps bulged through the sleeves of his grey flannel suit. Without his gum shield and the ringside haze of cigar smoke, he was clearly a very handsome animal indeed. This fact was not lost on a swoon of admiring females who leaned over our car begging for autographs. I recall one over-painted twittering female, her spectacles visibly steaming up, shrieking, 'Oh, you're just a living doll. I just gotta have your autograph. You can write it on my thigh if you like.'

'Oh Lord o'mercy,' grinned Ali, then a womaniser of some renown.

The banter was as misleading as his footwork in the ring. There was, and still is, a serious-minded character behind that mischievous, teasing persona. He stood accused at the time of being a draft dodger, refusing to go to Vietnam because of his Islamic beliefs. Nobody repeats that charge today. I certainly didn't buy it at the time. Walking with him through the largely black sections of Los Angeles as he kissed the kids, shook scores of hands and exchanged the occasional

Salaam aleichum I sensed this was no act. This was the genuine article. And no amateur at the spoken word: 'I'm happy, Allah's happy, Elijah Muhammad's happy because I'm standing up for what I believe. I got empty pockets now, but I'm a man. Better than having a million dollars and be "boy". Everywhere I go people recognise me, wanna help me. This car don't belong to me. I got brothers everywhere wanting to help me. I don't pay no hotel bills. My brothers provide the air tickets I need. Wherever I go the women prepare food for me. I'm getting' good and fat on food my followers cook for me. I've been invited to 25 Muslim countries. Kings have offered me their daughters in marriage...'

At which point this far from reticent hero went into overdrive about racial differences. I suspect he is more politically correct on that subject today. But on that sunny afternoon in Los Angeles we had, 'I'm learning that you can't mix the races. A tiger don't wanna know from mixing with a hyena. A lion don't wanna mix with a giraffe. And where do they get all this stuff about the black man being inferior? The blacker the berry the sweeter the juice. White sugar ain't good for nobody but brown sugar is healthy. They're trying to draft me and whup a million-dollar home. Well they can't whup me and they can't whup Allah. I'm proud you come to see me. Come to see me as Muhammad Ali, break my bread and hear my words. Am I gonna preach tonight? Yes sir! Am I gonna teach these people to be proud they're black? Yes sir! And now I'm gonna prepare my sermon.'

Beside me, in the back of the air-conditioned Cadillac with ivory telephone to hand, he began scribbling some notes. A smile broadened occasionally on those noble features. Then he read aloud, trying the sermon on for size: '"Then the Lord he asked Lot to save people from sinning like at Sodom and Gomorrah. But then Lot kicked the bucket so the Lord called on Noah to build him an ark to save the good people two by two but then Noah kicked the bucket so the Lord calls on Moses, but then Moses ups and kicks the bucket. And now there's evil upon the land and..."'

'That's good,' I said by way of ringing the bell. He said, 'It'll knock 'em cold' – which it did.

Boxer, preacher, poet and idol to men, women and especially children – if Muhammad Ali considered himself the greatest, who are we to argue?

Hollywood has always suffered a disproportionate amount of 'stick' usually from cynics, bitchy commentators and the just plain jealous: seventy-two suburbs in search of a city... a great place if you happen to be an orange... a city with all the personality of a paper cup...a trip through a sewer in a glass-bottomed boat... a place where you can be forgotten while you're out of the room going to the toilet...

But despite the gibes the 'dream factory' has bewitched the billions with its magic and created the legends who continue to enthral the world. Nothing defines their stature more incisively than their obituaries. (George Bernard Shaw said it better: 'Life levels all men. Death reveals the eminent.') I have written scores of such eulogies over the years. Some pieces were much harder to write than others. It was impossible to write about Judy Garland without a jolt of anger at the way she was hurt and exploited during her most troubled years. Marilyn Monroe presented other difficulties. There was much we suspected about her White House connections but it was a minefield journalists entered at their peril. So we wrote more about her sorrows than any of her sins, if indeed these ever existed. Cary Grant too earned himself a kind of diplomatic immunity. He was just too nice a guy for us to reveal – in his lifetime – the appalling hang-ups and family nightmares hidden behind the warmest smile in the west.

Most public figures, superstars in particular, have skeletons uncomfortably locked away in closets, even such unlikely candidates as Henry Fonda and Bing Crosby. But no such skeletons emerged to tarnish the incomparable image of the late Fred Astaire. When it comes to assessing this skinny, chinny phenomenon, it is prudent to toss all of Mr Roget's superlatives out of the window. That he was a dancing genius was never disputed, even by the great ballet stars of his generation. Robert Helpmann, Margot Fonteyn, Baryshnikov and Nureyev have all declared him to be the best, worshipping the ground he tapped on. What Nureyev told me he most admired about Fred was the originality of his choreography, the brilliant ideas behind those astonishing dance routines. But more than his dancing – and that spellbinding partnership with Ginger Rogers – was the happiness he purveyed in his monkey-faced grin, the easy, rubber-soled walk, and the sunshine in his songs. The musicals he brought to the world of motion pictures will keep his jaunty image alive into the next millennium.

Roberta, Top Hat, Easter Parade, The Story of Vernon and Irene Castle, The Barkleys of Broadway, Daddy Long Legs, Let's Dance, Funny Face, Silk Stockings – what a drab world it would have been without these singing, dancing masterpieces.

Then, when he could no longer hoof it as of yore, there were the more serious acting roles, like *On the Beach* and *The Towering Inferno*.

Throughout all his work he demonstrated the basic essentials of greatness: class, taste, finesse and style. He received an Academy Award in 1949 'for his unique artistry and his unique contribution to the techniques of motion pictures'. Leaving aside the glaring inadequacy of the tribute, it's worth recalling what the studio talent scout famously said of his first screen test: 'Can't act. Can't sing. Slightly bald. Can dance a little.'

The only meeting of any substance I had with him was at a party at the Beverly Wilshire Hotel. It was Ginger Rogers who piloted me over to the great man then left us both to talk. But not for long. 'I'd like very much to have a quiet chat with you some time,' I said.

'Why?' he asked.

'Well, for one thing, you're Fred Astaire.'

'So they tell me,' he laughed. But ever the gentleman he went on to explain, 'Look, I dance. I talk better with my feet. You probably know more about me than I do!' End of interview. I tried again at the racetrack. He tipped the winner but nothing about himself. I tried again on the golf course and he claimed I was putting him off his game. I did know of course that he was born Frederick Austerlitz Jr in Omaha, Nebraska, the son of a disgraced Austrian Army officer who came to America for an easier life. The date was 10 May 1899 – Queen Victoria was still alive and the nine-year-old Russian ballet prodigy Nijinsky was already practising vertical take-offs. In the early years it was Fred's elder sister Adele who was in the spotlight. She was a brilliant child dancer. Fred began to dance only when her teacher offered a package deal for the two of them. They became a double act in vaudeville doing their tap and soft-shoe shuffles around the major circuits. They brought their act to England and became the darlings of British royalty. It was the famous David O Selznick who saw Astaire's potential, observing shrewdly, 'I'm a little uncertain about the man. But I feel in spite of his enormous ears and bad chinline his charm is so tremendous that it comes through...'

It came through all right – mostly in top hat, white tie and tails – carrying with it those dream partners Ginger Rogers, Rita Hayworth, Cyd Charisse, Vera Ellen and Leslie Caron. But Fred became increasingly embarrassed about his baldness. He hated wearing a toupee. After completing *Blue Skies*, he flung off the hairpiece in front of the entire company and stamped on it. 'Never, never, never, never will I wear that blasted rug again.' But never is a long time in show business. When further romantic roles beckoned, that rug was brushed and dusted and ready for action.

When his first wife, Phyllis, died after 21 years of marriage – she was only 46 – Astaire vowed he would never marry again. But then, at the age of eighty, the old charmer took a fancy to a pretty young female jockey less than half his age named Robyn Smith. He died six contented years later. Hollywood honoured him as they did Clark Gable, as a king. The eulogies would have pleased him. But not quite as much as that verdict of the studio talent scout.

Maybe it was the way he did it.

Hollywood's greatest classics were made by film directors who, by tyranny or gentle persuasion, drew the best out of their stars. They were celebrities in their own right: Alfred Hitchcock, John Huston, George Stephens, Sidney Lumet, Vincent Minnelli, Josh Logan, William Wyler, and of course the late Billy Wilder, an Austro-Hungarian immigrant whose film classics included *Sunset Boulevard*, *Ace in the Hole*, *The Seven Year Itch*, *Witness for the Prosecution*, *The Apartment* and *Some Like it Hot*. (He was an uncompromising genius with a wicked tongue. I remember telling him in a supermarket on Santa Monica Boulevard in Beverly Hills that a mutual friend, the author Willi Frischauer, had committed suicide. 'Bloody fool!' was his only comment as he wheeled his groceries to his car.) But Wilder's films – and scores of others of equal calibre – are now analysed and discussed like sacred texts at film schools the world over.

The same respect is being paid to the collected works of Steven Spielberg. Just take three of his films, *Duel, E.T.* and *Schindler's List*, and marvel at his unerring eye and ear for the sensitive and the sinister in the human condition. With almost awesome versatility – we think of Orson Welles – he produces one blockbuster after another. And pretty unassuming he is about it too. With his films raking in upwards of an incredible one million dollars a day, he is arguably the most successful filmmaker on Earth, Mars or wherever else he puts his little green men. It was this slightly built, bearded genius who also created *Jaws* and *Close Encounters of the Third Kind*, bringing envious studio moguls kowtowing all the way to his executive suite.

When I saw him just after *E.T.* had broken every box-office record, he bestrode Hollywood like a colossus. He is respected, envied, and certainly feared by many – but not, be assured, by his mother Leah. This slim, no-nonsense Momma ran a delicatessen restaurant only a burp or two away from her son's gigantic extraterrestrial empire. One night, five minutes after closing time, Steven, with a friend, arrived outside the restaurant door. The CLOSED sign was up. The man who could buy half the studios of Hollywood, with plenty left over to buy the other half, bent his head to the letterbox.

'Mom, this is Steve.'

'So?' responded the mother of the director.

'So open up, we're hungry.'

'Listen, in the studios you're the boss,' declared Mrs Spielberg. 'Here I am the boss. Closed is closed. Tea is all you'll get.'

This may have sounded a shade ungenerous from a mother whose devoted son bought her a second luxury apartment because the windows in the first one, she said, were too high. He also fixed it for her to have unlimited credit in Beverly Hills's most exclusive stores and jewellers. But this breezy, powerhouse of a woman, formerly a concert pianist, hardly uses the cards. In fact this chic feisty lady – she was then 62 – decided to run the restaurant, she told me, just to let her rich and famous son know she could make it on her own. But pride shone out of her expressive eyes as we discussed her son the genius, over my bowl of chicken soup. She talked glowingly on and on until the broth turned cold. But I was not about to complain. Smart men, like actors and writers who want to go on eating, complain to the management at their peril.

Leah Spielberg is prouder still of Steve's post-*Schindler* dedication to creating and maintaining a permanent and authoritative record of the Holocaust. The scale of the operation – hundreds of survivors were interviewed around the world – has been rightly acknowledged by leading statesmen. This, together with his unrivalled record as a filmmaker, put Spielberg high on the list of Hollywood 'greats'. What kind of a character could achieve so much so quickly?

The short answer: a video-game fanatic and confessed hypochondriac with a lurking fear of being stuck between floors in elevators. He also suffers from what he calls 'my nocturnal paranoid fantasy'. He has this recurring nightmare that while he's sleeping a flood will wash him and his house into the Pacific. Snakes, sharks, space invaders and things that go shriek in the night – these and other childhood fantasies made Spielberg a legend in his thirties.

His parents (they were later divorced) bought him a movie camera when he was eleven. His first action shot was when a pressure cooker in which his mother was making Cherries Jubilee exploded. In the frantic stampede for police, firemen and smelling salts young Spielberg's camera focused on the crimson globs spattered over the walls and floor. The blood-tinted ocean in *Jaws* owes a lot to Mrs Spielberg's Cherries Jubilee. When Ma and Pa asked him to film a family group standing proudly in front of their new convertible, all they got was an art-house shot of a shining hubcap. 'Who knew this was genius?' said Leah.

It was Steven who pointed me in the direction of his mother's kosher restaurant. 'You have to admit my mother is really something,' he beamed. 'Full of spit and fire, always walking into the wind, as determined as hell to be useful, needed. All my drive I get from her. The great thing about her was that she diverted her gaze, turned a blind eye to the sort of tricks I'd pull, where most American mothers would have played the heavy. It may not have worked for others, but it worked for me.'

Maybe it is because of Leah that Spielberg has given some of the top jobs in his empire to women. The producer, assistant director, art director and film editor on *E.T.* were all women. 'I relate better to women in a working sense than I do to men. I think in a way it's softened me. I felt like I was back in my mother's kitchen in Phoenix, Arizona, watching her make matzo balls, which are good to eat but they sink you to the bottom of the sea.'

The vast range of Spielberg's films reflect the extent and intensity of his inner beliefs. But in the lottery of motion pictures even the best have their failures and these include Chaplin and Orson Welles. While Spielberg's *Schindler's List* defined the nightmare of the Holocaust with almost unbearable insight, his attempt to reawaken the American consciousness about the brutality of the slave trade in *Amistad* was, at best, a splendid failure. Similarly, his attempt to take the gung-ho gloss off modern warfare in *Saving Private Ryan* was much sound and fury signifying little. What matters is that Spielberg is never afraid to tilt at windmills. He has the guts to ignore occasionally the tyranny of the box office. In that sense, failure becomes an essential element of greatness. But, no matter what major issues will engage him in the future, the child in Spielberg will ensure that kids will have plenty to gasp, cheer or weep over. Even as he slumbers his mind still wanders through the galaxy, conjuring up other creatures to plod, squelch or bleep their way into our lives. But by day he is a filmmaker who, by all the accepted criteria, is probably the best there is. Add to that his immensely important Holocaust archives, the Shoah Foundation, and you have all the elements of greatness. A legend for sure. Almost in the class of his mother's chicken soup...

Question: Was Laurence Olivier the greatest actor ever?
Answer: Does it matter?

What matters is that by any criteria this consummate artist was the ultimate legend. On stage he could hook the back of a gallery with a flash of his eyes alone. Everything about him, his body, his gestures and that most imitated voice in the world, held an audience with the tenacity of a pit-bull terrier. When it came to acting he could play every trick in the pack. Almost every aspiring young actor, Richard

Burton included, parodied those Agincourt histrionics in Henry V but did everything short of falling on their knees to catch the Master's eye. I never knew an actor who churned so much of himself, entrails included, into his performances. He tore into those classic triumphs *Richard the Third*, *Hamlet*, *Othello* and as Archie Rice in *The Entertainer*, with a frenzy that made his trembling supporting players wonder whether it was worth the sweat. They scarcely dared to breathe when this verbal colossus was at full spate.

I remember seeing that freeze-you-with-a-stare routine on a film set when some remark of dangerous familiarity had got beneath his skin. The actor Peter O'Toole, who had once been on the receiving end, described it as 'that grey-eyed myopic stare that can turn you to stone'. I got a hint of it personally only once over beer and sandwiches with Olivier at the National Theatre. I had suggested that as an actor he might have been influenced somewhat by his friend, the great Shakespearean actor Sir John Gielgud. That affable smiling mask slipped. 'Not so, my friend!' he said icily, 'I am under no one's influence but my own.' (He did admit to borrowing a bit here and there from other actors. 'I've stolen from the best. We actors shop around.')

But for all his apparent self-assurance, Olivier, prior to a performance, was occasionally paralysed with fear. Even after winning three Oscars, and more glittering prizes than he could house, he told me that if he vomited only once before a major performance he reckoned he was holding up pretty well.

But, off-stage or away from the film set, worse agonies drove this immensely likeable man to despair. These centred on the almost horrific battles that preceded the final breakdown of his marriage to the actress Vivien Leigh. We in the press had a fair notion of what was going on: her drinking, her affairs, her manic depression. At theatrical parties and in Green Rooms around the country, 'Larry's nightmare' was the favourite topic of conversation. But loyalty (if not the laws of libel) persuaded us to give Larry a kind of diplomatic immunity. Theirs had been the kind of courtship that only heaven and Barbara Cartland could have dreamed up. With those classic oval features and expressive, large, blue-grey eyes, Vivien was regarded as the most beautiful actress in the country if not the world. Olivier, the tall, dashingly handsome giant of the theatre, was, in her terms, a lover and husband to die for. But she was a wilful, man-hungry virago not all that different from her Scarlett O'Hara in *Gone With the Wind*. She was a flirtatious female whose teasing eyes belied her chic, cool Mayfair image. The 21-year marriage, which at first had captivated the world, foundered on her near hysteria, violence, and sexual peccadilloes. But it was business as usual during altercations.

The actor in Olivier enabled him to contrive a buoyant smile in public while knowing that back home Vivien would be waiting in a dangerous emotional turmoil. It seemed miraculous to me that despite having to bear – in secret – this lacerating burden, Olivier could continue to work filming *The Prince and the Showgirl* with Marilyn Monroe. One day on the set at Shepperton studios I saw him standing there with Arthur Miller, then married to Marilyn. It was more than ironic. Here were the greatest living playwright and the greatest living actor both married to wives going through vastly different kinds of hell. Marilyn's problem was her pathological craving for reassurance. All Miller's wisdom and insight was directed towards keeping Marilyn from wilting physically and emotionally under Olivier's awesome presence.

Marilyn's mood swings were as wild as Vivien's. But they had a more benign and understandable source. She had a genuine fear of being professionally engulfed by Olivier's genius in front of and behind the camera. She should never have worried. Olivier told me he thought she was wonderful, 'intuitively brilliant', he said. (Remember Dame Sybil Thorndyke's highly audible comment on the set: 'That little girl is the only one here who knows how to act before a camera.') Whatever Miller talked about with Olivier, I suspect an element of mutual sympathy must have slipped in somewhere. But both men, with characteristic dignity, kept their silence.

It would take twenty years before Olivier revealed the full horror of living with the violent, sex-obsessed, mentally stricken Vivien. He was not merely concerned for his own life. In her most frenzied attacks on him he was genuinely fearful that he might kill her. As he recounts with wrenching candour in his autobiography *Confessions of an Actor*:

One night...in her manic state she slipped out of bed, fetched a wet face-cloth and started to slash me across the eyes with it. Enraged...I went quickly down the passage to the study-bedroom and managed to lock the door. She immediately started hammering on it. Something snapped in my brain. I threw open the door, grabbed her wrist...hurled her halfway across the room. Before hitting the bed she struck the outside corner of her eye on the corner of her marble bedside table top. I realized with horror that each of us was quite capable of murdering or causing death to each other.

Though he never talked about it, Vivien Leigh's affair with the late actor Peter Finch shattered him. The story goes that when he took Finch into the study of their Oxfordshire mansion Vivien breezed in with a glacial smile and demanded, 'Will one of you come to bed with me now?'

Vivien Leigh died of tuberculosis on 8 July 1967. She had not been Britain's greatest actress but she was certainly one of its biggest stars. At ten o'clock that night all the West End theatres extinguished their exterior lights for one hour as a mark of respect. She was 53. Married now to the serene and accomplished actress Joan Plowright, Olivier set himself a simple and decidedly mercenary target: to make as much money as possible to leave to Joan and the children he adored, Tarquin, Richard, Tamsin and Julie Kate. But as he grew older work became much harder. His battle against a whole array of crippling illnesses was painful to observe. I shook hands with him once and he winced. 'Careful, darling, that's the one that holds the glass.' First cancer, then pneumonia, a damaging coronary – 'what more', he wondered, 'am I required to endure?' The brutal answer was a crippling muscular disease, which made some movements difficult and a simple handshake an agony. When he was filming *The Boys from Brazil*, the pain he suffered was plainly visible in his eyes. At one point he called out to the director Franklin Schaffner, 'Could I have a cushion for my poor old bum.' All pain is unwelcome to all sufferers. But to deny Olivier the power of his gestures, to make raising an arm a stab of hell, was as malevolently hard-hearted as inflicting deafness on Beethoven. Three years before Olivier died in 1989 he received an award at the Los Angeles Film Festival. His friend Gregory Peck presented the statuette. Olivier almost broke down. 'For once in my life I wish that my days were a little longer so that I could enjoy this moment longer...'

All of us, I imagine, would have shared that wish. But then we would have wished no less for Humphrey Bogart, Marilyn Monroe, Grace Kelly, Judy Garland and all the others I've escorted through these pages. Legends are hard to come by. But be assured, more will emerge to dazzle us as the years and the cameras roll. At the Hollywood Wax Museum new effigies of the great will stare out at the queues replacing the lesser ones boiled down into oblivion. Along Hollywood Boulevard more gold-edged stars inscribed with the newly famous names will be embedded in the black, sun-baked paving, 1,775 at the last count. Tread carefully for you walk on the likes of Charles Chaplin, Ingrid Bergman, Bing Crosby, Jascha Heifetz, Ray Charles, yes, and Vivien Leigh. New 'overnight sensations' may just survive long enough to erect a Mexican hacienda on Coldwater Canyon and hope that the TV spin-offs will cover their prenuptial agreements. But the truly talented will add lustre to the phenomenon that began as a desert shack a century ago. The new video technology has boosted an already Croesus-rich industry into a multibillion-dollar bonanza. This was scarcely envisaged when moving pictures were first invented.

Cue August Lumiere, pioneer of cinematography in 1895 addressing his assistant: 'Young man, you can be grateful that my invention is not for sale, for it would undoubtedly ruin you. It can be exploited for a certain time as a scientific curiosity, but apart from that it has no commercial value whatsoever.'

Well, you can't lose them all.

Postscript

So this is where I came in. Or so it seems. The natives look the same. So does Los Angeles. The sun shines unremittingly upon what one cynic described as 'seventy-two suburbs in search of a city'. The tree branches continue to sag under the weight of oranges nobody bothers to pick. All the ingenious ways by which this town makes its billions function as brilliantly and as brazenly as ever. In the mandatory darkness of the famous Polo Lounge at the Beverly Hills Hotel, new moguls have replaced the old but the dialogue is still an eavesdropper's delight: 'The way I heard it the film is so bad they can't release it...Where we gonna find another de Niro...Sure I've read the script, what d'you want me to say?...Waiter, I said hold the mayo...'

Star watchers still congregate outside clubs and restaurants hoping to catch a glimpse of, say, Nicole Kidman gliding in or Michael Douglas and Catherine Zeta-Jones turtle-doveing back to their limousine. Out-of-towners buy Maps to Film Star Homes with about as much chance of spotting a celebrity as finding the Lost City of Atlantis. Meanwhile, Rodeo Drive, the richest little side street on earth, continues to reflect that most defiant credo of show business: 'If you've got it, baby, flaunt it!' The *Hollywood Reporter* and *Daily Variety*, the powerful bibles of the trade, are still avidly scrutinised by all the inhabitants to see if they've merited an 'item' – good or bad. 'Better to be damned than mentioned not at all,' wrote the satirist John Wolcot (1738–1819). They'd have paid him a fortune at MGM.

Away from motion pictures the town's heavily booked psycho-analysts stand ready to deal with father fixations, repetitive-dream syndromes, sex fantasies and good old-fashioned inferiority complexes. In short, it appears to be the mixture as before. A case of *plus ça change*.

Hollywood is still the same ongoing miracle, more prosperous than ever now its revenues are boosted by DVDs and vastly increased foreign markets. At the last count 84 films were in production with more than a hundred in preparation. Westerns, the mother lode of motion pictures, are back in fashion with several studios dusting down their boots and saddles. British actors retain their well-shod foothold in Hollywood, with Rowan Atkinson the hugely popular joker in the pack following the spectacular success of his spoof spy film *Johnny English*. 'Business as usual' seems to be writ large in those legendary 'dream factories' at Burbank, Culver City and the sprawling studios of downtown Hollywood.

But the confidence is illusory. The cataclysmic event of 9/11 in New York has had its reverberations here as with everywhere else in America. Prosperity and panic go hand in hand uneasily. 'What if...?' is the dark thought concentrating minds in studios, celebrity homes and the defiant skyscrapers of downtown Los Angeles and Beverly Hills's Century City. Until 9/11 Hollywood's only nightmare has been the fear of a 'Frisco-sized earthquake. But over the years it has developed a kind of grudging respect for the capricious San Andreas Fault, whose occasional subterranean fidgets set their champagne glasses atremble. Let's be 'stirred but not shaken' is all that Hollywood asks. The sheer unpredictability of the new terrorism is creating a siege mentality in this City of the Angels. When a suicidal gunman forced the evacuation of the CBS TV studios in Los Angeles in May 2002, Hollywood decided to pull up the drawbridge.

Actors are demanding, and getting, protection against stalkers. Safe rooms or 'panic pads' are being built in celebrity homes and executive suites offering protection against chemical and biological attack. Paranoia or not, the top people are shopping around for state-of-the-art bunkers that are blast-resistant, radiation-resistant, anthrax-proof and of course air-conditioned. The Rotweiler, the electric fence and the 'armed response' remain the standard welcome for intruders. But for a mere $500,000 you can get a nice little pad with reinforced-concrete walls, a generator and sanitary fitments of your choice. The fear of being stalked, mugged, anthraxed or even 'nuked' now clouds the blue horizon.

Yet the show, as it must, goes on. You can still be a soda jerk one day and a Rock Hudson the next; a hairdresser today, and a producer, Jon Peters, tomorrow. The decision by that amiable giant Arnold Schwarzenegger to run for governor of the State of California is simply – given the Ronald Reagan precedent – history repeating itself. Thus Hollywood encapsulates the American Dream. Its unique sorcery has touched the souls of billions. It has reshaped many lives – especially mine. I could have remained a crime reporter but serial killers are scarcely a breeze. I might have continued as a court correspondent. But, given a choice of palaces, I preferred the Victoria to the Buckingham. So I came to Hollywood, with all the familiar preconceptions; prepared to jeer but stayed to cheer.

Prolonged exposure to celebrity alone can be a sterile exercise. But close encounters with legends can teach one a thing or two about the human spirit. I had a great time with Humphrey Bogart on his yacht but think mostly of his brave, growling good humour in the painful hours before he died. Lee Marvin is remembered as a tough actor who drank a lot and raised hell. But I had the rare experience of catching this ex-Marine in perhaps the most eloquent two hours of his life. When he had finished speaking, there was nothing more that could be said about the barbarity of modern warfare. As I write this, Charlie Chaplin's greatest films are being repackaged on millions of DVDs. The world saw the laughable, lovable Tramp. My privileged access to the man at his home in Vevey, Switzerland, revealed a great man sadly out of step with its time. He wept real tears that day. But, as with Chaplin, every legend I ever knew imparted *something* beyond the world of show business. The most incisive account of the wretched Hollywood witch hunt of the 1940s was given to me by one of its most distinguished victims, the screenwriter the late Carl Foreman.

Then there was Marilyn Monroe. Most of the Seven Deadly Sins booby-trapped her short, sweet and ultimately catastrophic life. But

I prefer my vision of her that sunlit afternoon in her apartment in New York – a glowing, laughing, luscious peach of a woman enjoying a brief interlude of contentment.

Sinatra in rehearsal; Brando in his mischievous mode; the elegance of Grace Kelly; the splendid arrogance of Orson Welles – for these and other rarities over thirty years, I offer my gratitude to Hollywood. But especially to those immortals whose names gleam in the sunlight on that famous Boulevard.

The Author

Donald Zec is best known for his entertainment column in the *Daily Mirror*, which was syndicated worldwide. He entered journalism just before World War Two. On leaving the army in 1945, he returned to the paper as court correspondent and as a crime reporter before becoming film columnist. He has written biographies of Sophia Loren, Lee Marvin, Barbra Streisland (with Anthony Fowles), Cubby Broccoli of James Bond legend, and the late Queen Mother. He won a National Press Award in 1967 and holds an OBE for services to journalism. He lives in Holland Park, London, with his wife, Frances.

Bibliography

Barlett, Donald and Steele, James B, *Empire: The Life, Legend and Madness of Howard Hughes*. New York, 1979, Penguin Books.

Bragg, Melvyn, *Rich: The Life of Richard Burton*. London, 1989, Hodder and Stoughton.

Broccoli, Cubby (with Donald Zec), *When the Snow Melts*. London, 1998, Boxtree.

Davis, Andy, *The Beatles Files*. Surrey, 1998, Bramley Books.

Davis Jr, Sammy, with Boyar, Burt and Boyar, Jane *Why Me?* London, 1989, Michael Joseph.

Evans, Peter, *Peter Sellers*, London, 1969, New English Library/Times Mirror.

Friedrich, Otto, *City of Nets*. New York, 1986, Harper Row.

Frischauer, Willi, *Bardot: An Intimate Biography*. London, 1978, Michael Joseph.

Halliwell, Leslie, *Halliwell's Filmgoer's Book of Quotes*. London, 1978, Granada Publishing.

Koestenbaum, Wayne, *Andy Warhol*. London, 2001, Weidenfeld and Nicolson.

Hooper, David, *Public Scandal, Odium and Contempt*. London, 1984, Secker and Warburg, Coronet Books.

Kelley, Kitty, *Elizabeth Taylor*. London, 1981, Michael Joseph.

— *His Way*. New York, 1986, Bantam Press.

Lycett, Andrew, *Ian Fleming*. London, 1995, Weidenfeld and Nicolson.

Miller, Arthur, *Time Bends*. London, 1982, Methuen.

Olivier, Laurence. *Confessions of an Actor*. London, 1982, Weidenfeld and Nicolson.

Parker, John, *The Trial of Rock Hudson*. London, 1990, Sidgwick and Jackson.

Spada, James, *Grace: The Secret Lives of a Princess*. London, 1987, Sidgwick and Jackson.

Summers, Anthony, *Goddess: The Secret Lives of Marilyn Monroe*. London, 1987, Victor Gollancz.

Wayne, Jane Ellen, *The Lives and Loves of Grace Kelly*. London, 1991, Robson Books.

Zec, Donald and Fowles, Anthony, *Barbra: A Biography of Barbra Streisand*. London, 1981, New English Library.

Zec, Donald, *Marvin: The Story of Lee Marvin*. London, 1979, New English Library.

— *Sophia: An Intimate Biography*. New York, 1975, David McKay Co. Inc.

Index